The
Bengali
Five Spice Chronicles

The
Bengali
Five Spice Chronicles
Exploring the Cuisine of Eastern India

Rinku Bhattacharya

Hippocrene Books, Inc.
New York

For further information, contact:
HIPPOCRENE BOOKS, INC.
171 Madison Avenue
New York, NY 10016

www.hippocrenebooks.com

Library of Congress Cataloging-in-Publication Data

Bhattacharya, Rinku.
The Bengali five spice chronicles : food and memories / Rinku
Bhattacharya.
    p. cm
Includes bibliographical references and index.
ISBN-13: 978-0-7818-1305-1 (pbk.)
ISBN-10: 0-7818-1305-0 (pbk.)
1. Cooking, Bengali. 2. Spices. I. Title.
TX724.5.I4B499 2012
641.595492--dc23

                                        2012034314

Printed in the United States of America.

Dedication

This book is dedicated to:

The past

Bapi (father) and Dida (grandmother),
who form the foundation of my life

The present

Ma and Anshul and Khokon,
who help me stay grounded in this journey of life

The future

Deepta and Aadi, my children,
who help me find beauty in nature everyday

Contents

Foreword

by Stanley Elwood Brush

It's a pleasure to write a short introduction to a cookbook on Bengali cuisine. Particularly because it relates to the land of my birth, expatriate infant though I was, and the author is someone I have known since her graduate student days at a New England university where I taught Indian history. She is an expatriate, of sorts, too, belonging to Bengali parents employed by a transnational corporation in Africa.

I grew up in the Bengal railway colony town of Kharagpur, and my first breath was air mingled with the aromas emanating from the cook "house" on the back veranda of the Union Church parsonage. My milk bottles were filled with milk (boiled, of course) from local cows and water buffaloes and my favorite meal was the rice and dal lentils and chicken curry that our cook used to conjure up from a mysterious blend of ingredients that his wife ground up on a stone stained yellow from years of service for this purpose. The unpleasant part was having to witness the execution of the chicken and its unseemly de-feathering. As a boy I was unaware, of course, of the finer points of the stuff that went into curry, but I was very aware that the curry at Tamil wedding parties (there was a colony of Bengal-Napgur Railway Tamil employees who used the facilities at the Union Church compound) was pitched much higher on the *jhal* (hot pepper) scale than Bengali curry.

Rice and curry, dal and chapattis were clearly the favorite menu items on our boarding school menu in the hills. The flat, flexible whole wheat flour chapattis (called rotis in the north) were durable and useful as comestibles on two- and three-day hikes into the hills.

Now from the perspective of a well-nourished historian, I think it's fair to say that the re-conquest of their homelands by Indians and Pakistanis began at the table, with cooks and bearers and the dishes placed before their new rulers seated at dinner tables in Madras, Calcutta, Bombay, Lucknow, Delhi, and Lahore; in their hill station get-a-ways and in countless other stations on the plains! The charge of South Asian civilization into the West was launched from the kitchens of the Indian and Pakistani restaurants that circle the globe from Anchorage, Alaska, all the way around and down to Wellington, New Zealand. Who would have believed that it was not the ruling khans of the courts and armies but the khansamans, the "khans of the household," the "cooks," who would turn the tables on the West!

This cookbook fills a huge culture gap for me and others who know Bengal as a province of British India, with its Firpo's, Whiteaway Laidlaw's on Chowringee Road, the Howrah Station refreshment rooms, and Magnolia ice cream as representative of Bengali cuisine. We were well-acquainted with its flavorful pastries and candy, the curry puffs, *ludoos, gulabjamuns* and *russgullas*, and *barfi*, but the standard curry and rice and the mulligatawny soup of the foreigners' table did scant justice to the dining possibilities unexplored. Then there are others who are Bengali, but born and raised in a land far away, who want to re-create the food of their heritage. For them this book offers an answer and tool. For the cook who wants to explore innovative ideas, these original recipes tested and tried in Rinku's kitchen are the answer.

The Bengali Five Spice Chronicles is a welcome guidebook for gustatory explorers both old hands and new. I welcome it and am delighted to have a small role in its launching.

Stanley Elwood Brush
Lumberton, New Jersey

Preface

"There is a garden in every childhood, an enchanted place where colors are brighter, the air softer, and the morning more fragrant than ever again."

—Elizabeth Lawrence
(from "Through the Garden Gate"
column in *Charlotte Observer*)

The garden of my childhood is really the inspiration for this book.

I was born in Kolkata, India, to an adventurous father and a relatively traditional mother, on the cusp of the city's most favorite festival, the Durga Puja, thereby convincing my parents I was blessed. My father was full of energy, enthusiasm, and a strong passion to give his child the best of anything he could afford. He spent most of his time with me, encouraging me to dream, challenging my imagination, prompting me to wish on shooting stars, and at all times encouraging me to follow my interests and hobbies. He taught me to question and reason against the status quo. He introduced me to Rabindranath Tagore's work (the Bengali Nobel laureate who has shaped and continues to influence not only Bengali culture but the world at large). The poet's collection of music, poetry, and general writings are a guide to understanding nature, seasons, and the general beauty of our Earth. Like the Bard (as Tagore is nicknamed), my father loved India and dreamt of a world "that had not been broken into fragments by narrow domestic walls." My father also loved the simplicity of Bengali home food from his childhood. My father and I both shared a love of photography, food, and travel, as well as a deep passion for life and a firm belief that good does triumph over evil.

I get my love of reading and experimental cooking, however, from my mother. My mother had to re-create her home in various parts of the world, and she managed to keep her own Bengali kitchen alive and well, while adapting the best from other cultures around her.

I was also the first grandchild in my mother's family. My maternal grandparents doted on me and were a profound influence on my life. My name is an uncanny by-product of such dotage. When I was born, my grandmother wanted to acknowledge the birth and its coincidence with the Durga Puja by proposing several poetic and religious sounding names. None of these seemed to pass the vetting test of my father and other relatives; the shorter and comparatively modern names proposed by my father did not pass muster either. Luckily, all Bengali children have nicknames, usually referred to as their *daak naam* (call name). The formal or official name is called their *bhalo naam* (good name). In fact, how a person is addressed will often tell you about the relationship between the individual and the caller. So for years I was only called "Rinku" as my *daak naam*. By the time I started nursery school, they had finally settled on my *bhalo naam* of Jayeeta, meaning "the victorious one." At that point, however, it was too foreign to me and when I went to school, I told everyone my name was simply Rinku. This affinity for simplicity and exerting my independence about my destiny has remained with me throughout my life and it is reflected in my cooking.

As a very small child I unconsciously spent copious amounts of time shadowing my maternal grandmother, observing and learning how to cook the Bengali way. I had not realized the depth of this absorption until I actually began cooking Bengali food. In fact, several little facts of how to roll dough or chop vegetables often haunt me by way of instruction, almost as if Dida is just behind me helping me along.

When I was about eight years old, my father accepted a job that took him out of India to help build infrastructures in several developing countries, mostly in Africa. My parents and I spent two years in the East African countries of Tanzania and Kenya. Afterward, I came back to attend my old school, La Martiniere for Girls in Kolkata, India, as a residential student. Growing up in a residential school environment shaped my personality considerably. First, it allowed me to form deep friendships that have lasted over my lifetime. Second, it was also a time where I missed the comfort of kitchen sounds and the action of a home kitchen. I looked forward to holidays and weekends spent at home where I could dart around the kitchen chatting with my mother and grandmother while they cooked.

And while they cooked, they told me stories about life and mythology, and of course they talked about the food they were cooking. But interestingly, my mother discouraged me from active cooking as she felt it would discourage me from other academic pursuits. When I was eleven years old, I was blessed with a sibling, who has been a willing guinea pig for several of my recipes, and like my husband, my brother is an honest and keen critic.

I decided to travel to the United States to complete graduate studies in business and accounting, after which I embarked on a career in financial management. Here too I found a niche that nourished the mind and soul by applying my education to the non-profit sector. Once I was settled at work, like most Indian parents, mine began scouring the world for a suitable man for me. After four years of constant nagging from my parents to bring home an appropriate, intellectual Bengali son-in-law, I brought home a man who might fringe on satisfying the Bengali love for education but who unfortunately did not speak a word of Bengali. Sadly his Bengali language skills have not progressed, despite being married to me for well over a decade. He does, however, share my passion for food. And I have taught him the joys of savoring a well-made morning cup of Darjeeling tea. I felt that the closest and most practical way I could offer my husband an insight into the Bengali culture was through food.

The challenge to mastering Bengali cuisine was the lack of cookbooks that presented the cuisine in English. Certainly none were adapted to our fast-paced twenty-first-century lifestyle, where prepared ingredients blend easily with fresh ones. I wanted to translate traditional Bengali ingredients to commonly available ingredients in the West. This book is my attempt to document and chronicle this simple and practical approach to Bengali cuisine, that I hope will help others along the course of working through Bengali cuisine and discovering some Indian recipes that are off the beaten path.

I lost my father around the time I was completing the first draft of this book. As my interpretation of a culture and cuisine that he taught me to love, I had hoped this book would be a gift to him. Now I present it as a humble tribute to his influence and immense contributions to my life.

Introduction

Bengal is a region in the northeast of the Indian subcontinent that contains the Ganges and Brahmaputra river deltas and is often called "the land of rivers." In 1947, the province was divided into West Bengal, which has remained a state of India, and East Pakistan, also referred to as East Bengal. This partition was a painful divide, done mostly on the grounds of religion, forcing many families to leave their roots and possessions and migrate to what was considered their side of the border.

In 1971, the East Bengalis felt that culture and language were stronger factors than the religion that tied them to Pakistan, and so they fought for what is now the independent country of Bangladesh.

The culinary heritage of Bengal is the shared heritage of East Bengal and West Bengal. A heritage shared due to history, topography, and culture. There is, however, enough distinction between the cuisines of both these regions now, much like well-formed dialects of a land, for these sub-cuisines to claim their own identity. The essentials of rice, fish, greens, and grains are the same. The diversity lies in how these essentials are handled. The inhabitants of West Bengal are called Ghotis and their food is milder and often has a touch of sugar in its seasoning; the East Bengalis or Bangladeshis are called Bangals and have a predisposition for more fiery, sharper seasonings. Both, however, love fish, greens, rice, mustard, and desserts. This book focuses mostly on the Bengali cuisine of India, but there are some recipes included from my friends from Bangladesh to allow the reader to get some understanding of the diversity of both styles of Bengali cuisine. The culinary heritage of Bengal, in a broader sense, is the culinary heritage of Eastern India (a regional cuisine of India that is still unknown to the world).

If you are in West Bengal, the morning is heralded with the sound of a conch shell blown by the mistress of the house, and the day begins with an acknowledgement of the divine. To the Bengali, culture, music, and food are a way of life and indeed the reason for living. The music of conch shells also sounds to celebrate the arrival of the evening and the passing of a day well lived. The morning and evening noises also comprise Muslim prayers called the *namaz*, and sometimes the chiming of church bells. The primary religion of this region is Hinduism, but Islam and Christianity are strong and visible minority religions. The multi-religious influence can be seen in the foods and celebrations of the region.

Early morning prayers are followed by a visit to the market and then the task of preparing the meals of the day begins. Some of this routine has changed, since like in other parts of the world Bengali households are now more nuclear and both partners may work outside of the home. Though the routine changes, the importance paid to food in the Bengali homes has not diminished in the least.

Bengalis are probably one of the most food and culture obsessed people in India. They can actually be compared to the French in such passionate obsession.

1

Bengalis believe that certain foods are prescribed for specific occasions to assist with the mood and spirit of the occasion. For example, the Bengali child starts his or her life journey with milk and rice. A combination of milk and rice is considered the complete basic meal, since milk provides a balanced protein and rice provides starch.

Religious occasions also hold a place for vegetarian delights, and festive occasions such as weddings have different foods for the different moods of the celebration to allow you to satisfy all your senses. Occasions of sadness, such as death, are also acknowledged with prescriptions for simple vegetarian food (in the Hindu tradition) to allow the body to purify itself and thereby process grief quietly. And after the official mourning period, people bid farewell to the departed by partaking of the deceased's favorite foods.

The daily life and routine of the Bengali revolves around food and entertaining guests with food. The success of an event or celebration is based on the quality of food served. Bengali cuisine, however, does not use an excess of ingredients and spices. The variations and complexities in food are a result of practiced and delicate subtlety. The art of hospitality goes hand in hand with food; a true Bengali offering of food is complete only with the warmth of adequate presentation and indulgence of the visitor.

If you consider the full spectrum of Bengali cuisine, it offers you countless influences from the various invaders, traders, and in some cases international communities that have made Bengal their home. These include the Portuguese, the Chinese, the Jews, the Armenians, the Moghuls, and, of course, the British. The British were the last of the formal rulers and possibly left the strongest influence on the food, literature, and architecture of the region.

The inlet from the Bay of Bengal made the land accessible and therefore a popular entry point for travelers for the purposes of trade and invasions. The area now known as Bengal seemed to be its own agricultural society until it was later absorbed as a part of the Indus Valley civilization. The fertile land amid the rivers was home to the many greens and fish that are plentiful in the Bengali diet.

History indicates that the Indo-Aryan kingdom of Vanga was formed by the tenth century. For about 400 years, Bengal was ruled by Hindu rulers. These rulers came from Vanga as well as other parts of the country, such as the Gupta rulers from northern India and the Sen Dynasty from the south of India. Islam was introduced to Bengal through Arab Muslim traders. A relatively large number of people converted to Islam through Sufi missionaries around the twelfth century.

This was also the period when Bakhtiar Khilji, a general of the Slave Dynasty of the Delhi Sultanate, conquered large parts of Bengal. The Muslim rulers, followed by the Mughal rulers, conquered Bengal in the sixteenth century. The Mughals had their base in the northwestern parts of Bengal, in regions such as Murshidabad and Malda. The latter region is famous for its mango orchards. The inhabitants of these regions developed improvisations on the Bengali cuisine, initially to please their rulers but later these styles became a way of life. With the introduction of Islam, Bengali Muslims adopted dishes such as *kababs, koftas*, and *biryani* from their Moghul conquerors. There are also simpler influences, such as the addition of nuts and raisins, that otherwise might not come across as a simple Bengali homestyle dish.

Districts of West Bengal

N

State Capital
District Head Quarter
District Boundary
International Boundary

NEPAL
SIKKIM
BHUTAN
DARJEELING
JALPAIGURI
ASSAM
COOCHBEHAR
NORTH DINAJPUR
MEGHALAYA
SOUTH DINAJPUR
BIHAR
MALDA
BANGLADESH
MURSHIDABAD
BIRBHUM
BURDWAN
NADIA
PURULIA
BANKURA
24 PRGANAS NORTH
HOOGHLY
CALCUTTA
HOWRAH
ORISSA
24 PARGANAS SOUTH
MIDNAPUR
BAY OF BENGAL

Divergent sects of Hinduism, such as the Vaishnavs and Shaivaite sects, emerged to offer alternatives to the traditional caste-based segments of Hinduism, and these sects expressed a preference for vegetarian cuisine, often prescribing the elimination of garlic and onion also. A lot of vegetarian dishes are still cooked with ginger and asafetida rather than garlic and onion.

Portuguese traders arrived in the late fifteenth century, once Vasco da Gama reached India by sea in 1498. The Portuguese introduced chilies and vinegar into the Bengali cuisine and also shared influences such as a *vindaloo* and stuffed vegetables such as the *dolma*. Other new world vegetables introduced to the Bengali table were potatoes and tomatoes.

The British ties and rule were a very strong cultural force, particularly in Kolkata, and definitely impacted the cuisine in subtle ways through various westernized names for traditional Bengali dishes, and of course non-subtle ways in the plethora of Anglo-Indian dishes that are a part of the Bengali culinary repertoire. The British introduced several terms, such as the chop, cutlet, and *jhal ferazi* into the Bengali culinary lexicon. These have become popular dishes and indispensable to the culinary landscape of Bengal.

Bengali cooking is very frugal and environmentally friendly, and the Bengali plate offers a wonderful array of balanced vegetarian delights. Several components of the Bengali home meal may never be served to the outsider, because Bengalis consider some of these classic items too simple to serve to non-family members. Vegetables are usually boiled, steamed, or stir-fried. A traditional Bengali meal sequence involves eating through a rainbow assortment of vegetables, and then finishing off with non-vegetarian fare, usually fish. Since Bengalis rely on seasonal fare and usually eat what is available, the home food is produced in small quantities and cooking is a daily ritual.

The great river systems, heat, and humidity of Bengal combine with the fertile soil to allow rice and an abundance of vegetables to thrive and these in turn became the cornerstones of the Bengali diet. Mangoes, bananas, coconuts, and cane sugar grew in abundance; fish, milk, and meat were plentiful; and yogurt and spices such as ginger and black mustard were used to season the dishes. The northern most regions of Bengal are bordered by the Himalayas. These are also some of the finest tea-growing regions of the world, producing the famous Darjeeling tea and facilitating the Bengali passion for tea.

Rice, the staple of the Bengali diet since ancient times, has remained consistent and its preparation has been held to a continuing high standard. One crop a year is sufficient to sustain the people, providing ample leisure time for the Bengalis to pursue cultural ideals: folklore, music, and the culinary arts. The harvest season is marked by the winter festival called Sankranti, which is characterized by the preparation of several desserts collectively called *pithey*. Most of these desserts are made with rice and coconut.

Bengalis like to say that the twelve months of the calendar year include over thirteen festivals, in Bengali: *Baro Mashe, Tero Porbon*. It is almost impossible to travel into the region without bumping into some festival, particularly when considering the secular-religious universe of holidays. Bengali festivals that spread through the year also allow the capitalization of seasonal delights of the region; for example, the springtime fruit called *kool* is not eaten without being offered to the Spring Goddess Saraswati first, the summer mango too is similarly blessed, and winter delights such as date palm jaggery are incorporated into early sweets for the Goddess Kali before becoming a part of the everyday repertoire.

Other regional vegetables that are used extensively in Bengali cuisine are leafy greens, gourds, bitter melons, and bananas. The banana plant is essential to the Bengali existence and most parts of the plant—the flowers and the fruit—are eaten in different dishes. The leaves are used as plates and also as a receptacle for steaming fish or vegetables. The thicker parts of the stalks are used for decorations and food receptacles. Bengalis certainly give a place of importance to this plant: in the most prominent festival of the region, the Hindu festival of Durga Puja, the banana plant is the symbolic wife of the Lord Ganesh, who is a son of Dugra. The banana tree is often seen adjacent to Ganesh who is dressed in a traditional white and red silk sari. The colors white and red are symbolic and considered auspicious colors and are typically used for decoration.

Panch Phoron: Bengali Five Spice Blend

Every existence—no matter how simple—is in some way tinged with the myriad flavors of life. This is often a composition of sweet, sour, bitter, savory, and the astringent, much like the five-spice blend we Bengalis call *panch phoron*. The Bengali Five Spice Blend is a blend of five whole spices in equal proportions: cumin seeds, mustard seeds, nigella seeds, fenugreek seeds, and fennel seeds. The fenugreek is a substitution for the spice called *radhuni* (a form of celery seed relatively uncommon outside of India). The actual *panch phoron*, however, is available in most Indian stores, often transliterated as *panch puran*. It is almost impossible to prepare a Bengali meal without using the *panch phoron* blend, and the individual spices are also important and form the basis of the Bengali pantry.

The Bengali kitchen is typified by the scent of the mustard oil heating, followed by the crackling sound of the essential five-spice mixture. The crackling is almost immediately followed by the fragrance of cumin, nigella, and fennel merging into a union of scents. The popping of whole seeds in oil to add flavor to a dish is a hallmark of Indian cooking. This process adds a nutty taste to the seeds and mellows and matures their flavor.

BENGALI FIVE SPICE BLEND
Panch Phoron

1 teaspoon fennel seeds
1 teaspoon cumin seeds
1 teaspoon nigella seeds
1 teaspoon black mustard seeds
1 teaspoon fenugreek seeds

Mix the seeds together evenly.
Store in an airtight container and use as needed.

Chapter One:
Ingredients, Techniques and Tools

The Essential Bengali Pantry

ASAFETIDA (Hing): This spice is like the quiet smart person at the back of the room, who suddenly surprises you when they speak. Asafetida is an unusual smelling spice that does not look especially pretty. It is a resin of a tree and is used mostly in vegetarian cooking as a substitute for garlic and onion and sometimes to enhance the flavors of these seasonings. It is used sparingly and once you learn how to use it, it too will feature on your spice short list.

BANANA LEAVES (Kolapata): The banana plant is essential to the Bengali culinary repertoire and the plant is used in its entirety. To acknowledge this importance, the banana tree is the symbolic wife of the Elephant God Ganesh, who is worshipped as the son of Durga, the Mother Goddess. The leaves of the banana plant are used for steaming food. Frozen banana leaves are available in the U.S. in Mexican grocery stores, as well as in some Asian stores.

BAY LEAVES (Tej Patta): These familiar leaves of the cassia tree impart a sweet, peppery flavor and are used in stews, rice, and sometimes desserts. We usually break them into a few pieces when adding to a dish. Bay leaves are not usually eaten, so depending on your preference, they can be removed prior to serving a dish.

BLACK PEPPERCORNS (Kalo Morich): Black peppercorns are one of the most versatile of spices. Native to the southern coast of India, black peppercorns are used to add heat to Indian food. They impart a different kind of heat than the red or green chilies that are more commonly used in Indian cuisine.

BORI (Lentil Nugget): These tiny small rounds of dried lentil cakes are readily available in most Indian groceries and might be named *vadi* on the packaging. They are essential in Bengali cooking, particularly for vegetarian recipes where additional protein is needed.

CHICKPEA FLOUR (Besan): This is a fine, chalky flour that is made of ground chickpeas. It is completely gluten-free and used in Bengali cooking for thickening purposes as well as for batters and bindings. The flour is high in protein and very nutritious and results in a light textured crisp coating when fried.

CHILIES: *See* Green Chilies; Red Chilies, Dried

CILANTRO (Dhoney Pata): Cilantro is an Americanized term for this herb, also commonly called coriander leaves as the leaves are from the coriander plant. They are used extensively as a fresh garnish in Indian cooking. It is important not to use the dried variety for the recipes in this book.

CINNAMON (Darchini): This is the dried, curled fragrant bark of the cinnamon tree. Cinnamon is used much like cloves in Indian cooking, either powdered or whole for seasoning curries and stews. When using cinnamon sticks we usually crush them slightly with a rolling pin or mortar and pestle to break them into a few smaller pieces.

CLARIFIED BUTTER. *See* Ghee

CLOVES (Lobongo): Cloves are actually tiny dried flower buds. Aromatic cloves are used in powder form or whole in spice blends.

COCONUT (Narkol): The coconuts used in cooking are the fruit of the large coconut palm. Coconut trees line the landscape of West Bengal and their fruit and milk are used to add a touch of creaminess to curries. Good frozen coconut is readily available and an acceptable substitute for freshly grated in most cases.

CORIANDER SEEDS (Dhone): These small, round, brown seeds are typically used in conjunction with cumin seeds in Indian cooking. Coriander seeds are rarely used whole in Bengali cooking.

CUMIN SEEDS (Jire): Cumin seeds, with their slightly smoky, lightly peppery taste, are one of the most versatile seasoning spices. Roasted or toasted cumin seeds are significantly more flavorful than plain powdered cumin.

DALS: See pages 67-68 for a list of different varieties and their uses.

FENNEL SEEDS (Mauri): These are the seeds of the oval, green or yellowish-brown dried fruit of *Foeniculum vulgare*, a member of the parsley family. They have a sweet, anise-like flavor and are used for tempering as well as in pow-dered form in Bengali cooking. Fennel seeds are a very versatile spice in the Bengali kitchen, used in both sweet and savory recipes.

FENUGREEK SEEDS (Methi): These bright yellow seeds are shaped like a multi-dimensional polygon. Fenugreek seeds are naturally bitter and have a faint smell of maple. Like mustard seeds, they acquire a mellow and nutty flavor when toasted in oil.

FIVE SPICE BLEND (Panch Phoron): This sorceress of spice blends consists of equal parts of the following seeds: fennel, nigella, cumin, fenugreek, and mustard. See page 5 for basic recipe. This flavorful mixture originated in eastern India and is used in the states of Assam and Orrisa as well. It is usually toasted in a little oil before use to mellow and marry the flavors of the seeds, resulting in a nutty, nuanced seasoning.

GHEE (Clarified Butter): Ghee yields a nice rich taste and is used as a flavoring medium in cooking. Ghee is often poured over hot rice to add a richness and also is found in a lot of festival cuisine, both for its taste and for its perceived qualities of purity. For health reasons, it is best used in moderation as a finishing medium.

GREEN CARDAMOM (Elach): Cardamom has a strong, unique taste with an intensely aromatic fragrance. Cardamom is best stored in pod form, because once the seeds are exposed or ground they quickly lose their flavor. The pod is the dried un-ripened fruit of the plant. The small, brown-black sticky seeds are contained in a pod in three double rows with about six seeds in each row. Cardamom pods are generally green but are also available in bleached white pod form. There are also black cardamom pods that are used in moderation in some Bengali recipes.

GREEN CHILIES (Kacha Lonka): Spicy finger chilies such as the green cayenne pepper are used fresh in Indian cooking for heat and flavor. If you cannot find these, you may substitute with the long Italian peppers or jalapeños if they are more readily available.

GREEN MANGOES (Kancha Aam): The delicate unripe green mango is used in Bengali cuisine to add a tang to lentils, paired with mustard as a relish or a base for steaming fish, and sweetened and eaten in chutneys. Green mangoes are available in Indian stores and should be bought as young and tender as possible.

LENTILS (Dals): See pages 67-68 for a list of different varieties and their uses.

MANGOES: *See* Green Mangoes

MUSTARD OIL (Shorsher Tel): This sharp, golden yellow oil is the cooking oil of choice in Bengal. It is available in most Indian stores. If you are unable to obtain it, add a pinch of powdered mustard to regular vegetable oil.

MUSTARD SEEDS (Sorshe): These are the tiny black seeds of the mustard plant. When crushed, they impart the creamy paste that is the base of familiar prepared mustards. When heated in oil, mustard seeds actually pop slightly and develop a nice nutty flavor. A small amount of whole mustard seeds is sometimes all that is needed for a powerhouse of flavor.

NIGELLA SEEDS (Kalo Jire): These very tiny black seeds are used whole to flavor stir-fries and more frequently, dry curries. They are often also used, much like poppy seeds, to decorate breads.

OILS: The two core cooking mediums traditionally used in Bengali cuisine are mustard oil and ghee (clarified butter). For the purposes of accessibility and taste, plain vegetable oil (shada tel) is also used. In this book, where there is no specific reference to the type of cooking oil, a mild neutral tasting vegetable oil such as canola oil should be used.

PANCH PHORON (Five Spice Blend): See page 5.

RED CHILIES, DRIED (Lal Lonka): Dried whole red chilies, sold in packages, are used in stir-frying to impart both heat and flavor. I recommend using the long, red variety of chili found in most Indian groceries. If additional heat is desired, these chilies can be very lightly crushed before adding them to a dish and this can be applied in the recipes in this book.

SAFFRON (Kesar): This expensive and elegant spice is not used extensively in Bengali cuisine, but some of the recipes for rice and a few desserts call for it. Saffron is derived from the stamen of the saffron flower and a little goes a long way in coloring and flavoring food.

TAMARIND (Tetul): Tamarind is a naturally sour fruit used in Bengali cooking for an assortment of dishes. These days, I am happy to see that there are several brands of readily available tamarind pastes. I usually get one of these jars and use as needed.

TURMERIC (Haldi): This simple yellow powder is also one of the must-haves in an Indian pantry, although I admit I do not use it as extensively as some people. It is actually regarded both for its color and for its anti-inflammatory qualities. I tend to use it somewhat sparingly with brightly colored vegetables since I think that these vegetables shine wonderfully on their own merit.

YOGURT (Doi): Natural yogurt is used in cooking and is also sometimes eaten with a sprinkling of sugar to finish off a meal. Natural yogurt is either made at home or bought at the sweet shops. This yogurt is usually set in earthen pots and is thick and relatively free of whey. Low-fat Greek-style yogurt is a good option for Bengali cooking.

Spice Pastes and Blends

Bengali cooking is distinguished by the use of relatively smooth ground spice pastes to form the base for sauces and dry curries. The smoothness of Bengali sauces is created through fine processing of the ingredients. This method also allows a thick paste to form naturally. Meal preparation in a Bengali kitchen often begins with *moshla bata*, the art of grinding spice pastes.

In Bengali kitchens, spice pastes are hand ground using a grinding stone. Intuitively you might think a blender would do a better job, but this is not necessarily true. A blender is better for large quantities of spices, but I have gotten the best results using a wet/dry grinder or in certain instances a hand grater. All these pastes (with the exception of the mustard paste) freeze well and can also be kept up to a week in the refrigerator.

GRATED OR GROUND ONIONS
Piyaj Bata

Onions are usually coarsely ground and then used for the base of many sauces and curries. The best way to obtain the right consistency is to cut off the top of the onion, peel it, and grate the onion using a hand grater. In many of the recipes, however, this can be conveniently done through the use of a food processor which yields a somewhat coarser but acceptable texture. In recipes where a large number of onions are needed this is the preferred method. Red onions are most suitable for Bengali cooking.

GINGER PASTE
Aada Bata

Fresh ginger is peeled and ground to a smooth paste for use in Bengali dishes. Look for ginger that is relatively young, smooth, and without much fiber. The ginger paste can be made by processing ginger in a blender or wet/dry grinder.

GARLIC PASTE
Roshoon Bata

Garlic is actually used somewhat sparingly in Bengali cooking, but is essential in meat and certain other dishes. Garlic paste can also be made in a grinder, but I usually use a garlic press and have found that the consistency of pressed garlic works well with most of the recipes.

GINGER-CUMIN-CORIANDER PASTE
Ada Dhone Jire Bata

This essential wet spice blend is integral to most Bengali cooking. It takes the form of curry powder in other Indian cooking or is similar to Thai curry pastes. This recipe freezes well and can be stored in the refrigerator for up to 2 weeks.

Prep/Cook Time: 10 minutes | **Makes:** ½ cup

INGREDIENTS
2-inch piece fresh ginger, peeled
2 tablespoons cumin seeds
2 tablespoons coriander seeds
1 or 2 green chilies

PREPARATION
Place all the ingredients and ¼ cup warm water in a blender and blend till smooth. To get the right consistency, you will need to pulse this and blend in intervals. Save and store in the refrigerator and use as needed.

POPPY SEED PASTE
Posto Bata

This delicate creamy white paste makes a lovely-tasting addition to foods. Soaking the seeds in warm water makes the difference. The seeds can be kept soaked in water for up to 3 days in the refrigerator before using.

Prep Time: 3 hours (mostly for soaking seeds) | **Makes:** ½ cup

INGREDIENTS
⅓ cup white poppy seeds, soaked for at least 2 hours in warm water
2 or 3 green chilies
½ teaspoon salt

PREPARATION
Place all the ingredients and ¼ cup warm water in a blender and blend till smooth. To get the right consistency, you will need to pulse the mixture a few times and then blend it smoothly for 5 minutes. Save and store in the refrigerator for a few days (but it will turn slightly darker due to oxidation).

MUSTARD SEED PASTE
Shorshe Bata

This delicate, pungent paste is one of the most beloved cooking essentials of Bengali cuisine. The best texture is derived with hand grinding on a grinding stone in order to bruise and process the mustard seeds to a rich creamy aioli-like texture. To compensate for the lack of room in a mechanical grinder, it is important to soak the seeds for a long time in warm water to get the right creamy texture. It is also essential to use the green chilies or you will get a paste with a rather bitter taste.

Prep Time: 6 to 7 hours (mostly for soaking seeds) | **Makes:** ½ cup

INGREDIENTS
⅓ cup black mustard seeds, soaked for at least 6 hours in warm water
2 or 3 green chilies
½ teaspoon salt

PREPARATION
Place all the ingredients and ¼ cup warm water in a blender and grind till smooth. To get the right consistency, you will need to pulse and blend the mixture in intervals. But do not over blend. The finished paste is a creamy yellow with brown and green flecks. The sharpness of the mustard increases too much on sitting and therefore this cannot be made ahead and stored for more than a day or two.

QUICK PREPARED MUSTARD I
Chot Pot Shorshe Bata I

There are times when you do not have the time to soak the mustard seeds to prepare the paste, so this recipe offers an acceptable substitute. The brand of mustard that I have found works best for this recipe is Grey Poupon, a mild and creamy Dijon mustard.

Makes: ¼ cup

INGREDIENTS
4 tablespoons prepared Dijon mustard
2 green chilies
½ teaspoon salt

PREPARATION
Place all the ingredients in a blender and blend until smooth. Place in a cup and use as needed.

QUICK PREPARED MUSTARD II
Chot Pot Shorshe Bata II

Imagine my surprise when I was watching a Bengali cooking show in Kolkata last year and I saw countless advertisements promoting powdered mustard. The problem sometimes with being away from India is that it is hard to keep up with the modernization trends in the country. Those advertisements gave me permission to try the mustard paste with mustard powder. Use a brand from your Indian grocer such as Swad for this variation.

Makes: ¼ cup

INGREDIENTS
2 tablespoons mustard powder
3 green chilies
½-inch piece fresh ginger, peeled
1 teaspoon salt

PREPARATION
Place all the ingredients and 6 tablespoons of water in a blender. Blend until it makes a smooth paste. Let the paste rest for about 10 minutes before using. Use this paste as a substitute for the regular mustard paste as needed.

ROASTED SPICE BLEND
Bhaja Masala

I paid attention to my mother's recipe for this spice blend for the first time when she visited my graduate school apartment. I returned home and was quite surprised to find a strong but familiar fragrance wafting from my kitchen. I walked in to uncover another secret of the Bengali kitchen, the roasted spice mixture. This spice blend is used as a finishing spice.

Makes: ¼ cup

INGREDIENTS
8 to 10 whole dried red chilies
1 tablespoon cumin seeds
1 tablespoon fennel seeds
2 bay leaves

PREPARATION
Roast all the ingredients for about 1 minute in a dry skillet till they are darker and aromatic. Grind to a powder and store and use as needed.

FRAGRANT SPICE BLEND
Garam Masala

It is worth noting that there are several variations of this fragrant spice blend across India. The Bengali garam masala is simpler that other garam masala blends and consists of equal portions of cardamom seeds, cloves, and cinnamon powdered together. This is a little different from the commercial pre-mixed varieties of garam masala which are closer to the blend of garam masala from northern India.

Makes: ¼ cup

INGREDIENTS
4 (2-inch) cinnamon sticks
1 tablespoon cardamom seeds
1½ tablespoons cloves

PREPARATION
Place the cinnamon sticks, cardamom seeds, and cloves in a dry pan and lightly roast for 1 to 2 minutes. Place in a coffee grinder or spice mill and grind till powdered. Store in an airtight jar and use as needed.

CUMIN-CORIANDER POWDER
Dhone Jire Guro

Another versatile all-purpose spice blend, this powder can definitely be created by mixing pre-ground cumin and coriander powders, but please do take the time to grind these spices yourself—your taste buds will thank you.

Makes: ¼ cup

INGREDIENTS
3 tablespoons cumin seeds
3 tablespoons coriander seeds

PREPARATION
Lightly roast the cumin seeds and coriander seeds in a dry small skillet for 1 to 2 minutes until just fragrant. Place the spices in a spice grinder and grind until a smooth powder is formed. Store in an airtight jar and use as needed.

Cooking with Green Mangoes

There are a couple of ways to cut and use unripe or green mango, depending on the purpose of the preparation. With lentils, you usually use just the flesh of the mango. For chutneys (*jhols*), however, the mango is peeled and the hard seed removed. This leaves a thinner shell at the base of the mango that can be cut with a knife. The mango is then cubed or cut into wedges for the chutney recipes.

Grating and Preparing Coconut

Frozen shredded coconut and canned coconut milk work for a lot of the recipes in this book. For the desserts, however, if possible use freshly grated coconut, which has a softer texture and taste. Select a coconut from the Indian grocer or the tropical section of the market and shake it to ensure that there is still some water in it. Carefully crack the coconut. Using a sharp knife, cut off the flesh of the coconut and scrape off the outer brown coating and grate the white flesh using a fine microplain grater. The grated coconut can also be frozen and I have found that home-grated coconut, even when frozen, tastes sweeter and fresher than some of the commercial varieties.

Preparing Channa (Cottage Cheese)

Channa (cottage cheese) is made at home by curdling fresh milk with lemon or lime juice. To make about 1 cup cottage cheese, bring ½ gallon of milk, usually the 2% fat variety, to a boil on medium heat. When the milk begins to boil, squeeze in the juice of 1½ limes. The milk and whey usually separate in less than 15 seconds. Remove from heat and pour the mixture into a cheesecloth-lined colander and allow to drain. The curds of cheese will collect on the cheesecloth. Then tie the cheesecloth into a ball and squeeze the mixture over a bowl to remove any residual liquid. For most recipes in Bengali cooking, draining this for about 30 minutes works, however longer draining is needed for the desserts. While paneer, store-bought cottage cheese sold in blocks, is an acceptable substitute for use in the curries, the homemade variety is the best option for dessert recipes.

Essential Tools and General Tips for Bengali Cooking

Translating traditional Bengali kitchen tools to more practical options has taken a little bit of trial and error, but I have managed to cull it down to some essential items. While the actual core concepts need translation, most cooks have their own methods of cooking and can find ways to make a kitchen their own space.

I've heard several jokes about how it takes more than one man to do the work of one woman—well, it takes at least three small tools to capture the full range of functionality of a hand grinding stone called a "*sil nora.*" It is possible to find such a grinding stone outside of India—in fact, well-stocked Bengali stores in Little India in Queens sell them. The challenge with the grinding stone and the *boti*, a traditional cutting blade, is that these tools are based on the concept of working on the floor and this is not what most people tend to do any more.

COCONUT SCRAPER OR GRATER: Coconut is used quite extensively in Bengali cooking. While I list frozen grated coconut in several recipes for convenience, it is definitely preferable to have the sweet softness of freshly grated coconut, especially for desserts.

HAND GRATER: The simple hand grater is an indispensable tool in the kitchen. In particular, the grater actually yields the best texture for onions used in Bengali curries. It is difficult to actually grate onions without some tears, so I hesitate to suggest this method in recipes, but hand grating does indeed offer the texture that is closest to the one created by the Bengali grinding stone.

SPICE GRINDER: A coffee grinder or spice grinder is essential for powdering whole spices. The seasoning mixes in this book are still not readily available in mass markets and I cannot stress enough the difference in quality and taste between freshly powdered spices and commercial varieties that have been sitting on shelves indefinitely. I have found most coffee grinders to be hardy and extremely well-suited for spice grinding.

MORTAR AND PESTLE: A mortar and pestle are useful to have around because in many Bengali recipes whole spices are gently bruised to release greater flavors. I have personally found that metal mortars are more useful for the purposes described in this book.

PRESSURE COOKER: There are a few recipes in the lentils section that could benefit from the use of the pressure cooker. If you are new to the pressure cooker, try to find a small one (usually the Indian variety available online).

SLOTTED SPOON (Jhajri): A good sturdy metal slotted spoon is essential, especially when frying things such as the *luchis* or other fried fritters in the book.

SLOW COOKER: A slow cooker is not used in most homes in India; however it works well with Bengali recipes, which reach their true depth of deep flavor through slow cooking. In the traditional Bengali kitchen of yore, coal and brick stoves called *unoons* allowed the food to cook on slow and consistent heat. I have adapted several of my recipes for the slow cooker to achieve the same depth of flavor without all the attention or fuss.

WET/DRY GRINDER: Bengali cuisine relies on a selection of spice pastes to form the base of several curries. This is fairly typical of most Indian regional cuisine. In fact, Indian blender sets, or "mixies" as they are called, typically come with three attachments: a blender for liquids and smoothies; a spice grinder for dry powders; and an in-between chutney jar for wet mixing. I have found mixers such as the Magic Bullet or the Rival wet/dry grinder very useful and effective for spice pastes.

WOK (Korai): A cast-iron wok or even hard anodized non-stick wok are very useful in the Bengali kitchen for cooking vegetables and frying food, since the curved shape of the wok is effective for distributing the heat. The shape also allows for frying without excessive oil.

Basic Bengali Culinary Terms

ACHAAR: Pickles and relishes are popular accompaniments to Indian meals. Most are made with spices, such as salt and turmeric, and oils. The fruit or vegetables are seasoned with spices, sun-dried, and then preserved in oil. Bengali pickles are both sweet and savory. Sweet pickles are usually seasoned with jaggery.

AMBOL: This term usually refers to chutneys that are predominantly tart as it broadly means "acidic." The term *tok* meaning "acidic" is also sometimes used to refer to this variety of dishes and is used interchangeably with *ambol*.

BHAJA: Fried food is called "*bhaja*" in Bengali cuisine. The fried creations can be deep-fried or shallow-fried and are usually served at the beginning of a meal with lentils or even a rice-and-lentil porridge (*khichuri*). Most *bhajas* are either coated with turmeric and salt and fried plain, or coated with chickpea flour batter before frying.

BHAPA: The style of Bengali cooking where ingredients are steamed. Fresh fish or seasonal vegetables are rubbed delicately with salt, mustard oil, and turmeric and steamed in either a sealed metal container or wrapped in banana leaves. The steamed dishes are often cooked over rice to allow the dishes to cook together.

BHATEY: A traditional style of cooking where ingredients such as vegetables and lentils are boiled and then eaten with rice. The vegetables are often wrapped in cheesecloth or placed in a "tiffin container," and then cooked together with the rice. When the vegetables are boiled separately from the rice, the dish is called a *sheddo* (or *shiddo*). Bengali cooking techniques are based upon maximizing energy and fuel. So if a pot of rice was already boiling on the coal stove, other items would be cooked over and around it.

BHUNA or KOSHA: A method of slow and careful cooking of meat where very little water is added. The meat is slow-cooked to perfection enveloped by caramelized onions to keep it moist. *Kosha Mangsho* (slow-cooked dry lamb or mutton) is a classic Bengali dish using this technique.

CHORCHORI: A style of cooking where ingredients are braised or stir-fried. A good *chorchori* is a medley of balanced vegetables cooked to soft perfection and seasoned with a sharp biting amount of seasoning. It is a good way to use up leftover vegetables. Despite its frugal nature, much like the French ratatouille a good *chorchori* is testimony to the talent of a good cook.

CHAATNEY: The Bengali *chaatney* or *chutney* is probably the cousin or ancestor of the anglicized sugary condiment that is synonymous with Indian food. Bengali chutney is part of a full course meal and serves as the intermezzo, transitioning the palate from the savory to the sweet. It is close to *ambol*, but chutneys tend to be more varied and are made with seasonal ingredients including mangoes, tomatoes, dates, pineapples, and papayas.

CHANCHRA: A method of cooking similar to a *chorchori* with the presence of fish bones and leftovers. Leftover fish bones are put to good use here and the end result is a dry, oily, and spicy dish that goes well with rice.

CHECHKI: The *chechki* is similar to a *chorchori* but usually made with a single vegetable or just a combination of two vegetables. The base seasoning for this is the Bengali Five Spice seasoning called *panch phoron* (page 5), or sometimes nigella seeds called *kalo jire*.

CHOKKA: A Bengali dish in which vegetables, commonly pumpkin or taro, are sautéed with spices, chickpeas, and ghee (clarified butter). The resultant dish is slightly sweet to taste and often eaten with *luchis*.

DAALNA: A thick and spicy gravy for vegetarian entrees such as cauliflower or *channa* (Indian chickpeas). The *daalna* is characterized by frying onions and ginger with an assortment of spices to create a thick base. A *daalna* is usually considered an elaborate main dish.

DOLMA or DORMA: This is a process of stuffing a vegetable with meal or Indian cheese and then simmering it in a nice, thick, almost dry gravy. This is most often done by stuffing the *potol* (a pointed green gourd), but can also be done with bell peppers.

GHONTO: A drier, relatively rich and usually vegetarian preparation. There are a few typical vegetables that lend themselves to this preparation, such as the bottle gourd (*lau*), banana blossoms (*mocha*), and carp heads.

ISHTEW or STEW: A lightly spiced, soupy medley. It is one of the terms that owe their existence to the English influence.

JHAAL: This word literally means "hot and spicy." It usually refers to a relatively thin and spicy preparation of fish that is spiced with mustard paste (prepared with fresh mustard and spicy hot green chilies). Turmeric and seeds such as nigella are also added for additional flavor.

JHOL: A mild Bengali stew prepared with various vegetables or with fish, seafood, and meats. The *jhol* has plenty of gravy and is called *patla jhol* (literally "thin stew"). *Jhols* made with carp or prawns are highly appreciated on Bengali tables during summer, and are excellent for convalescents.

KAALIA: A *kaalia* is a deep rich preparation where the base is prepared with slow-cooked onions and seasoned with assorted fragrant spices. The *kaalia* is best suited to heavier fishes such as carp and is essential Bengali festive fare. These days the same preparation is also prepared with goat meat for the carnivorous palate.

KOFTA: *Koftas* are dumplings made of minced meat, fish, and paneer, or vegetables like cabbage and raw bananas. The *koftas* are also called *muthiya* (fistful), because of the method of shaping and fashioning them with one's hands.

KORMA: A *korma* is a flavorful and rich curry mostly made with meat or fish. The gravy includes ghee as well as yogurt, together with bay leaves, coriander, cumin, chilies, and raisins. The *korma* sauce is usually cooked at a low temperature to avoid curdling.

PATURI: *Paturi* is a method of preparing food by wrapping it in a banana leaf and then steaming. Substituting other leaves or synthetic material (such as aluminum foil) for the banana leaf does not do justice to the unique flavor embued by the banana leaf, however it still captures the delicate softness created by this gentle method of steaming.

PORA: The Bengali word for "charred" or "burnt," to make *pora*, vegetables such as eggplant and taro and even fruits such as the green mango are first grilled after mixing in mustard oil and spices. The grilled items are then crushed and garnished with onions and green chilies before serving.

Chapter Two:
The Bengali Meal

A favorite Bengali folktale tells of a spice merchant named Dhanapati who lost his treasured bird. A woman named Khullana found it and when the merchant returned to get the bird, he fell in love with the maiden and married her. The traditional order of the Bengali meal follows what Khullana cooked for her new family as her first home-cooked meal. The first meal a bride cooks in her groom's house is called *Bou Bhaat* (Bride Rice). It is worth mentioning that in the legend Khullana's maid needed two men to carry the groceries for the day. It would be reasonable to assume that nowadays we do not have the time and large families to do justice to such a large food repertoire.

After years of teaching students how to cook, I have realized that some people relish structure in this area. To that end I have pieced together a collection of menus and offer suggestions for occasions, planning, and beverages that I believe will be helpful as you use this book. This should not, however, prevent the reader from trying the dishes individually, especially if desired to add to a menu. There are also suggestions for Bengali foods, such as chutney and cheese assortments, that make good appetizers or starters for any type of meal. I encourage the reader to experiment and develop your own combinations. My intention is really for you to try the dishes, enjoy their uniqueness, and make them a part of your life either as a Bengali platter or a part of a cosmopolitan table.

EATING THE BENGALI WAY

Kolkata is home to an amazing diversity of restaurants including authentic Bengali, Moghlai, Indo-Chinese, Continental (also known as Anglo-Indian), and Indo-Thai cuisine. This is reflective of the interesting history of Bengal as well as the cosmopolitan love of food shared and enjoyed by most Bengalis. The Bengali judges the success of an event, such as a wedding or any other social gathering for that matter, based on the quality of the food offered.

In *Eating India*, food writer Chitrita Banerji notes, "The Bengali meal, whether it is a wedding banquet or an ordinary day's repast, is structured in a sequence." This sequence moves the order of the dishes from the lighter to the heavier dishes, breaking with the sweet tart, and finally completing the meal with dessert.

The proper homestyle Bengali meal commences with *bhat* (rice), *dal* (lentils), and some *tetho* (bitter). These items are then complemented with vegetables, for instance a preparation of greens such as spinach or some vegetable medley such as a *chorchori*, and then there are the fish and/or meat dishes. While people tend to overemphasize the importance of fish in Bengali cuisine, the fish is much like the small diamond in a multi-gem setting, encircled by the amazing cornucopia of seasonal vegetables cooked in delicate and complex ways depending on the occasion. Bengali cuisine is frugal in its use of energy, so vegetables are often steamed with rice to maximize the energy used and food is sometimes slow cooked on the embers of dying coals.

Fish and meat dishes are followed by a sweet-and-sour chutney accompanied by crisp *papor* (lentil wafers), and the meal is finally finished with dessert. As in other parts of India, these items are served on large plate with small bowls. The *misti* (dessert) is very close to a Bengali's heart and often the quality of a formal meal, such as a wedding, is judged solely by the quality of the sweets offered. There are sweet shops literally on every block of the city so regularly buying sweets is part of the ritual of Bengali eating.

While some parts of India like stainless steel for their traditional dining plates, the Bengali metal of choice used to be bell metal, an alloy of brass and copper. Festive meals used to be served on fresh banana leaves, available in abundance in Bengal. In fact, it is a shame that such an earth-friendly tradition is losing out in popularity to paper plates. Also usually served on the leaves are wedges of lime, some green chilies, and a small amount of salt to allow the diner some flexibility and moderation in seasoning their food. Traditionally Bengalis eat with their hands; it is believed that this allows a deeper connection to the food.

There are variations between lunchtime and evening meals. I tried to make these distinctions in the menu section. The differences are usually very apparent during multi-day weddings. For example, the traditional dish called *shukto*, a vegetable medley that incorporates bitter gourds, is typically a lunchtime offering, and whole wheat flatbreads or crisp-fried *luchis* are usually evening offerings. In addition to the general distinction between morning and evening fare, there are a lot of foods that vary with seasons and festivals.

Outside of the regular meals, the Bengali foodie pays homage to street vendors and indulges in a multitude of snacks and foods ranging from the classic *jhal muri* (a mixture of puffed rice with tamarind, diced cooked potatoes, peanuts, minced cilantro, and green chilies) to the decadent *moghlai paratha* (a rich, flaky flatbread with a topping of beaten spiced eggs), and Bengali teatime comes with its own platter of special snacks. In fact I could write an entire book just on the teatime snacks of the Bengalis.

PRACTICAL EVERYDAY MENUS

I have not included any desserts in some of these menus, mostly because it is not very common to whip up a dessert on an everyday basis, despite the infamous Bengali sweet tooth. Bengalis usually rely on roadside confectionaries for their sweets. Typically natural yogurt with some sugar is preferred at home. As time permits, however, please do make recipes from the dessert section to satisfy your sweet tooth.

LUNCH
Lunch almost always features rice, usually in its simplest form—steamed white rice with a touch of ghee—but more festive varieties are also acceptable. The rice is accompanied by lentils and some form of palate-cleaning bitter vegetable, which is then usually followed by a fish or meat dish. When serving a regular course Bengali meal, I often tend to pick a baked main dish (mostly to accommodate my time allotment for the kitchen) that can be made in tandem with the rest of the meal.

Lunch Menu One

Yellow Rice *Turmeric Rice*
Orange Split Lentils with Caramelized Onions *Masoor Dal*
Spicy Crisp Bitter Melon Circles *Jhal Tauk Korolar Jhuri*
Fiddlehead Ferns with Potatoes and Nigella Seeds *Dheki Shaager Chorchori*
My Aunt's Lamb Casserole *Chotomashir Manshor Caserole*

Lunch Menu Two

Fine-Grained Refined White Rice *Kala Jeera Atap Chaal*
Roasted Yellow Split Lentils Tempered with Fennel Seeds
     Mouri Phoron Diye Bhaja Moong Dal
Creamed Spinach with Mustard *Shorshe Saag*
Tempered Mashed Potatoes with Eggs *Alu Dimer Bhortha*
Baked Fish in a Green Poppy Seed Paste *Dhone Posto Diye Bhapa Maach*

Lunch Menu Three

Spring Onion Pilaf *Piajkolir Pulao*
Yellow Split Peas with Cauliflower and Radishes
     Mulo ar Kopir Data Diye Motor Dal
Fish Roe Fritters *Macher Dimer Bora*
Creamed Spinach with Mustard *Shorshe Saag*
Chicken with Poppy Seed Sauce *Posto Murgi*

DINNER

The evening meal is a lighter meal and, if you are from West Bengal, this typically includes some form of bread. Lentils are not very common for the evening meal, with the exception of the cholar dal or Bengal gram lentils. To compliment the breads dishes, drier thicker sauces are selected.

Dinner Menu One

Unleavened Puffed Whole Wheat Flatbreads *Ruti*
My Uncle's Yellow Bengal Gram Lentils *Mesho's Cholar Dal*
Oven-Crisped Winter Squash *Kumro Bhaja*
Golden Cauliflower in Orange Mustard Sauce *Kamala Shorshe Phulkopi*
Rich Yogurt and Tomato Chicken *Kaasha Doi Tomato Murgi*

Dinner Menu Two

Mashed Smoked Eggplant *Begun Pora*
Eggs Cooked with Black Pepper and Fenugreek *Dim Morich*
Triangular Whole-Grain Flatbreads with Nigella Seeds
    Kalo Jire Diye Tekona Porota
Green Papaya Chutney *Plastic Chutney*

Dinner Menu Three

Spicy Multi-grain Flatbreads with Eggs *Anda Porota*
Dry Spiced Kohlrabi with Shrimp *Chingri Maach Diye Olkopir Ghanto*
Lamb or Goat Curry with Mint *Pudina Diye Mangshor Jhol*

SPECIAL OCCASION MENUS

Since I discuss festivals, culture, and general lifestyle in some detail through the course of this book, the next segment of menus is for times of joy and festivity.

A Sunday Morning Brunch
Robibarer Jhol Khabar

Fried Puffy Bread with Green Pea Filling *Matarshutir Kachoris*
Sweet Bengal Gram Lentils with Coconut and Raisins *Misti Cholar Dal*
Spicy Omelet Curry *Omelet Dalna*
Delicate Spongy Pancakes with Pineapple *Anaras Diye Chanar Malpoa*

A Relaxed Sunday Dinner or Luncheon
Robibarer Feast

Fine-Grained Refined White Rice *Kala Jeera Atap Chaal*
My Grandmother's Festive Rice with Vegetables *Didimar Fried Rice*
Yellow Split Peas with Cauliflower and Radishes
   Mulo ar Kopir Data Diye Motor Dal
Poppy Seed and Green Chili Fritters *Posto Bora*
Creamed Spinach with Mustard *Shorshe Shaag*
Creamy Shrimp Curry *Chingri Maacher Korma*
Mutton or Lamb Curry with Potatoes and Bell Peppers
   Alu Capsicum Diye Mansho
Tomato, Cranberry and Date Chutney *Tomato, Cranberry ar Khejurer Chaatney*
Almond, Maple and Tapioca Pudding *Badam Doodher Payesh*

A Classic Festive Vegetarian Meal
Pujor Kabar

Yellow Lentil Risotto *Moonger Daler Khichuri*
Julienne Pan-Fried Potatoes *Alu Bhaja*
Onion Rings with Nigella Seeds *Gol Piyaji*
Fried Squash Blossoms *Kumro Phul Bhaja*
Roasted or Fried Lentil Wafers *Papor*
Fresh Pineapple Chutney *Anaraser Chaatney*
Cottage Cheese Cakes *Sandesh*

A Vegetarian Feast
Niramish Kabar

Essential Bengali Festive Rice *Ghee Bhaat*
Deep-Fried Puffy Breads *Luchis*
Orange Split Lentils with Tomatoes and Cilantro
  Tomato Dhoney Pata Diye Masoor Dal
Lightly Spiced Pan-Fried Eggplant *Begun Bhaja*
Fresh Sauteed Okra with Mustard *Shorshe Bhindi*
Green Plantain Cakes in a Creamy Sauce *Kach Kolar Kopta*
Channa Pudding *Channar Payesh*

A Tired Traveler's Meal
Klanto Pothiker Kabar

Fine-Grained Refined White Rice *Kala Jeera Atap Chaal*
Spicy Mashed Potatoes or Taro *Alu ba Kochu Sheddo*
Orange Split Lentils with Caramelized Onions *Masoor Dal*

My Grandmother's Lunchtime Meal
Didimar Dupoorer Kabar

Fine-Grained Refined White Rice *Kala Jeera Atap Chaal*
Yellow Split Lentils with Fish Head *Macher Muro Diye Moong Dal*
Lightly Spiced Pan-Sauteed Okra *Bhindi Bhaja*
Malabar Spinach with Vegetables and Shrimp *Pui Chingri Chorchori*
Baked Curried Tamarind Swordfish or Hilsa *Tetul Diye Ilish Maach*
Fish in a Light Ginger Gravy *Halka Pabda Maacher Jhol*
Roasted or Fried Lentil Wafers *Papor*
Green Papaya Chutney *Plastic Chutney*

A Muslim-Inspired Festive Meal
Nobabi Kabar

Saffron Rice with Meatballs *Moti Churi Biryani*
Spicy Multi-grain Flatbreads with Eggs *Anda Porota*
Turnips and Green Peas in Coconut Sauce *Salgam Monoroma*
Lemon, Chickpea and Cucumber Salad *Soshar Salad*
Vermicelli Pudding with Almonds and Pistachios *Simoyer Payesh*

An Anglo Indian Inspired Christmas
Baro Diner Ranna

Anglo-Indian Rice and Lentil Pilaf with Fish *Reclaimed Kedgeree*
Roasted Chicken Marinated with Lemon, Chilies, and Molasses *Moorgir Roast*
Ground Lamb Stuffed Mini Peppers in Onion Cardamom Sauce *Choto Capsicumer Dolma*
Anglo-Indian Fruit Cake

Spice One: Mustard Seeds

Black mustard seeds are a key component of the Bengali Five Spice Blend (*panch phoron*; see page 5). The mustard seed is black in color with a yellow inside, and the spice in its very basic form is bitter to taste but mellows to a nutty flavor when warmed and popped. It is essential to the Bengali cuisine, much like the staple rice. The mustard seed features in the famous mustard paste and golden mustard oil, which no Bengali table is without. Unlike in certain other regional cuisines, however, the mustard seed is not usually used whole for cooking outside of the *panch phoron* blend.

Grinding and working with mustard seeds seems so effortless when watching the Bengali cook grind them on the grinding stone, but it has taken me a lot of trial and error to achieve a consistency that cuts the bitterness and yields the sharp creamy taste that works for mustard-based sauces. The real trick is to soak the mustard seeds for an adequate period and to use a good, sharp variety of green chili for the paste. The long soaking period softens the seeds, to avoid over-processing by the mechanical grinder which tends to cause a bitter taste.

After a lot of effort, I realized that there are now mustard powders that can help one out in a bind. There is a difference, however, in texture, taste, and appearance when you use the powdered variety.

(See recipes for mustard pastes, pages 15-16.)

Chapter Three:
Rice and Breads
Bhaat ar Ruti

Rice is the staple grain in the Bengali diet. In fact, the colloquial way to inquire if someone has eaten is to ask whether they have eaten their rice: "*Bhaat Khecho*?" A simple invitation to join the family for rice and lentils (*dal bhat*) is akin to a Middle Eastern host inviting a guest to break bread. Bengalis consider it inauspicious for the home pantry to run out of rice. There is usually a small amount of rice placed near the Goddess Lakshmi who is usually depicted as the household goddess of wealth and prosperity and is a common fixture in Hindu Bengali households. In fact, in some traditional Bengali households, the afternoon meal, including the rice, is cooked early so that the "bread (or should I say rice?) winner" is fed before he or she leaves for work, at around ten in the morning.

In some houses, the refined rice of choice is the parboiled rice known as *sheddo chaal*. This is a healthier rice option, since it is unpolished and has more nutrients, much like brown rice. Parboiled rice is partially boiled in the husk. The three basic steps of parboiling are soaking, steaming, and drying. These steps also make rice easier to process by hand, boost its nutritional profile (other than its vitamin-B content which is denatured), and change its texture to a coarser one. I have to confess it is not very popular in my own family.

The other white rice of choice is the tiny-grained and very fragrant rice *govinda bhog* or *kala jeera*. It is available in most Indian stores and some specialty stores. The more commonly available basmati rice can be substituted if you cannot find the *kala jeera*, which is usually reserved for fancier rice dishes rather than being eaten in its simpler steamed form.

LEARNING THE ROPES AWAY FROM HOME

When I left home for graduate school, I did not have a clue about making rice. I had no idea that the steaming plate of fragrant, white goodness that accompanied most mealtimes needed precision or timing. I tried to put whatever culinary know-how I had to work, but I was floundering.

By my third week in the U.S., homesickness partly manifested itself as a craving for rice and other familiar foods. This led me to spend extra time talking to other Indian students. Finally, after sharing my plight with a fellow rice-eating South Indian student (yes, rice is the staple in most parts of South India, too), I was given a decent tutorial on how to make the short-grained variety of rice (which is interestingly sold in the U.S. as "fine long grain rice"). I am happy to note that I have since learned how to cook rice like a true Bengali and can guide you through this wonderful journey.

Rice Ceremony
Annaprashan

When a child is six months old, the introduction of the first solid foods, usually rice in the form of rice pudding, is a formal event called *annaprashan.* The ancient name for this rice pudding used to be *paramanna* or "the ultimate food" and this combination of rice, milk, and sugar was considered auspicious. Rice puddings are also the traditional birthday offering, once it has been blessed and offered to the divine deity.

The first feeding of solid food to the infant is usually done by the child's maternal uncle (*mama*), or if the uncle is not available the child's maternal grand-father. There are other interesting rituals, like offering a child an assortment of items to choose from, such as a pen, money, or soil. The child's choice in turn determines their life's direction. My brother was present for both my children's rice ceremonies and I was lucky to also have my parents for my son's rice ceremony. In fact, my mother had made the rice pudding for his *Annaprashan* herself.

Other rituals emphasize the importance of rice during religious ceremonies. The un-husked grains of rice called *dhan* are essential in prayer offerings. The *dhan* is also used during the *Ashirbad* blessing ceremony in which prospective brides and grooms are blessed by all the senior members of their families.

COOKING AND SERVING RICE

Plain white rice is preferred with Bengali food. When fancier variations of rice are prepared, some plain white rice is also served. This is not the case with meat-based rice dishes or the rice and lentil risotto-like porridges (*khichuri*) since these are considered one-dish meals.

BASIC RICE

The Bengali way of cooking rice is to ensure that the grains are just a shade softer than the consistency we call al dente. While I do have one rice cooker recipe in this collection of recipes, Bengalis prefer not to cook rice by letting it absorb all the water, but rather prefer cooking it in a lot of water and draining out the remaining liquid. I have seen this draining process done all my life by placing a loose lid or plate over the top of the rice pot and sliding this very slightly, creating a space that is small enough to block the rice, but comfortable enough to let the water slide out. The pot is usually held with a kitchen towel and tilted on the side of the opening to let the water drain out. But after dropping a pot of rice once, I learned to use a colander for this purpose!

My grandmother would use the term "*jhor jhore*" which in culinary parlance means that the grains are soft, but separate. Actually, much like the texture of pasta in Italian cooking, getting the texture of rice correct is the signature of a good Bengali cook.

PARBOILED RICE
Sheddo Chaal

This parboiled variety of rice cooked with some of the husk left is preferred in Bengali households, especially those in the countryside. The fans of this variety of rice argue that its more earthy taste lends character to the meal.

Cook Time: 25 minutes | **Makes:** 4 servings

INGREDIENTS
1 cup parboiled rice (such as ponni rice sold in Indian grocery stores)

PREPARATION
Place the rice and 6 to 8 cups water in a large pot and bring to a simmer. Cook on medium low heat for about 25 minutes. Drain the rice thoroughly in a colander and serve hot.

FINE-GRAINED REFINED WHITE RICE
Kala Jeera Atap Chaal

This refined white rice is really what features commonly on the Bengali table. A few varieties of white rice are commonly used, however, *govinda bhog* or the *kala jeera* rice is what I grew up with. These varieties are available just like basmati rice in large bags at Indian groceries.

Prep Time: 5 minutes | **Cook Time:** 13 minutes | **Makes:** 4 servings

INGREDIENTS
1 cup kala jeera rice
1 teaspoon ghee (clarified butter; optional)
1 teaspoon salt (optional)

PREPARATION
Place the rice and 4 cups of water in a large pot and bring the water to a simmer. Cook on medium-low heat for about 12 minutes, until the rice is soft but not mushy. Drain the rice thoroughly in a colander and serve hot with the ghee and the salt if you choose to use them.

> **Note:** If you choose to use basmati rice, cook the same way as the kala jeera, but it needs about 5 extra minutes to cook. I tend to use basmati rice fairly frequently and it does not impact the taste when used as a basic white rice. It used to be more expensive and therefore treated more as a luxury rather than an everyday rice item in Bengali cuisine.

FRAGRANT BROTH (FOR COOKING BENGALI PILAFS)
Aakhni

Prep/Cook Time: 1 hour (mostly unattended) | **Makes:** about 4 to 5 cups

INGREDIENTS
10 bay leaves
2 large black cardamom pods
4 to 6 green cardamom pods
10 to 12 cloves
2 or 3 cinnamon sticks, broken into pieces
2 teaspoons salt

PREPARATION
Place all the ingredients and 6 to 8 cups of water in a large pot and simmer the mixture for 1 hour. If you have more time you can do this for 3 to 4 hours. Cool and strain the fragrant water and use as needed to cook rice (see following recipe).

ESSENTIAL BENGALI FESTIVE RICE
Ghee Bhaat

Ghee bhaat literally translates to "rice cooked with clarified butter." It is usually served alongside plain rice for weddings and other festive occasions. The rice is cooked in a broth called *aakhni* (see above) made with fragrant spices. If you don't have time to make the *aakhni*, you can just use water, which is what I do fairly often.

Prep Time: 5 minutes | **Cook Time:** 25 minutes (not including *aakhni* prep)
Makes: 6 servings

INGREDIENTS
1½ cups kala jeera rice
1 teaspoon salt
¼ teaspoon lime juice
2 tablespoons ghee (clarified butter)
3 or 4 green cardamom pods
2-inch cinnamon stick, broken into pieces
2 or 3 dried bay leaves
2 or 3 cloves
1 teaspoon sugar
½ cup cashew nuts
2 cups Fragrant Broth (*Aakhni*, see above) or water
2 tablespoons raisins

PREPARATION

Place the rice, 4 cups of water, and salt in a large pot. Bring to a boil and add the lime juice. Cook for 3 to 5 minutes. Drain the rice thoroughly in a colander.

In a small skillet, heat the ghee and add the cardamoms, cinnamon stick, bay leaves, cloves, and sugar and stir well. Add the cashew nuts and cook for about 1 minute, stirring frequently. Add the parboiled rice and broth and bring to a simmer. Add the raisins, cover, and cook for 10 minutes. Turn off the heat and leave the rice undisturbed for 5 to 10 minutes before serving.

MY GRANDMOTHER'S FESTIVE RICE WITH VEGETABLES
Didimar Fried Rice

This extremely fragrant mixed vegetable fried-rice dish is made with basmati rice. I "adapted" the recipe based on memories of watching my maternal grandmother prepare it. Her recipes were never written out in specific measurements, so I really had to rely on my memory. Sometimes I add small shrimp and caramelized sliced onions to it.

Prep Time: 15 minutes (plus 1 hour for pre-soaking the rice)
Cook Time: 45 minutes | **Makes:** 4 to 5 servings

INGREDIENTS
1½ cups basmati rice, pre-soaked for about 1 hour
3 tablespoons ghee or butter
1 teaspoon salt
1 teaspoon turmeric
1 teaspoon sugar
2 or 3 bay leaves
1 star anise
4 green cardamom pods
4 cloves
4-inch cinnamon stick, broken into pieces
1½ cups mixed fresh chopped vegetables (use a colorful mixture such as carrots, beans, peas, cauliflower)
⅓ cup broken cashews
⅓ cup raisins

PREPARATION
Rinse the rice and drain thoroughly. Heat 2 tablespoons ghee or butter in a saucepan on medium heat for about 1 minute. Add the rice, salt, turmeric, sugar, and whole spices and fry well for at least 10 minutes, until the rice changes color to beige.

In a separate skillet, heat the remaining 1 tablespoon ghee and add the vegetables, cashews, and raisins. Cook for 5 to 7 minutes. Add to the rice along with 2 cups of water and cover. Cook on low heat for 18 minutes. Turn off the heat and let the rice rest for 10 minutes before serving.

RICE PILAF WITH CHICKEN
Murgir Nobabi Pulao

This multi-layered and fragrant rice dish with aromatic spices is a close cousin of the *biryani*, an elaborate multilayered casserole of marinated meat and rice. This recipe is a little drier and a little simpler to make and does not require marinating the chicken in yogurt. Recipes such as this are generally inspired by the Muslim style of cooking.

Prep Time: 25 minutes (plus 1 hour for pre-soaking rice)
Cook Time: 45 to 50 minutes (largely unattended) | **Makes:** 6 to 8 servings

INGREDIENTS
2 cups basmati rice, presoaked for about 1 hour
⅓ cup oil
1 medium red onion, finely chopped
1 teaspoon fresh ginger paste (page 13)
3 or 4 cloves garlic, pressed
1 teaspoon turmeric
2 teaspoons salt
2 green chilies, finely chopped
2 teaspoons cumin-coriander powder (page 17)
¾ teaspoon cayenne pepper powder
3 tomatoes, finely chopped
2 pounds chicken, skinned and cut into pieces (with bones)
3 green cardamom pods
4 cloves
4-inch cinnamon stick, broken into pieces
1 tablespoon ghee (clarified butter)
⅓ cup broken cashew nuts
1 recipe brown onions (see page 42)

PREPARATION
Drain the rice. Heat the oil in a saucepan and add the onion, ginger paste, and garlic. Cook the mixture for about 6 to 8 minutes until the onions soften and begin to turn a pale golden color.

Add the turmeric, salt, green chilies, cumin-coriander powder, cayenne pepper powder, tomatoes, and chicken. Cook, stirring frequently, until any liquid evaporates and the chicken is well browned, about 10 to 12 minutes.

Mix in the cardamom pods, cloves, cinnamon stick, 2 cups water, and rice and bring to a simmer. Reduce the temperature and cover and cook the rice on low heat for about 25 minutes.

Remove the cover, add the ghee and cashews, and stir gently. Mix in the brown onions before serving.

BROWN ONIONS
Bhaja Piyaj

Prep Time: 10 minutes | **Cook Time:** 15 minutes | **Makes:** ½ cup

INGREDIENTS
⅓ cup oil
1 teaspoon sugar
2 onions, thinly sliced

PREPARATION
Heat the oil in a medium wok or skillet. Add the sugar and onions, cook on low heat, stirring occasionally, until the onions soften and wilt and gradually begin to curl at the edges. Continue cooking until the onions turn golden and crisp, watching carefully so onions do not burn. Gently remove the onions from the pan and drain on paper towels. (Use in the pilaf recipe on page 41.)

SPRING ONION PILAF
Piajkolir Pulao

A truly light and elegant pilaf, this is an understated and delicate recipe that complements most meals, from simple to elaborate. The spring onions (*piaj koli*) are the greens of the onion plant— you can usually find them in farmers markets, but can substitute scallions if needed.

Prep Time: 5 minutes | **Cook Time:** 25 minutes | **Makes:** 4 to 6 servings

INGREDIENTS
1 tablespoon ghee (clarified butter)
1 cup chopped spring onions
1 cup kala jeera rice
1 teaspoon garam masala (page 17)
2 or 3 whole bay leaves
½ teaspoon turmeric
1 teaspoon salt
1 teaspoon sugar

PREPARATION
Heat the ghee in a saucepan; add the onions and rice and cook the mixture stirring constantly for 5 minutes. The onions should soften and begin to turn pale golden.

Add the garam masala, bay leaves, turmeric, salt, sugar, and 1½ cups water. Bring to a boil and then cook covered on low heat for 20 minutes. Turn off the heat and let this rest for another 5 minutes, fluff the rice and serve.

MY MOTHER'S FISH HEAD PILAF WITH VEGETABLES
Muro Bhaat

The simple vestiges of tradition and commonality one retains in life are often what become "culture" in the larger sense. The traditional word for mother in Bengali is *Ma*. One of these little traditions for me was my insistence on being called "*Ma*" by my children, even though that name is not typically used in America anymore.

This is my Ma's recipe for fish head pilaf. Rich in flavor and full of omega 3 oils, fish heads are quite the delicacy in Bengali cooking. In fact, they are considered a source of brain power. My Ma's *muro bhaat* included more rice than some recipes do, as well as richer flavors and an assortment of my favorite veggies. This recipe was revived when my parents visited me from India when my babies were born. Ma would get carp from the local Chinese store, make the *muro bhaat* with the head, and use the rest of the fish for everyday food. This can be made with the head of any fish, with the exception of salmon or fish like it. The lemon and chopped cilantro are optional—they are really garnishes that I prefer as healthy substitutes for the clarified butter that typically finishes the dish.

Prep Time: 15 to 20 minutes | **Cook Time:** 45 minutes | **Makes:** 4 to 6 servings

INGREDIENTS
1 medium fish head
1 teaspoon turmeric
2 teaspoons salt
3 to 4 tablespoons oil
1 onion, thinly sliced
1 teaspoon minced fresh ginger
2 or 3 cloves
3 green cardamom pods
2-inch cinnamon stick, broken into pieces
2 bay leaves
1 teaspoon cayenne pepper powder
¾ cup rice (preferably kala jeera)
1 cup chopped cauliflower
1 cup green peas (fresh or frozen)
1 lemon (optional)
1 tablespoon chopped cilantro (optional)

PREPARATION
Rub the fish head with turmeric and 1 teaspoon of salt and set aside for 15 minutes. Heat half the oil in a wok on medium heat and cook the fish head for 6 to 8 minutes on each side, until browned and soft and crisp at spots. Break into pieces (you should be able to do this with a regular wooden spoon which is an indicator of the doneness of the fish head) and set aside.

Add the remaining oil to the wok and add the onion and ginger and sauté for less than a minute. Add the cloves, cardamoms, cinnamon stick, bay leaves, cayenne pepper powder, and remaining teaspoon of salt, and stir well and roast for about 2 minutes. Add the rice and mix well and cook for another 4 minutes.

Add the fish head pieces and mix well. Add the cauliflower and green peas and mix well. Add 1½ cups water and bring to a simmer on medium heat. Cover and cook the mixture for 20 minutes until the water has been absorbed and the rice is soft. Remove from heat and let rest for about 10 minutes. Cut the lemon in half (if using) and squeeze in the lemon juice and stir in the cilantro.

SAFFRON RICE WITH MEATBALLS
Moti Churi Biryani

I created this dish for my father. He loved recipes that were authentic in style but had been tweaked by me. I used to buy store-bought ground chicken, but lately I have been grinding my own in a food processor. This allows me to use good-quality free range chicken, which I find more flavorful and healthier too.

Prep Time: 15 minutes (plus 30 minutes for soaking rice)
Cook Time: 50 minutes | **Makes:** 4 to 6 servings

INGREDIENTS
Meatballs
1 small onion
1-inch piece fresh ginger, peeled
2 cloves garlic
2 green chilies
1 pound ground chicken
1 teaspoon turmeric
1 teaspoon salt
1 teaspoon garam masala (page 17)
1 teaspoon cumin-coriander powder (page 17)

Rice
3 to 4 tablespoons oil
1 teaspoon ghee (clarified butter)
3 green cardamom pods
2 cloves
2-inch cinnamon stick, broken into pieces
1 large onion, thinly sliced
1 teaspoon sugar
2 cups basmati rice, soaked for about 30 minutes and drained
2 teaspoons salt
1 cup low-fat Greek yogurt, beaten till smooth
½ cup frozen peas
1 teaspoon saffron strands

PREPARATION
Make meatballs:
Preheat the oven to 350 degrees F. Process the onion, ginger, garlic, and green chilies in a food processor until finely chopped. Mix this with the ground chicken and add the turmeric, salt, garam masala, and cumin-coriander powder, and mix well (I like to use my hands for this purpose to get this evenly mixed). Grease a baking sheet with oil or cooking spray. Shape the chicken mixture into walnut-size meatballs and place on the baking sheet. Bake for 7 to 8 minutes, turning over once. (It is important to cook the meatballs thoroughly, but make sure they do not dry out.)

Make the rice:
Heat the oil and ghee in a saucepan and add the cardamom pods, cloves, cinnamon stick, and onion. Stir in the sugar and cook on low for 10 to 15 minutes. Stir in the rice, salt, yogurt, peas, and 2 cups water and cook on low heat for 25 minutes. The rice should be fluffy and cooked through at this point. Carefully mix in the saffron and check seasonings.

Gently mix the meatballs into the rice, cover, and let simmer for at least 5 to 7 minutes on low heat. Turn off heat and let rice rest for 5 minutes before serving.

RICE WITH BEETS AND GREEN PEAS
Beet diye Ghee Bhaat

An important part of the Bengali cultural identity is the writings, songs, and thinking of the Bengali poet and nobel laureate Rabindranath Tagore. I have tried to teach my children some of his music, which I love, and I hope that in time, they'll want to explore more of this rich heritage.

One of our favorite Tagore songs describes *Shiter Haowa* (the winter breeze). Late fall weather in New York is close to the Indian winter, and in fact, the beets that we grow in our garden are also a winter hallmark in the Bengali garden. This beautiful creation is perfect for a cool fall day—pretty, nutritious, and fragrant.

Prep Time: 10 minutes (plus 1 hour for pre-soaking rice)
Cook Time: 40 minutes | **Makes:** 4 servings

INGREDIENTS
2 teaspoons ghee (clarified butter)
1 small white onion, finely chopped
4 cloves
3-inch cinnamon stick, broken into pieces
3 green cardamom pods
1 tablespoon coarsely chopped cashew nuts
1 tablespoon raisins
1 beet, peeled and grated
1 teaspoon salt
1 cup kala jeera rice, soaked for 1 hour and drained
½ cup frozen peas

PREPARATION

Heat the ghee in a saucepan on medium heat. Add the chopped onion and cook for 4 to 5 minutes, until soft and beginning to turn golden. Lightly crush the cloves, cinnamon stick, and cardamom pods in a mortar. Add to the onions along with the cashew nuts and raisins and cook until the nuts are lightly browned.

Add the beet, salt, and rice, and mix well. Add 1 cup water and cook on low heat for 10 minutes. Stir well, add ½ cup water and the peas and cook on low for another 10 minutes, until the rice is cooked through and not sticky. Turn off the heat and let the rice rest for another 10 minutes. Fluff and serve.

SLOW-COOKED RICE WITH SAFFRON, SHRIMP AND ROSEWATER
Kacchi Biryani

I picked up a lot of recipes of various origins during my graduate school days, often by watching visiting parents of fellow students cook. I firmly believe that the best, most authentic cooking occurs at home, at least that is the case with regional Indian cooking.

This recipe was learned by watching Mrs. Siddhique, a parent of one of my fellow students from Bangladesh. It is simpler than most *biryani* recipes and has a wonderful flavor. The original version was rather rich and took a long time and precision to make, since it was made with fatty goat meat. I loved the flavors, especially the combination of saffron and rosewater, so I have adapted it for a more manageable version using large shrimp. A *kacchi biryani* essentially means that raw meat (or in my version shrimp) is marinated and then cooked along with the rice. (In a lot of versions of *biryani* you parboil the meat or lamb before adding it to the rice, hence the term *kacchi* which means "raw.") The key to this dish is marinating the shrimp well and having patience during the process of slow and gentle cooking.

Prep Time: 1½ hours (includes 1 hour to marinate shrimp and soak rice)
Cook Time: 1½ hours (mostly unattended) | **Makes:** 6 servings

INGREDIENTS
Shrimp
1-inch piece fresh ginger, peeled
5 or 6 garlic cloves
1 teaspoon cayenne pepper powder
1 teaspoon fennel seeds
1½ teaspoons coriander seeds
1½ teaspoons garam masala (see page 17)
1½ cups sour cream
2 teaspoons salt
2 pounds jumbo shrimp, shelled

Biryani
Oil for frying
2 potatoes, peeled and quartered
2 teaspoons salt
Orange food coloring (optional)
4 onions, thinly sliced
1½ cups white basmati rice, soaked for at least 30 minutes and rinsed well
1 teaspoon cardamom seeds
2 or 3 cloves
3-inch cinnamon stick, broken into pieces
1 teaspoon black peppercorns
3 or 4 bay leaves
1 teaspoon saffron threads
2 tablespoons milk
2 tablespoons ghee (clarified butter)
2 to 3 teaspoons rosewater
Sliced almonds for garnish

PREPARATION
Prepare shrimp:
Place the ginger, garlic, cayenne pepper powder, fennel seeds, coriander seeds, garam masala, and sour cream in a blender and blend for a good 5 minutes until the mixture is smooth and well mixed. Pour this mixture into a large bowl; add the salt and shrimp and let marinate for an hour at room temperature (60 degrees F. or below). I usually continue preparing the rest of the dish while the shrimp is marinating.

Prepare the biryani:
Heat some oil in a wok or skillet, add the potatoes and fry until crisp and golden. Sprinkle with salt and a little food coloring, if using, but do not mix the food coloring in thoroughly since this later mixes with the rice to give it a streaked appearance. Remove potatoes from pan and set aside.

Add the onions to the wok or skillet, in batches if needed, and fry until they soften and turn crisp and golden. Drain on paper towels.

In a heavy-bottomed pot with a tight-fitting lid, heat 3 tablespoons oil. Add the rice and fry for about 2 to 3 minutes. Add the cardamom seeds, cloves, cinnamon stick, peppercorns, and bay leaves. Lightly mix in the shrimp mixture along with 1¾ cup water. Cover the pot and cook this mixture on very low heat undisturbed for 45 minutes.

Soak the saffron strands in the milk for a few minutes. Remove the cover from the rice and sprinkle in the saffron milk and rosewater. Add the ghee and cook for another 20 minutes.

Stir the rice mixture gently and mix in the fried potatoes and onions. Garnish with the sliced almonds before serving.

RICE AND LENTIL PILAF
Bhuni Khichuri

The combination of rice and lentils is called *khichuri* in Bengal. The more common varieties are usually wet but I have given here a *bhuni* (dry) version that is more like a pilaf or festive rice.

My grandmother told me that the ideal *bhuni khichuri* should retain the shape of the lentils, but they should be separate and cooked through, so they are soft and powdery to touch. I use chicken broth in this recipe to enhance the flavor without adding more ghee, but the traditional Bengali version would not include broth.

Prep Time: 5 minutes | **Cook Time:** 40 minutes | **Makes:** 4 servings

INGREDIENTS
2 tablespoons oil
1 teaspoon cumin seeds
1 small red onion, finely chopped
1 teaspoon fresh ginger paste (page 13)
1 or 2 bay leaves
2 or 3 cardamom pods
2-inch cinnamon stick, broken into pieces
¼ teaspoon turmeric
¾ cup dried yellow split lentils (moong dal)
2 cups chicken broth or water
1 cup basmati rice
¾ teaspoon salt

Garnish
3 tablespoons finely chopped cilantro
Juice of 1 lime
1 teaspoon ghee (clarified butter)

PREPARATION
Heat the oil in a saucepan. Add the cumin seeds and sizzle for a few seconds. Add the onion, ginger paste, remaining spices, and yellow lentils. Sauté this well for 3 to 4 minutes, until the lentils begin turning light brown.

Add 1 cup chicken broth and cook on high until well absorbed. Add the rice, remaining 1 cup broth, and salt. Stir well, cover, and cook for 20 more minutes on very low heat until rice is fairly soft.

Remove from heat and let sit undisturbed for about 5 minutes. Remove the lid and gently fluff the rice. Stir in the cilantro. Squeeze in the lime juice and add the ghee. Fluff the rice before serving.

ANGLO-INDIAN RICE AND LENTIL PILAF WITH FISH
Reclaimed Kedgeree

Anglo-Indians (people of mixed British and Indian heritage) contribute an interesting dimension to the cuisine of India. This recipe is a re-hash of a dish called *kedgeree*, an Anglo-Indian adaptation of *khichuri* (rice and lentils) made with a combination of rice, cream, eggs, and smoked fish. One afternoon, I had some good sea bass that I cooked up with eggs, and this recipe was born. My friend Julianna once asked me about the name of this recipe. I named this "Reclaimed Kedgeree" because *kedgeree* is an Anglo-Indian take on an Indian dish, and this one is an Indian take back. The mild flavors of this recipe make it very popular for the brunch table.

Prep Time: 20 minutes | **Cook Time:** 40 minutes | **Makes:** 4 servings

INGREDIENTS
2 tablespoons oil
2 bay leaves
2 cloves
3 green cardamom pods
2-inch cinnamon stick, broken into pieces
1 red onion, finely chopped
1 teaspoon grated fresh ginger
½ cup cooked and flaked fresh white fish
1 teaspoon salt
1 teaspoon sugar
1 teaspoon cumin-coriander powder (page 17)
1 teaspoon cayenne pepper powder
¾ cup dried orange/red split lentils (masoor dal)
1 cup kala jeera rice
½ cup half and half
Juice of 1 lime
2 tablespoons chopped cilantro
1 teaspoon ghee (clarified butter)
3 hard-boiled eggs, chopped
Lots of freshly ground black pepper

PREPARATION
Heat the oil in a saucepan. Add the bay leaves, cloves, cardamom pods, and cinnamon stick and sauté for 30 seconds. Add the onion and ginger and cook for 3 to 5 minutes. Add the fish, salt, sugar, and powdered spices and cook for another 3 to 5 minutes.

Add the lentils and rice and stir until the rice is well coated with the spices. Add 1½ cups water and bring to a boil. Reduce heat and simmer for 12 minutes. Stir in the half and half and lime juice and cook for another 6 to 7 minutes. Turn off the heat, add the cilantro, ghee, and eggs and gently stir. Let the rice rest for 10 minutes. Add lots of freshly ground black pepper before serving.

YELLOW LENTIL RISOTTO
Mooger Daler Khichuri

This recipe is a traditional variation of the rice and lentil porridge called *khichuri*. The key to a good Bengali *khichuri*, much like a risotto, is to ensure that the consistency is creamy and that the grains are cooked through but not mushy. It is also important that the proportion of lentils is greater than the amount of rice by about one-third.

This *khichuri* (made with yellow split lentils) first surfaces in Bengal during the spring festival of Saraswati Puja. This festival marks the beginning of spring and is celebrated with a prayer and invocation to Saraswati, the Goddess of Learning. Several spring fruits, including an Indian berry called *kool,* are first offered to the Goddess before being eaten for the season.

Prep Time: 15 minutes | **Cook Time:** 30 to 40 minutes | **Makes:** 4 to 6 servings

INGREDIENTS
¾ cup dried yellow split lentils (moong dal)
½ cup kala jeera rice
¾ teaspoon salt
½ teaspoon turmeric
1 tablespoon ginger-cumin-coriander paste (page 14)
1 small potato, peeled and cut into small pieces
½ cup chopped cauliflower
1 tablespoon ghee (clarified butter)
1 teaspoon cumin seeds
2 or 3 bay leaves
2-inch cinnamon stick, broken into pieces

PREPARATION
Roast the lentils in a pot over medium heat, stirring frequently, for about 5 minutes, until very fragrant and pale golden. Add about 1 cup water and cook on medium heat until the water is evaporated. Add another 1 cup water, the rice, salt, turmeric, ginger-cumin-coriander paste, potato, and cauliflower and cook, covered, on low heat for about 20 minutes. Gradually add another 2 cups of water as needed until the rice and dal are soft but still intact (in other words it should not be too mushy or thick, the finished dish should have a creamy porridge or rissoto consistency).

In a small skillet, heat the ghee and add the cumin seeds, bay leaves, and cinnamon stick and cook until the cumin seeds sizzle and the bay leaves and cinnamon stick darken. Pour this over the *khichuri* and enjoy!

Handwriting Ritual

Another tradition associated with the Saraswati Puja festival is the handwriting ritual called *hate khori* (literally meaning "chalk in hand"). Little children who haven't learned to write yet come in with a slate and chalk and the priest helps them write the alphabet and then blesses it. The slate is cleaned with a milk-dabbed cloth a few days later and the student is ready to commence writing.

My daughter began writing in-between two Saraswati Pujas and hence began her education without the benefit of such blessing. She has now migrated to the computer and I sometimes think modern-day children should actually get their kiddy laptops blessed instead of the chalkboard, particularly since many of them tend to learn to type before actually writing!

RED LENTILS AND RISOTTO
Masoor Daler Khichuri

Our daughter Deepta arrived three weeks early, our first signal that life would need to be planned around our children, rather than expecting them to conform to our schedules. I happened to spend the snowy day before she was born at home making *khichuri*. My husband very diligently froze the leftovers, and this was what we ate once I returned from the hospital with the baby, so the dish always reminds me of her arrival. In this version I've added tomatoes and cilantro to give a contemporary touch to the recipe.

Prep Time: 15 minutes | **Cook Time:** 50 minutes (mostly unattended)
Makes: 6 servings

INGREDIENTS
1 cup dried orange/red split lentils (masoor dal)
½ teaspoon turmeric
⅔ cup rice (preferably kala jeera)
1 tablespoon ginger-cumin-coriander paste (page 14)
2 tomatoes, finely chopped
3 or 4 green chilies, slit halfway lengthwise
1 teaspoon sugar
1 teaspoon salt
3 tablespoons oil
1 medium red onion, finely chopped
2 tablespoons chopped cilantro
1 tablespoon ghee (clarified butter)
1 teaspoon cumin seeds

PREPARATION

In a large, heavy-bottomed pan put the red lentils and about 3 cups water and bring to a simmer over medium heat. Add the turmeric and simmer for about 20 minutes. Add the rice, 3 more cups water, ginger-cumin-coriander paste, tomatoes, green chilies, sugar, and salt and simmer for about 25 minutes on medium heat, stirring occasionally. The rice and lentil mixture should be a porridge-like consistency (add more water if too thick).

While this is cooking, heat the oil in a wok or skillet and add the onion and cook on medium heat until soft and pale golden. Stir the onions into the rice and lentil mixture and cook for about 5 minutes. Turn off the heat and stir in the cilantro.

Heat the ghee in a small skillet and add the cumin seeds and cook for about 40 seconds until the cumin seeds darken and turn fragrant. Pour the spice mixture over the rice and lentils. Stir lightly and serve the mixture hot.

SOPHISTICATED MIXED LENTIL KHICHURI
Stylish Char Mishali Khichuri

The appeal of this lentil porridge rests in the relative complexity of its ingredients. I use split Bengal lentils (*cholar dal*) with a mixture of three other lentils. The *khichuri* is pre-cooked, seasoned, and then finished off in the slow cooker. If you do not have a slow cooker, it can be done on a stove top on very low heat, but this will need more attention from the cook. This recipe has become quite a hit and people often ask me to make it, so I have enhanced it with elegant garnishes such as fresh radishes and micro greens.

Prep Time: 20 minutes | **Cook Time:** 6 hours (mostly unattended in slow cooker)
Makes: 10 to 12 servings

INGREDIENTS
¾ cup dried yellow Bengali gram lentils (cholar dal)
⅓ cup dried yellow split lentils (moong dal)
1 cup dried orange/red split lentils (masoor dal)
⅓ cup dried yellow split peas (motor dal)
1 tablespoon salt
1½ cups white rice
2 potatoes, peeled and quartered
⅓ cup oil
3 onions, finely chopped
6 tomatoes, finely chopped
1 tablespoon fresh ginger paste (page 13)
1½ tablespoons cumin-coriander powder (page 17)
1 teaspoon turmeric
1 teaspoon cayenne pepper powder

3 cups large cauliflower florets
2 carrots, peeled and chopped
1 cup green peas

For tempering
2 tablespoons ghee (clarified butter)
2 teaspoons cumin seeds
4-inch cinnamon stick, broken into pieces
3 cloves, coarsely ground
3 dried red chilies

Garnishes
Juice of 1 or 2 lemons or limes
4 tablespoons chopped cilantro
Grated fresh radishes
Grated fresh carrots

PREPARATION
Place all the lentils except ½ cup of the orange lentils in the base of a pressure cooker and roast lightly for about 3 minutes on medium heat until the lentils are fragrant and very lightly browned. Add 6 cups of water and the salt and cook under pressure for about 5 minutes. Cool and transfer this mixture to a slow cooker. (Note: This step can be eliminated as it just gives a jump start to the recipe; you can just add the uncooked lentils, water, and salt to the slow cooker if desired.) Add the rice and potatoes to the slow cooker.

Heat the oil in a wok on medium heat till it is hot but not smoking. Add the onions and cook for about 6 minutes, stirring frequently, until soft and pale golden. Add the tomatoes and cook for another 3 to 4 minutes. Add the ginger paste and cumin-coriander powder and cook for about 1 to 2 minutes, until the mixture is fragrant. Add this spice base to the mixture in slow cooker along with the turmeric and cayenne pepper powder and stir well. Cook on low for about 4 hours, and if you are around stop by to occasionally stir it.

At this point the mixture should be a rich yellow orange color and have a thick porridge-like consistency and be simmering briskly. Add in the remaining ½ cup of orange lentils and the cauliflower and carrots and continue cooking for another 30 to 40 minutes. Stir in the green peas.

Heat the ghee for tempering in a small skillet on medium heat for about 1 minute. Add the cumin seeds, cinnamon stick, cloves, and dried red chilies and cook for another minute until the spices darken (when tempering spices it is important to cook them but not burn them). Pour the seasoned ghee into the *khichuri* and let it simmer for about 15 minutes.

Squeeze in the lemon or lime juice (the option to use a second lemon or lime depends on your personal taste). Stir in the cilantro. Serve topped with the grated radishes and carrots.

BENGALI LEMON AND YOGURT RICE
Gondhora Lebu Diye Doi Bhaat

This lovely and delicate recipe is from the cuisine of Bangladesh or East Bengal. I adapted this recipe from a Bengali cooking site. The fragrance of the lemon is headier than lime in my opinion—hence the name *gondhoraj* (king of fragrance) is reserved for lemons. I use lemons and limes interchangeably in certain cases, but in this recipe the lemon rules.

Prep Time: 1 to 2 hours (for marinating) | **Cook Time:** 25 to 30 minutes
Makes: 4 servings

INGREDIENTS
1 cup kala jeera rice
Juice of 2 lemons
1½ teaspoons salt
4 tablespoons low-fat Greek yogurt, beaten until smooth
1 tablespoon oil
1 tablespoon ghee (clarified butter)
1 teaspoon nigella seeds
1½ teaspoons fresh ginger paste (page 13)
⅛ teaspoon asafetida
2 teaspoons sugar
4 green chilies, slit halfway lengthwise
2 dried red chilies
½ cup dry roasted peanuts
2 tablespoons chopped cilantro

PREPARATION
Place the rice and 4 cups of water in a cooking pot and simmer on medium heat for about 13 minutes, until the rice is almost tender. Drain the rice thoroughly and spread out to dry.

Mix the lemon juice, salt, and yogurt together and then mix lightly with the rice and let the rice marinate for at least 1 hour.

Heat the oil and ghee in a saucepan on medium heat for about 1 minute. Add the nigella seeds and saute until the seeds begin sizzling. Add the ginger paste, asafetida, and rice mixture and mix well. Add the sugar, green chilies, and red chilies and cook for about 3 to 4 minutes. Stir in the peanuts and cook for another minute. Garnish with the cilantro before serving.

YELLOW RICE
Turmeric Rice

This Anglo-Indian recipe is typically paired with ball curry, a lightly curried version of meatballs, or even *vindaloo* for festive and special occasions. I recall this rice from my convent school days. Students used to go to church on Sundays; however, unlike certain forms of parochial education, this was an optional activity. Sunday lunch was uniformly savored by all and would typically consist of ball curry and yellow rice. I prefer the richer tasting coconut rice, but coconut milk is optional.

Prep Time: 5 minutes | **Cook Time:** 40 minutes | **Makes:** 4 to 6 servings

INGREDIENTS
2 tablespoons oil
2 tablespoons butter
1 medium onion, thinly sliced
1 large bay leaf, broken
1 or 2 star anise
1½ cups basmati rice
½ cup light coconut milk (optional; increase the amount of water if not using)
½ teaspoon turmeric
1 teaspoon salt

PREPARATION
Heat the oil and half of the butter in a saucepan on medium heat. Add the onion and cook until nicely browned, about 10 minutes, stirring frequently.

Add the bay leaf pieces and star anise and cook for about 1 minute. Add the rice and cook for about 1 minute. Add the coconut milk, if using, and bring to a simmer. Add the turmeric, salt, and 2½ cups water and cover and cook on medium low heat for about 10 minutes.

Remove the cover and continue cooking until the water is absorbed and the rice is soft and separate, about 10 minutes.

Turn off the heat and cover and let the rice rest for about 5 minutes. Remove the cover and fluff and serve.

UNLEAVENED PUFFED WHOLE WHEAT FLATBREADS
Ruti

These basic flatbreads are the usual fare in Bengal at dinnertime. In Bangladesh, however, Bengalis find the use of wheat in place of rice quite a breach of tradition. As with everything, Bengali cooks are rather particular in how they make *ruti*. The Bengali versions of these flatbreads are made as thin as possible, and are relatively small in comparison with their North Indian counterparts.

I remember watching my grandmother roll these beauties. She explained that the dough should not be too moist and not too dry before it is rolled out. Her flatbreads would move easily around the rolling board in a circular motion.

Prep Time: 1½ hours (including 30 to 40 minutes for dough to rest)
Cook Time: 25 to 30 minutes | **Makes:** 4 to 5 servings

INGREDIENTS
2 cups whole wheat flour (atta), plus extra flour for rolling
½ teaspoon salt
2 tablespoons oil

PREPARATION
Sift the flour into a mixing bowl, add the salt and 1 tablespoon of oil and mix well. Gradually mix in ½ cup water a little at a time, kneading well, squeezing and molding the dough to form a nice round mound. Shape into a ball and coat with the remaining tablespoon of oil. Cover the dough and let it rest for about 30 minutes in a warm place.

Break the dough into walnut-size balls, and roll them out to 6-inch to 7-inch circles. (It is important to try to roll these out as thin as you can without breaking the dough. It is fine to use a lot of flour on the surface when working with the dough at the beginning; just shake the flour off before placing the bread on the cooking pan.)

Heat a flat griddle pan (called a *tawa*). Place the dough circles on the hot pan (working in batches) and cook for 1 to 2 minutes; turn and cook on the other side for another 1 to 2 minutes. If you are working on a gas stove, remove each flatbread with tongs and place over the open flame until the bread puffs up and darkens some, being careful not to burn it. Remove from flame and serve. (If you do not have a gas stove, an alternate method of cooking these flatbreads is to use a clean tea towel to press lightly in spots while the bread is on the griddle pan to allow the bread to lightly brown and puff up in spots.)

DEEP-FRIED PUFFY BREADS
Luchis

A *luchi* is the Bengali version of the puffed Indian bread called *poori*. My first job was in the Lower Eastside of New York City, which boasts a lot of Indian restaurants. In every office where I have worked, one of my tasks has been educating my co-workers about the world of Indian food. One day my supervisor came to me and asked if I knew the balloon bread, and I gave him a look of bewilderment. When we ordered the *luchis* at a restaurant, I realized what he meant, since the restaurant served these puffed delicacies much larger than you would normally see at home and they did indeed look like balloons.

Prep Time: 45 minutes | **Cook Time:** 30 minutes | **Makes:** about 20

INGREDIENTS
2 cups all-purpose white flour
½ teaspoon salt
2 tablespoons ghee (clarified butter)
Oil for frying

PREPARATION
Sift the flour and salt into a bowl. Mix in the ghee with your hands. Gradually add about ¾ cup water and knead after each addition. Make sure that the dough does not become too wet. It should be firm, springy, smooth, and manageable.

Put a little oil in a small bowl. Divide the dough into about 20 walnut-size balls. Dip each dough ball into the oil and then roll out to a 5-inch circle. Keep the rolled out circles under a damp cloth while you are rolling out the rest.

Heat about 2 cups of oil in a medium wok. Test the temperature of the oil with a breadcrumb, the crumb should rise immediately to the top.

Gently place a dough circle into the hot oil, it should rise to the surface and puff up in about 30 seconds. Carefully turn it over and cook the other side for 30 seconds. Use a slotted spatula to remove it from the oil, allowing the excess oil to drain off the *luchi* and back into the wok. Repeat this process with the remaining *luchis* and serve hot.

LENTIL-STUFFED PUFFY BREADS
Radha Ballabhi

The name of these puffed breads provides insight into the role of food in Bengali culture. The love of food and its importance to the people runs deep, hence several food items have exalted names. For instance, every-day rice is called *Govinda bhog*, which translates to "Krishna's food." *Radha Ballabhi* essentially translates to "Radha (Lord Krishna's consort) and Krishna." The name was inspired by its colors, the darker filling representing Krishna's blue complexion and the lighter outer crust, Radha's. I have used a combination of whole wheat and white flour in this recipe, but you can use just white flour for a richer bread.

Tea shops in Kolkatta make this bread fresh in the evening, and they are usually sold with potato curry. They can be eaten with most of the dry vegetable dishes in this book and of course with the Bengal gram lentils.

Prep Time: 90 minutes (plus 3 to 4 hours for soaking lentils)
Cook Time: 35 minutes | **Makes:** 10

INGREDIENTS
Outer crust
1 cup all-purpose white flour, plus additional for rolling
1 cup whole wheat flour (atta)
1 teaspoon salt
1 tablespoon ghee (clarified butter)

Filling
¾ cup dried white split lentils (kalai dal), soaked in water for 3 to 4 hours
1 teaspoon salt
1 teaspoon chili powder
½ teaspoon fennel seed powder
½ teaspoon cumin-coriander powder (page 17)
5 tablespoons oil

Oil for deep frying

PREPARATION
Make crust:
Mix the flours with the salt and ghee. Gradually add about ¾ cup water, making sure the dough does not become too wet. Knead until smooth.

Make filling:
Pulse the lentils with the salt and spices in a food processor until coarsely chopped. Heat the 5 tablespoons oil in a non-stick wok or skillet and fry the filling until it is dry and beginning to turn brown. Set aside to cool.

Assemble and fry:
Divide the dough for crust into lime-size balls. Make deep pouches in the balls and stuff each with about 1½ teaspoons of the filling. Seal well and place on a

greased tray and allow to rest for about 20 minutes. Begin rolling the balls out into 6-inch circles on a floured surface, starting with the first one made, taking care not to break open the outer crust of dough.

Heat some oil in a wok. Test readiness by dropping a breadcrumb in the oil — it should immediately come up to the surface if the oil is hot enough. Working in batches, gently lower each dough circle into the hot oil and cook until puffed and pale brown, about 1 minute. (It is important to maintain the temperature at medium heat otherwise the breads will not puff up.) Turn and cook for another minute or so on the other side. Use a slotted spatula to remove the breads from the oil, allowing the excess oil to drain off and back into the wok. Serve hot.

FRIED PUFFY BREADS WITH GREEN PEA FILLING
Matarshutir Kachoris

To understand the essentials of regional Indian cooking, the devil, as they say, is in the details. *Kachoris* are filled breads that puff when they are deep fried. The Bengali *kachori* differs slightly from the North Indian variety in its texture. This *kachori* is meant to be softer as opposed to the slightly crisper coating of its Northern cousin. The green pea filling is also a unique variation that is typical of the Eastern regions. The pre-stuffed dough packets can actually be prepared up to two days in advance and kept in the refrigerator. If prepared in advance, they should be removed from the refrigerator and kept at room temperature to warm for about 30 minutes prior to rolling and frying.

Prep Time: 1½ hours (includes time for dough to rest)
Cook Time: 30 to 40 minutes | **Makes:** 16

INGREDIENTS
Dough
3 cups all-purpose white flour, plus extra for rolling
1 teaspoon salt
2 tablespoons ghee or oil
¾ cup cold water

Filling
1 cup frozen peas, thawed
1 tablespoon oil
½ teaspoon nigella seeds
1 teaspoon fresh ginger paste (page 13)
½ teaspoon cayenne pepper powder
¾ teaspoon fennel seed powder
¾ teaspoon salt
1 teaspoon sugar

Oil for frying

PREPARATION
Prepare dough:
Sift the flour and salt into a mixing bowl. Gently mix the ghee or oil into the flour, resulting in something that looks like a pie crust dough. Gradually mix in the cold water to form a smooth elastic dough. (The dough should not feel sticky and it should have a smooth pliable texture.) Set the dough aside to rest.

Make the filling:
Place the peas in a food processor and process until smooth. Heat the oil in a wok or skillet, add the nigella seeds and wait for these to sizzle. Add the ginger paste, cayenne pepper powder, fennel seed powder, salt, and sugar and mix well. Add the pureed peas and cook for about 6 to 7 minutes, stirring frequently, until the mixture is cooked through and separating from the sides of the pan. Cool the mixture slightly.

Assemble and fry:
Divide the dough into 16 portions. Shape a portion into a ball and roll out, using some flour, into a 3-inch disc. Place about 1½ teaspoons of the filling onto the center of the circle. Shape the circle into a round package by covering the filling with the dough, carefully ensuring that the dough covers the filling comfortably without any tears. Place the dough packet seal side down on a greased tray and continue with remaining dough portions. Keep the dough packets organized on the tray so you can roll them out in the order they were made.

Place some oil in a wok and set the heat to medium high. Test readiness by dropping a breadcrumb in the oil; it should immediately come up to the surface if the oil is hot enough.

Take a sealed dough packet and roll out on a floured surface to a circle about 3 to 4 inches in diameter. It is critical to try to roll these out as thin as possible without tearing the dough. Gently place the rolled dough into the hot oil and wait until disc rises to the surface and then puffs up. Cook briefly on the first side for about 1 minute and then turn and cook for a couple of minutes on the other side (the finished bread should be puffy and pale golden in color). Use a slotted spatula to lift it out and drain the oil on the side of the wok. Continue this process with all the remaining dough packets. Serve hot.

TRIANGULAR WHOLE-GRAIN FLATBREADS WITH NIGELLA SEEDS
Kalo Jire diye Tekona Porota

It is the small nuances such as the triangular shape of these flatbreads (as opposed to the more popular circular version) that make any food unique. I have never seen triangular *porothas* outside of people's homes, but they are really the only way that they were made in my house. I have added the nigella seeds to give some flavor as well as a contrasting appearance.

Prep Time: 1 hour (including time for dough to rest) | **Cook Time:** 30 minutes
Makes: 8

INGREDIENTS
1½ cups whole wheat flour (can substitute all-purpose flour)
½ cup all-purpose white flour, plus extra for rolling
1 tablespoon ghee (clarified butter)
1 teaspoon nigella seeds
1 teaspoon salt
½ cup buttermilk
Oil for frying

PREPARATION
In a bowl, mix together with your fingers the flours, ghee, nigella seeds, and salt. Gradually mix in the buttermilk and ½ cup of water until you have a smooth but pliable dough. It should spring back to touch. Let the dough rest for 30 minutes.

Divide the dough into lime-size balls. Take one and roll out to a disc about 3 inches in diameter. Fold this into a semi-circle and roll the semi-circle to stretch slightly. Fold over to form a triangular shape and roll out the dough carefully to form a triangle about 4 inches on each side. Repeat with remaining dough balls.

Heat a flat pan or griddle. Place the dough triangles on the pan and cook for 1 to 2 minutes on one side until the bread darkens slightly and then turn and continue to cook for another minute or so (the dough will begin to form puffy circles). After the breads have been dry roasted on both sides, add a little oil to the pan and fry on both sides until the breads are a pale golden color with darker brown spots.

SPICY MULTI-GRAIN FLATBREADS WITH EGGS
Anda Porota

This interesting variation of the *porota* is largely Ango-Indian inspired. It makes a great brunch dish or a balanced accompaniment for any meal. These flatbreads are made with white whole wheat flour, which results in a soft, light-tasting bread, and thus ends up being a great hit with kids.

You would think that something like this would be called *dimer porota* (*dim* is the Bengali word for "egg"), but the Anglo-Indians take great pride in contorting the lingo to produce a speech that is neither Indian nor English. In fact, one of the amusements of my school days was to listen to some teachers mangle elaborate and carefully thought out Bengali names when they spoke.

Prep Time: 1½ hours | **Cook Time:** 25 to 35 minutes | **Makes:** 10

INGREDIENTS
1 cup white all-purpose flour
1 cup whole wheat flour (atta)
½ teaspoon baking soda
1 teaspoon salt
1 tablespoon ghee (clarified butter) or butter, melted
3 eggs
1 small onion, finely chopped
2 or 3 green chilies, finely chopped
2 tablespoons finely chopped cilantro
Oil or ghee for frying

PREPARATION
Sift the flours with the baking soda and salt. Rub the ghee into the flours. Add the eggs, onion, green chilies, and cilantro. Knead well, adding a little water as needed to make a soft pliable dough that springs back when touched. Place in a greased container and let sit in a warm place (room temperature) to rest for about 30 to 45 minutes.

Break the dough into 10 large balls and roll out on a little flour into 8-inch circles. Heat a non-stick skillet and cook the dough circles on one side for about 1 minute until the dough darkens slightly. Turn and cook for another minute on the other side, until the bread puffs up slightly and light brown spots appear. Then add a little oil or ghee to the pan and spread evenly and gently brown the porotas, turn and add a little more oil or ghee and crisp lightly on the second side. Repeat with remaining dough circles. Serve with sweet pickles or butter and jam for an authentic experience.

LAMB-STUFFED FLATBREADS
Maanshor Porota

Recipes like this are traditionally made with all-purpose white flour. However, over the years I've come to realize that with the exception of some breads like *luchis*, whole wheat flour works just as well. While I do not believe in compromising taste for the sake of nutrition, I do think a happy medium can often be found. The ground lamb filling for this recipe is versatile and can be used as a filling in other dishes such as fritters.

Prep Time: 1 hour | **Cook Time:** 1 hour | **Makes:** 8

INGREDIENTS
Dough
2 cups whole wheat flour (atta)
½ teaspoon baking powder
2 tablespoons ghee (clarified butter)

Lamb filling
3 tablespoons oil
1 onion, chopped
1 teaspoon fresh ginger paste (page 13)
2 garlic cloves, pressed
1 teaspoon cayenne pepper powder
½ pound ground lamb
1 teaspoon salt
1 teaspoon sugar
1 teaspoon garam masala (page 17)
2 teaspoons chopped cilantro

Oil for frying

PREPARATION
Prepare dough:
Mix the flour and baking powder. Knead in the ghee and gradually add ¾ cup of water to form a firm, pliable dough. Let the dough rest while making the lamb filling.

Make filling:
Heat the oil in a wok or skillet. Add the onion, ginger paste, and pressed garlic and cook for a few minutes. Add the cayenne pepper powder and ground lamb. Stir in the salt and sugar and cook the lamb on medium heat until the juices evaporate and the meat begins to brown. Add the garam masala and chopped cilantro. Let the mixture cool slightly.

Assemble and fry:
To assemble the *porota*, divide dough into 16 small round pieces. Gently roll 2 pieces out to 3-inch discs. Place about 2 tablespoons meat filling on one disc and cover it with the other. Roll out the sandwiched discs until thin and sealed.

(This needs to be done delicately to ensure that there are no breaks or holes in the dough.) Continue making stuffed discs until all the dough is used.

Heat a flat skillet (*tawa*). Place some of the filled flatbread on the pan. Cook for about 2 minutes on each side. The flatbread should dry out and puff up a little. Add some oil and fry until crisp on both sides. Repeat until they're all cooked and enjoy!

MULTI-LAYERED FLAKY FLATBREADS
Dhakai Porota

When I first learned about the queen bee, I was rather impressed and fascinated by her exalted status and wanted to sample the royal jelly that she lived on. This never did happen, although I do love a good natural honey. In the world of Bengali flatbreads, the *dhakai porota* is definitely the queen bee. It is rich, takes time to prepare, and is reserved for eating with a good preparation of goat meat or rich, sweet *cholar dal*.

The artistry of this bread lies in its layered crispness. The more layers that can be built in, the better testimony to the chef's talent.

Prep Time: 75 minutes (including time for dough to rest)
Cook Time: 25 to 30 minutes | **Makes:** 8

INGREDIENTS
2 cups all-purpose white flour
2 tablespoons ghee (clarified butter)
1 teaspoon salt
Oil or ghee for frying and rolling

PREPARATION
Place the flour in a mixing bowl and rub the ghee into it, much like when making pastry dough. Add the salt and gradually add ¾ cup water to form a smooth, elastic dough. Cover the dough and let it rest for about 20 to 30 minutes in a warm place.

Divide the dough into 8 pieces. Grease your hands and shape one piece into a long rope. Starting on one end gradually begin rolling the dough rope into a tight spiral (similar to a cinnamon bun), the objective is to get as many rings from the coil as possible. Place the rolled coil on a flat surface and gently flatten. The objective here is to get a circular flatbread without completely flattening out the coils. If this is done correctly, you will still be able to see them. Continue making more coiled flatbreads with the remaining dough pieces.

Heat a griddle (*tawa*). Place a few of the flatbreads on the hot griddle and roast for 1 to 2 minutes on each side. Add a little ghee or oil to the griddle and cook until the flatbreads are crisp and golden. Remove the finished *porota* from the heat and continue this process until all the flatbreads are cooked.

Chapter Four:
Lentils
Dal

The second layer of the Bengali meal is lentils or dal. As in other parts of India the term "lentils" is used rather loosely for both lentils and certain beans. Lentils are one of the first plants cultivated in civilization.

The Bengali preparation method ensures that lentils are soft, but that they still retain their shape. Lentils are cooked to a much thinner, soupier consistency than in other parts of India. Most of the lentils used in the Bengali kitchens are the split, husked variety. My mother maintains a certain order in selecting which lentils to cook. Certain types of lentils are strictly used as an accompaniment with rice dishes, others are more appropriately combined with vegetables, and some are best eaten with the fancier Bengali breads.

The pressure cooker is a common appliance in the Bengali kitchen, although not used as extensively as in some of the other parts of India. It is mostly used for some of the more complex lentils, such as split peas, or the Bengali gram lentils (*cholar dal*), and yellow pigeon peas (*arhar*). I also offer conventional and slow-cooker measurements for these lentils in case you do not want to work with a pressure cooker.

Following is a list of typical lentils used and cooked in the Bengali kitchen. Each of these lentils has its own method of tempering (*shombara*) and its own prescription for how it is combined with other recipes. The tempering of the lentils is done right at the end of cooking, and it is a culinary faux pas to not attend to this at the appropriate time and ensure the appropriate balance. Lentils are usually served with some type of pan-fried vegetables or fritters, and I've included recipes for those in this book as well.

I must mention that I like to add tomatoes and cilantro to lentils as well as to other recipes in this book—reflecting a rather contemporary approach on my part. While these additions are gaining acceptability in Bengali households, they are not typical of the original cast of ingredients as they were not native to the land.

LENTILS (DALS) USED IN BENGALI COOKING

ARHAR/TOOR DAL (Yellow Split Pigeon Peas): These lentils are similar to yellow Bengali gram lentils but have a slightly darker ochre-like color. These lentils have a very distinct, earthy taste. They work well with tart flavors and are usually cooked with a souring agent such as tamarind, lime, or green mango.

CHOLAR DAL (Yellow Bengali Gram Lentils): These small golden yellow lentils are considered the elite lentils of Bengali cuisine. They do take a little longer to cook and should be cooked in a pressure cooker if possible. They are usually reserved for festive occasions, formal meals, and relaxed breakfasts with complex Bengali breads.

KABULI CHOLA (Chickpeas): Chickpeas are added to certain dishes as a texture and protein enhancer; they are also combined with cucumbers and potatoes for lighter salads in summer. They are mostly eaten by themselves as a heavier snack or light meal, such as the *ghoogni*, rather than as one of the dishes on a Bengali table. White chickpeas are the variety used in Bengali cooking. They can be found dried in most supermarkets and, of course, in Indian stores. It is a good idea to soak the chickpeas overnight before using them as this removes some of the loose and harder to digest starches as well as softens the dried peas so they cook faster. I cook chickpeas using either a pressure cooker or a slow cooker for convenience.

KALAI/URAD DAL (White Split Lentils): These small split white lentils look like a dainty, pale cousin of yellow split lentils. They tend to be a little sticky, so are usually roasted before cooking. While they have their place on the Bengali table, they are not an everyday lentil like the masoor dal or moong dal.

MASOOR/MASUR/MUSHORIR DAL (Orange/Red Split Lentils): These lentils are orange in color and cook up to a buttery soft consistency and are the Bengali comfort lentils. They are now sold in packages by Goya and in Indian stores. The delicate buttery taste of these lentils make them a favorite to be enjoyed alone with just a final tempering rather than subjecting them to a more complex preparation.

MOONG DAL (Yellow Split Lentils): Bengali cooks use the split-husked variety of these sunny yellow lentils. They are usually roasted in a dry skillet or wok until wonderfully fragrant, and then cooked in the usual way. These light lentils pair well with summer vegetables such as the bottle gourd.

MOTOR (Whole Dried Peas): These whole dried peas are almost white in color. They tend to have a milder taste than chickpeas and are usually preferred for certain curried creations. They may be found in Indian groceries labeled as *vatana*. These dried peas should be soaked before cooking and I cook them in either a pressure cooker or slow cooker for convenience.

MOTOR DAL (Yellow Split Peas): The yellow split peas used in the recipes in this chapter are an approximation of the lentils we like to call *motor dal*. They take a little longer to cook and work well if soaked and then cooked in a pressure cooker. With their mild flavor, these lentils also pair well with vegetables.

TOOR DAL: *See* Arhar/Toor Dal

URAD DAL: *See* Kalai/Urad Dal

MY UNCLE'S YELLOW BENGALI GRAM LENTILS
Mesho's Cholar Dal

In India, the term "uncle" is not really a catch-all one, at least used in the context of relatives. Every uncle, aunt, and grandparent has a specific name, carefully denoting the nature of the relationship and birth order to keep it nice and simple. The only challenge here is that these attributes are also added to family friends, so a mother's friends are often *mashi* (mother's sister) and a father's friends are *kaka* (father's brother), confusing an outsider as to where the family lines begin and end.

So the *mesho* that I refer to in this recipe's name is my mother's sister's husband. His cooking is the simple, practical kind. He retains a vision of the India that he left thirty years ago and in his spare time he entertains himself reading old Bengali literature and watching Bollywood films from the sixties. A conversation with him can almost make you feel that you have gone back through a time machine.

Prep Time: overnight (to soak lentils) | **Cook Time:** 45 to 50 minutes in saucepan; or 10 minutes in pressure cooker | **Makes:** 4 to 6 servings

INGREDIENTS
⅔ cup dried yellow Bengali gram lentils (cholar dal), soaked
  overnight in 2 to 3 cups water
1 teaspoon turmeric
1 teaspoon salt
½ teaspoon cayenne pepper powder
1 teaspoon fresh ginger paste (page 13)
2 cloves garlic, finely chopped (optional, this is my addition)
2 tomatoes, chopped
1 teaspoon ghee (clarified butter)
¾ teaspoon cumin seeds
2 or 3 dried whole red chilies

PREPARATION
Drain and rinse the lentils and place in a cooking pot with 3 cups water. Bring the lentils to a simmer. Add the turmeric, salt, cayenne pepper powder, ginger paste, garlic, and tomatoes and simmer on medium-low heat for about 35 to 40 minutes. The lentils should be soft and easily mashed with the back of a spoon; the mixture should be creamy and fairly thick but the lentils should retain their shape.

Heat the ghee in a small skillet and add the cumin seeds and chilies. When the seeds begin to sizzle pour the mixture over the lentils and serve.

ORANGE SPLIT LENTILS WITH TOMATOES AND CILANTRO
Tomato Dhoney Pata Diye Masoor Dal

This is a weeknight variation of orange split lentils which are extremely versatile because of their quick cooking time and naturally mild and adaptive taste. They are comforting, simple, and as basic as it gets. Everyone in my family, including my children, loves this lentil. This light variation is a summertime favorite but can be enjoyed as a soup in winter, if desired, with some hot buttered whole wheat toast.

Prep Time: 5 minutes | **Cook Time:** 25 minutes | **Makes:** 6 servings

INGREDIENTS
½ cup dried orange/red split lentils (masoor dal)
½ teaspoon turmeric
1 teaspoon salt
4 green chilies, slit lengthwise
2 ripe tomatoes, chopped
2 teaspoons ghee (clarified butter)
1 teaspoon cumin seeds
2 tablespoons chopped cilantro

PREPARATION
Put the lentils and 3 cups of water in a saucepan and bring to a boil. Add the turmeric, salt, and green chilies and cook for about 15 minutes. While the lentils are boiling a scum may form on the surface, gently remove this while the lentils are cooking.

Add the tomatoes and cook for another 5 minutes. Mix the mixture well—it should have a nice soupy consistency that is not too thin or too thick.

Heat the ghee in a small skillet on medium heat for about 1 minute and add the cumin seeds and wait till the seeds begin to sizzle. Pour this seasoned ghee over the lentils and stir in the cilantro.

YELLOW SPLIT PEAS WITH CAULIFLOWER AND RADISHES
Mulo ar Kopir Data Diye Motor Dal

Yellow split peas can be used in lieu of the lentils that we call *motor dal* in India. I personally think that the texture is close, but not identical. These lentils have a naturally creamy texture and can be effectively cooked in a pressure cooker. They are often cooked with vegetables; my mother makes these with the fuzzy green broad beans called *sheem* in India.

The cauliflower stalks and radishes in this recipe are the addition of my friend Shapna, who in turn got the idea from her mother-in-law. You can also use tender, farm fresh broccoli stalks instead of, or along with, the cauliflower stalks.

Prep Time: 4 to 5 hours (to soak split peas) | **Cook Time:** 15 minutes in pressure cooker; or 45 to 50 minutes in saucepan (mostly unattended)
Makes: 4 to 6 servings

INGREDIENTS
¾ cup dried yellow split peas (motor dal), soaked for 4 to 5 hours in warm water
1 teaspoon salt
½ teaspoon turmeric
1 cup chopped cauliflower stalks and tender leaves (not florets)
½ cup thinly sliced red or white radishes
1 teaspoon ghee (clarified butter)
1 teaspoon oil
1 teaspoon finely grated fresh ginger
⅛ teaspoon asafetida or hing (optional)
½ teaspoon nigella seeds

PREPARATION
Rinse the soaked yellow split peas thoroughly. Place the yellow split peas, 2 cups of water, salt, and turmeric in either a pressure cooker or saucepan. Cook under pressure for 15 minutes, or in the saucepan on medium-low heat for about 40 to 45 minutes, adding the cauliflower stalks and radishes about halfway through the cooking. (This cooking can be done with minimal attention and just occasional stirring to ensure that the water has not evaporated.)

Remove the cover and mix the lentils with a wooden spoon until smooth.

Heat the ghee and oil in a small skillet. Add the ginger and cook lightly. Add the asafetida, if using, and the nigella seeds and wait till they sizzle. Pour the seasoned oil over the lentils and stir well. Turn off the heat and let the flavors settle for 2 to 3 minutes. Serve with rice.

ORANGE SPLIT LENTILS WITH CARAMELIZED ONIONS
Masoor Dal

These are wonderfully comforting, homey orange lentils. I love this dish on a snowy New York night over steaming white rice. It calms both body and soul.

Please note that this recipe requires attention to timing as you sauté and brown the onions. It is important to start the browning process simultaneously with simmering the orange lentils.

Prep Time: 5 minutes | **Cook Time:** 25 to 30 minutes | **Makes:** 4 servings

INGREDIENTS
½ cup dried orange/red split lentils (masoor dal)
¾ teaspoon turmeric
1 teaspoon salt
3 green chilies, slit halfway lengthwise
4 tablespoons oil
1 medium red onion, very thinly sliced
1 teaspoon ghee (clarified butter)

PREPARATION
Place the lentils and 2 cups of water in a cooking pot. Place the pot on medium heat. Add the turmeric, salt, and green chilies and bring to a simmer. Lower the heat to low and continue cooking about 20 minutes, until the lentils are soft and smooth. The liquid should be smooth and fairly thick.

While the lentils are cooking, heat the oil in a small wok on medium-low heat for about 1 minute until fairly hot. Add the onion and cook until crisp and golden. This process takes some time and needs care during the final 5 minutes to ensure that the onions brown but do not burn.

Gently pour the oil and onions into the lentils. Add the ghee and cook until the ghee has melted into the lentils. Serve with rice or a bread of your choice.

YELLOW SPLIT LENTILS WITH FISH HEAD

Macher Muro Diye Moong Dal

This traditional recipe—a festive dish reserved for special lunches—is adapted from my mother's culinary collection. Recently I discovered that my fish seller will actually cut the fish heads into two or four parts for me, very helpful if it is a large fish head and you only want to use part of it.

Prep Time: 15 to 20 minutes | **Cook Time:** 35 minutes | **Makes:** 6 servings

INGREDIENTS

⅓ cup plus 2 tablespoons vegetable or mustard oil
1 medium fish head (preferably from a white fish)
2 teaspoons turmeric
2 teaspoons salt
¾ cup dried split yellow lentils (moong dal)
1 onion, thinly sliced
1 teaspoon fresh ginger paste (page 13)
½ teaspoon cayenne pepper powder
1 teaspoon cumin-coriander powder (page 17)
1 teaspoon sugar
Juice of 1 lime (optional)
1 tablespoon chopped cilantro

PREPARATION

Place the ⅓ cup oil in a wok and heat over medium flame for about 2 minutes, until very hot and almost smoking. Rub the fish head with half the turmeric and half the salt and place in the oil and fry over a steady medium-low flame until nice and crisp, turning once during cooking, about 10 minutes.

While the fish head is cooking, place the lentils in a heavy-bottomed pan and dry roast lightly until they turn very pale golden and are very aromatic.

In a separate saucepan, heat the remaining 2 tablespoons oil on medium-low heat and add the onion and ginger paste and sauté for about 5 minutes, until the onion wilts and begins to curl and crisp lightly on the sides. Add the cayenne pepper powder, cumin-coriander powder, sugar, roasted lentils, 3 cups of water, the remaining 1 teaspoon salt, and and remaining 1 teaspoon turmeric. Bring to a simmer and cook for about 15 minutes, until the lentils are almost cooked through.

Break the fried fish head into 2 to 3 pieces and lower into the lentils. Simmer the lentils with the fish head for another 10 minutes, gently breaking the fish head further until the pieces are fairly small. Squeeze in some lime juice, if using, and sprinkle with the cilantro before serving.

MIXED LENTILS WITH SPINACH FOR A CROWD
Palong Saag Diye Barobari Dal

The term *barobari* literally means "twelve houses." I often heard my grand-mothers use it in reference to festivals such as Durga Pujas. For their generation, these events used to be extended family affairs, comprised of a dozen or so households. Nowadays the Puja can be a public, more commercial event. In any case, whether you have twelve families or twenty over, this recipe of lentils enriched with spinach is sure to be a crowd pleaser!

Prep Time: 15 minutes | **Cook Time:** 25 minutes if using a pressure cooker; 75 minutes if using a saucepan | **Makes:** 15 servings

INGREDIENTS
⅓ cup each of 3 or 4 types of lentils (a mixture of masoor, yellow moong, and arhar/toor works well)
1 red onion, finely chopped
¾ teaspoon turmeric
1 teaspoon salt
1 teaspoon cumin-coriander powder (page 17)
2 tomatoes, chopped
1 green chili, finely chopped
3 cups finely chopped fresh spinach
1½ tablespoons ghee (clarified butter)
1½ teaspoons fresh ginger paste (page 13)
2 dried red chilies
¼ teaspoon asafetida
½ teaspoon panch phoron (page 5)

PREPARATION
Place the lentils, 6 cups of water, red onion, turmeric, salt, cumin-coriander powder, tomatoes, and green chili in a pressure cooker and cook under pressure for about 15 minutes. (Alternately, put the ingredients in a pot and bring to a simmer and cook lentils for about 1 hour, stirring occasionally, until the mixture is smooth and soft.)

Remove the cover and add in the spinach and cook for another 10 minutes, until the spinach is nice and soft.

Heat the ghee in a small skillet and add the ginger paste and sauté lightly for 1 to 2 minutes. Add the red chilies and asafetida and cook for a few seconds. Add the panch phoron and wait till the spices begin to crackle. Pour the mixture over the lentils and mix well.

WHOLE PEAS WITH TOMATOES AND TAMARIND
Nirameesh Ghugni

Ghugni is a stew cooked with whole dried peas, which are as essential to the Bengali kitchen as chickpeas are to the Punjabi kitchen. There are meat-based variations of *ghugni*, usually made with minced goat meat, that are somewhat similar to American-style chili. This vegetarian version is something that I have devised to keep the flavor of the whole peas and tamarind more pronounced.

Prep Time: 10 minutes (plus 5 hours soaking time for peas)
Cook Time: 2¼ hours in saucepan; or 30 minutes in pressure cooker
Makes: 8 servings

INGREDIENTS
¾ cup whole dried peas (motor/vatana), soaked in hot water for about 5 hours
2 to 3 tablespoons oil
2 cardamom pods
2 cloves
2-inch cinnamon stick, broken into pieces
2 or 3 bay leaves
1 onion, very finely chopped
1½ teaspoons cumin-coriander powder (page 17)
1 cup diced tomatoes
2 green chilies
2 cloves garlic
1½-inch piece fresh ginger, peeled
1 teaspoon salt
1 teaspoon sugar
3 tablespoons strained tamarind paste
1 tablespoon chopped cilantro
½ teaspoon bhaja masala (page 16) or garam masala (page 17)

PREPARATION
Rinse and wash the soaked whole dried peas.

In the base of a pressure cooker, heat the oil and add the cardamom pods, cloves, cinnamon stick, and bay leaves and cook for about 15 to 20 seconds, until the spices swell up and darken slightly. (If you are not using a pressure cooker, a heavy-bottomed pan will work.) Add the onion and cook on low, stirring in the cumin-coriander powder, until the onions soften and begin to turn gently golden on the edges.

Grind the tomatoes, chilies, garlic, ginger, salt, and sugar in a food processor to a smooth paste and add to the onions and cook for 5 minutes. Mix in the soaked peas and 4 cups of water and cook under pressure for 20 minutes. (Alternately, if using the heavy-bottomed pan, cook undisturbed except for the occasional stirring until the peas are nice and soft, about 2 hours.) Remove the lid and add the tamarind paste. Garnish with cilantro and bhaja or garam masala and enjoy.

RED LENTILS WITH BOK CHOY
Bok Choy Diye Dal

Some people might be appalled that I would add bok choy to lentils and call it a Bengali dish. If you try this lovely fresh green vegetable in a Bengali culinary context, however, I'm sure you will really not care about its origins. I love the crunch and fresh taste of bok choy, and often buy more than I know what to do with, so these lentils are one of the ways I use up the green. Spinach is a good substitute if you don't have bok choy.

Prep Time: 5 minutes | **Cook Time:** 25 minutes | **Makes:** 4 to 6 servings

INGREDIENTS
¾ cup orange/red split lentils (masoor dal)
1 teaspoon salt
½ teaspoon turmeric
1 teaspoon minced fresh ginger
1 teaspoon minced garlic
2 or 3 green chilies, slit
2 to 3 tablespoons oil
1 small shallot, thinly sliced
1 head bok choy, finely chopped (about 1 cup)
1 teaspoon ghee (clarified butter)
1 teaspoon cumin seeds

PREPARATION
Put the lentils, 4 cups water, salt, turmeric, ginger, garlic, and green chilies in a large pot and cook for 15 minutes, until the lentils are nice and soft.

Heat the oil in a small skillet and add the shallot and bok choy and saute for 5 minutes until the shallot is wilted and the bok choy is tender crisp. Add to the lentils and simmer for 5 minutes.

Heat the ghee and add the cumin seeds and when they sizzle and are brown pour over the lentils and stir in. Cover and let the flavors mesh together for a few minutes before serving.

ROASTED YELLOW SPLIT LENTILS TEMPERED WITH FENNEL SEEDS
Mouri Phoron Diye Bhaja Moong Dal

The lentils are first roasted until pale golden and then cooked in the typical Bengali manner. This was a dish often found on our table when I was growing up, and I still find the smell of these lentils roasting one of the most nostalgic fragrances. One whiff brings me back to childhood.

Prep Time: 5 minutes | **Cook Time:** 30 minutes | **Makes:** 4 servings

INGREDIENTS
½ cup yellow split lentils (moong dal)
½ teaspoon turmeric
1 teaspoon salt
2 green chilies, slit lengthwise
1 teaspoon ghee (clarified butter)
½ teaspoon fennel seeds
⅛ teaspoon asafetida

PREPARATION
Dry roast the lentils in a heavy-bottomed saucepan for 5 minutes, till very fragrant and pale golden in color. Add the turmeric, salt, green chilies, and 2 cups of water and bring to a simmer. Cook the lentils for about 15 minutes, unattended, adding a little more water if needed to keep to a light soupy consistency.

Heat the ghee in a small skillet. Add the fennel seeds and cook for 30 seconds. Add the asafetida and pour mixture over the lentils. Stir the seasoned oil into the lentils and serve over rice.

TART PIGEON PEAS AND GREEN MANGOES
Tauk Aam Diye Dal

Yellow split pigeon peas (called *arhar dal* in Bengali and *toor dal* in Hindi) tend to work well with tart seasonings. A handful of assorted fresh vegetables can be added to this recipe if desired. Fresh green mangoes are available in Indian stores as are packages of frozen green mangoes, and the latter works very well for this recipe. The frozen mango is usually available with the skin on, and it can remain on during cooking and be removed later.

Prep Time: 10 minutes | **Cook Time:** 25 minutes in pressure cooker; 45 minutes in saucepan | **Makes:** 4 servings

INGREDIENTS
½ cup dried yellow split pigeon peas (arhar/toor dal)
1 green mango, peeled and cut into pieces (*see note above*)
½ teaspoon turmeric
¾ teaspoon salt
2 green chilies, slit lengthwise
1 teaspoon ghee (clarified butter)
1 teaspoon cumin seeds

PREPARATION
Put the pigeon peas, green mango, turmeric, salt, green chilies, and 2 cups of water in a pressure cooker or large saucepan (you may need more water for the saucepan) and cook until the lentils are very soft but not mushy (25 minutes under pressure; 45 minutes in pan on stove). Remove the cover and stir well, mashing in the mango pieces. Heat the ghee in a small skillet and add the cumin seeds. When they sizzle pour onto the lentils and mix well.

YELLOW SPLIT LENTILS WITH BITTER MELON
Tetor Dal

Bengalis have a fondness for bitter foods, such as the bitter melon. It is right up there with their love for sweets, and actually works well since the benefits of one may offset the damages of the other.

These lentils are somewhat thick in their cooked consistency and the bitterness of the bitter melon is not very pronounced.

Prep Time: 10 minutes | **Cook Time:** 30 minutes | **Makes:** 4 to 6 servings

INGREDIENTS
½ cup dried yellow split lentils (moong dal)
3 to 4 tablespoons oil
1 small red onion, chopped
2 small bitter melons (called karela in Indian groceries), seeded and sliced
½ teaspoon cumin powder
1 teaspoon grated fresh ginger
1 tomato, chopped
1 teaspoon salt
½ teaspoon turmeric
4 green chilies, slit lengthwise
2 teaspoons ghee (clarified butter)
1 teaspoon cumin seeds
½ teaspoon mustard seeds

PREPARATION
Place the lentils in a pan and dry roast for 3 to 5 minutes until they are pale golden and very fragrant.

Heat the oil in a separate pot and add the onion and bitter melons and saute for 4 to 5 minutes. Add the cumin powder, ginger, tomato, salt, turmeric, chilies, and 4 cups water and bring to a boil. Simmer the mixture for 20 to 25 minutes.

Heat the ghee in a small skillet and add the cumin seeds and mustard seeds and wait till the mustard seeds pop. Pour the seasoned oil over the lentils and serve.

YELLOW SPLIT LENTILS WITH CAULIFLOWER
Kopi Diye Moong Dal

Lentils have their champions in a household. I am a fan of the yellow split moong lentils especially when pairing them with vegetables. However, my brother and mother tend to prefer the orange/red lentils (*masoor dal*). This recipe can be prepared with either. If using the orange/red lentils you can skip the step of roasting them.

Prep Time: 5 minutes | **Cook Time:** 25 minutes | **Makes:** 4 servings

INGREDIENTS
½ cup yellow split lentils (moong dal)
½ teaspoon turmeric
½ teaspoon cayenne pepper powder
¾ teaspoon salt
1 cup cauliflower florets, cut into small pieces
1 tablespoon oil
1 teaspoon ghee (clarified butter)
1 teaspoon cumin seeds
1 or 2 bay leaves, broken into pieces

PREPARATION
Place the lentils in a cooking vessel and dry roast them for 3 to 4 minutes, stirring constantly, until the lentils smell toasty and fragrant and darken a few shades.

Put the roasted lentils, 2 cups of water, turmeric, cayenne pepper powder, and salt in a pot and cook for 10 minutes.

Add the cauliflower and cook till it is soft, about another 5 to 7 minutes. (The lentils should now have a nice soft consistency and the cauliflower should be cooked through.)

Heat the oil and ghee in a small skillet on medium heat until almost smoking and then add the cumin seeds and bay leaves. Cook for about 1 to 2 minutes until the cumin sizzles and darkens along with the bay leaves. The spices should turn fragrant but not be too hot. Pour over the lentils and mix in and enjoy with rice and any other dish of your choice.

SWEET BENGALI GRAM LENTILS WITH COCONUT AND RAISINS
Misti Cholar Dal

This is a festive recipe for special occasions, when you might actually get a fresh coconut and chop it yourself into tiny, delicate pieces. But I must confess I often make do with frozen shredded coconut, and in fact wrote this recipe with the frozen variety in mind. Either way it is up to you, but the fresh coconut does yield a nice crunchy sweet taste.

I have on occasion made small *Matarshutir Kachoris* (Fried Puffy Breads with Green Pea Filling, page 59) and arranged then on an appetizer platter to serve with this dal. It is a modern twist on a very traditional combination.

Prep Time: 7 to 8 hours (to soak the lentils) | **Cook Time:** 25 minutes in a pressure cooker; 45 minutes in a saucepan | **Makes:** 4 to 6 servings

INGREDIENTS
½ cup yellow Bengali gram lentils(cholar dal), soaked overnight
3 green chilies
½ teaspoon turmeric
½ teaspoon cayenne pepper powder
1 teaspoon salt
1½ teaspoons sugar
1 teaspoon raisins
½ cup finely shredded coconut
2 teaspoons ghee (clarified butter)
2 cloves
1-inch cinnamon stick, broken into pieces
2 cardamom pods
1 bay leaf

PREPARATION
Put the lentils, chilies, turmeric, cayenne pepper powder, salt, sugar, raisins, and 2½ cups water in a pressure cooker or large saucepan (you may need more water for the saucepan). Cook till the lentils are very soft but still retain their original shape, about 25 minutes under pressure or 45 minutes in pot on stove.

Gently toast the coconut in a small skillet (I do this without oil, since the coconut has quite a bit of oil). Stir the coconut into the lentil mixture and taste for salt. (It should have a creamy appearance and slightly sweet taste).

Heat the ghee in the small skillet and add the cloves, cinnamon stick, cardamom pods, and bay leaf and cook for 20 seconds. Pour over the lentils and gently stir in and simmer for another 5 minutes before serving.

ROASTED WHITE SPLIT LENTILS WITH FENNEL AND FIVE-SPICE SEASONING
Mauri Diye Kalair Dal

I learned this dish from the lady who helped with the cooking at my mother's house in India. I really liked the unusual flavors in these lentils. The lime in this recipe is my addition, but I think that it contrasts well with the sweetness of the fennel seeds.

Prep Time: 5 minutes | **Cook Time:** 35 to 40 minutes (mostly unattended)
Makes: 4 to 6 servings

INGREDIENTS
½ cup dried white split lentils (kalai/urad dal)
½-inch piece fresh ginger, peeled
2 tablespoons fennel seeds
1 teaspoon salt
½ teaspoon turmeric
½ teaspoon cayenne pepper powder
2 teaspoons ghee (clarified butter)
1 teaspoon panch phoron (page 5)
Juice of 1 lime

PREPARATION
Place the white lentils in a pan and dry roast for about 5 minutes, until they are nice and fragrant. Place the ginger and fennel seeds in a wet/dry grinder and grind until smooth. Add the spice paste to the lentils and mix in 3 cups of water, salt, turmeric, and cayenne pepper powder and bring the mixture to a boil. Turn the heat down low and simmer for about 20 minutes.

Heat the ghee in a small skillet and add the panch phoron and wait till the spices splutter. Pour the seasoned ghee over the lentils. Squeeze the lime juice into the lentils and serve.

My Mother's Fish Head Pilaf with Vegetables (*Muro Bhaat*), page 43

Saffron Rice with Meatballs (*Moti Churi Birayani*), page 44

Yellow Split Lentils with Cauliflower (*Kopi Diye Moong Dal*), page 79

Onion Rings with Nigella Seeds (*Gol Piyali*), page 89

East Bengali Creamy Vegetable Medley (*Shapnar Shukto*), page 105

Mixed Seasonal Greens with Garlic and Fennel (*Rasun Phoron Diye Shaag*), page 106

Stir-Fried Mixed Vegetables (*Labra*), page 112

Potatoes with
Poppy Seeds
(*Alu Posto*),
page 122

Curried Cabbage with Potatoes and Green Peas (*Badha Kopir Ghanto*), page 124

Turnips and Green Peas in Coconut Sauce (*Salgam Monoroma*), page 139

Chili Basil Paneer (*Lanka Tulsi Diye Channar Dalna*), page 141

Winter Squash and Red Chard Curry (*Kumro Diye Lal Shager Ghanto*), page 142

Spicy Omelet Curry (*Omelet Dalna*), page 149

Eggs with Onions and Bell Peppers (*Dimer Jhal Ferazi*), page 150

Fish with Yogurt and Fresh Herbs (*Methi Dhone Pata Diye Doi Maach*), page 168

Mustard-Coated Fish Wrapped in Banana Leaves (*Macher Paturi*), page 165

Creamy Shrimp Curry (*Chingri Macher Korma*), page 176

Super-Quick Mustard Coconut Shrimp (*Shorse Narkol Chingri*), page 175

Childhood Mutton or Lamb Curry (*Chelebelar Mangshor Jhol*), page 207

Grilled Marinated Lamb Kababs (*Kababs*), page 241

Fresh Pineapple Chutney (*Anarasar Chaatney*), page 223
with Roasted or Fried Lentil Wafers (*Papor*), page 253

Banana Blossom Croquettes (*Mochar Chop*), page 244

Cottage Cheese Cakes (*Sandesh*), page 257

Almond, Maple and Tapioca Pudding (*Badam Doodher Payesh*), page 262

Delicate Spongy Pancakes with Pineapple (*Anaras diye Chanar Malpoa*),
page 273

Chapter Five:
Bhaja

Bhaja literally means "fried" and there are many fried offerings in Bengali cooking—usually served in small quantities along with lentils. The *bhaja* category encompasses plain vegetables, usually coated with salt and turmeric and fried, as well as a whole assortment of chickpea-batter fritters.

Simple, lightly seasoned lentils pair amazingly well with crisp, fried vegetables and fritters. The preferred vegetables for *bhaja* are potatoes, pumpkin, and okra. In general, serving sizes are small as these are starters to the Bengali meal. The more conventional fritters are made with lentils and poppy seeds, but all kinds of leftover bits and pieces of fish and vegetables can be used. And really, almost anything tastes good when it is spiced and fried, doesn't it?

I have learned over the years that these fritters actually get done much more quickly when fried in a deeper skillet. My experience has been that a heavy-bottomed anodized skillet requires less oil than a wok and is almost as good at controlling the heat.

Bhajas are the accompaniment of choice with lentil and rice porridges (*khichuris*). In fact, for religious festivals like Durga Pujas, this is still common fare. *Bhajas* are also a perfect appetizer to mix and match with other types of cuisines. As accompaniments or snacks these fritters work well with chutneys or even ketchup. My condiment of choice with *bhajas* is coconut mint chutney (page 224).

JULIENNE PAN-FRIED POTATOES
Alu Bhaja

At a bare minimum, these tiny, crisp, spiced potato straws are served with lentils. Just these tiny morsels with lentils and rice is enough to make most Bengalis happy. It is important to note that the *bhajas* and *boras* are usually one element of other assorted offerings, so they are served in small amounts.

Prep Time: 10 minutes | **Cook Time:** 15 to 20 minutes | **Makes:** 4 servings

INGREDIENTS
2 large potatoes (Yukon Golds work well)
½ teaspoon turmeric
Oil for frying
Salt
Freshly ground pepper

PREPARATION
Peel the potatoes, cut in half and then cut into thin matchstick-size pieces. Wash thoroughly in plenty of water. Dry the potatoes. (Note: Cut the potatoes immediately before frying so they don't turn brown.)

Heat some oil in a deep skillet and add the potatoes and fry till crisply golden, taking care not to brown them too much. Remove from pan with a slotted spoon and drain on paper towels. Sprinkle generously with salt and pepper and serve with rice and lentils.

CRISP TURNIP AND WINTER SQUASH STIR-FRY
Salgam ar Kumro Bhaja

I so miss the pumpkin flowers that we had in India! To this end, I made my husband grow every conceivable squash in our garden in order to use their blossoms. And with the flowers, there is always the fruit. This recipe is a healthier variation of wonderful potato fries. Turnips also work well for this recipe, making me realize just what an underappreciated vegetable the turnip is.

Prep Time: 15 to 20 minutes | **Cook Time:** 20 minutes | **Makes:** 4 to 6 servings

INGREDIENTS
¾ cup thinly sliced turnips (matchstick-size pieces)
¾ cup thinly sliced butternut squash or winter squash (matchstick-size pieces)
1 teaspoon salt
1 teaspoon cumin powder
½ teaspoon cayenne pepper powder
1 tablespoon rice flour
Oil for shallow frying

PREPARATION

Place the julienned vegetables in a large mixing bowl and add the salt, cumin powder, and cayenne pepper powder and mix well. Coat very lightly with the rice flour.

Heat some oil in a deep skillet and fry the vegetables until they are very lightly browned. Remove with a slotted spoon and drain on paper towels and serve.

LIGHTLY SPICED PAN-SAUTEED OKRA
Bhindi Bhaja

My kids love this simple okra dish. Okra or lady's fingers are readily available these days, but this recipe can be made with other vegetables of your choice, including the pointed gourd called *potol* in Bengali. If the okra is very fresh, I often skip adding turmeric to allow the vegetable's bright green color to show.

Prep Time: 10 to 15 minutes | **Cook Time:** 10 minutes | **Makes:** 4 to 6 servings

INGREDIENTS
2 pounds okra, trimmed, washed, and cut into 1-inch pieces*
½ teaspoon turmeric (optional)
1 teaspoon salt
4 to 6 tablespoons mustard oil
1 teaspoon panch phoron (page 5)

PREPARATION
Rub the okra with the turmeric (if using) and salt and set aside. Heat the oil in a wok or skillet and add the panch phoron and wait till the seeds begin to crackle. Add the okra and stir lightly for about 5 minutes until lightly crisp. Add ¼ cup water* and cover and cook for about 4 minutes. Remove the cover and cook until the water is completely absorbed. It is important the okra is cooked through but not mushy.

*Note: It is important to dry the okra thoroughly before cutting it.
If the okra is very fresh, water is usually not needed for cooking since it cooks through without it.

LIGHTLY SPICED PAN-FRIED EGGPLANTS
Begun Bhaja

Though the spices and techniques of this recipe are not very different from others, here the natural, soft flesh of the eggplant transcends to amazing gastronomical proportions. A good *begun bhaja* (fried eggplant) is worth all the calories. I have tried cooking it in the oven, but I have to confess that nothing comes close to the taste of the soft, sensuous fried variety. It is imperative to use young, tender eggplants.

Prep Time: 7 to 8 minutes | **Cook Time:** 10-15 minutes | **Makes:** 4 servings

INGREDIENTS
4 medium eggplants
1 teaspoon turmeric
1 teaspoon salt
Mustard oil for frying

PREPARATION
Cut the eggplants into quarters lengthwise and then into 2-inch wedges. Rub the eggplants with the turmeric and salt.

Heat some oil in a wok or skillet until it is smoking. Add the eggplant pieces (in batches) and fry for about 5 minutes. Remove gently with a slotted spoon and drain on paper towels to remove excess oil before serving.

LENTIL FRITTERS WITH GINGER AND GREEN CHILIES
Gaan Didar Daler Bora

Sometimes when a large fresh fish is cut into steaks, the smaller pieces are set aside and fried to a nice golden crispness to be served with lentils. My music teacher, Gaan Dida (meaning "musical grandmother"), tells me how her brother loved these lentil fritters more than the fried fish they were served with, so she usually traded her fritters for his fish and they were both happy.

Prep Time: 10 minutes (plus 2 to 3 hours for soaking lentils)
Cook Time: 25 minutes | **Makes:** 4 to 6 servings

INGREDIENTS
¾ cup yellow split lentils (moong dal) or white split lentils (kalai/urad dal),
    soaked in warm water for about 2 to 3 hours
1-inch piece fresh ginger, peeled
1 teaspoon cumin seeds
3 or 4 green chilies
1 teaspoon salt
2 tablespoons onion, finely chopped (optional)
Oil for shallow frying

PREPARATION
Drain the lentils and place in a blender with ¾ cup of water, the ginger, cumin seeds, chilies, and salt and blend until very smooth. Mix in the chopped onions if using.

Heat some oil in a skillet and add the lentil mixture by tablespoonfuls to the oil (working in batches) and fry for about 5 minutes until the side facing the heat is nice and crisp and uniformly golden brown. (With these and any other fritters, it is important to let them fry undisturbed.) Turn and cook for another 3 to 4 minutes on the other side. Remove with a slotted spoon and drain on paper towels. Serve hot.

SPICY CRISP BITTER MELON CIRCLES
Jhal Tauk Korolar Jhuri

The presentation of bitter melon in Indian cooking is comprised of two extremes: there is the simple, boiled format like in Bengali cuisine where the vegetable is used as a palate cleanser, and there are North Indian versions where the vegetable is cooked almost like a pickle to the point where very little of its original taste remains. This recipe strikes a middle ground by seasoning the vegetable with a lighter touch.

I strayed by adding mango powder (amchur) rather than the traditional Bengali tamarind in this recipe, but managed to add enough character to get this vegetable ready for prime time. In this form it can be used to accompany most meals.

Prep Time: 1 hour (for soaking and marinating) | **Cook Time:** 15 minutes
Makes: 4 servings

INGREDIENTS
5 young bitter melons
4 cups ice water
2 teaspoons coarse salt (such as kosher salt)
1 teaspoon amchur powder
½ teaspoon cayenne pepper powder
¾ teaspoon salt
½ teaspoon turmeric
¾ cup vegetable or mustard oil for frying

PREPARATION
Slice the bitter melons into thin slices. Mix the ice water and kosher salt and soak the bitter melon in this water for about 25 minutes. Drain thoroughly on paper towels.

Mix together the amchur powder, cayenne pepper powder, salt, and turmeric and rub into the bitter melon slices and set aside for about 30 minutes.

Heat some oil in a wok or skillet on medium for about 5 to 6 minutes, until almost smoking. Add the bitter melon (in batches if needed, as there should be enough room to allow the vegetables to move around freely to turn golden brown and crisp). Cook for about 6 to 7 minutes until the bitter melon is nice and crisp. Remove with a slotted spoon and drain on paper towels before serving. Before each new batch is added to the oil, clear the oil of any crumbs with a slotted spoon and make sure that it is nice and hot.

ONION RINGS WITH NIGELLA SEEDS
Gol Piyaji

These onion fritters are a well-loved roadside food in Bengal—hot and crisply fried, wrapped lovingly in newspaper bags.

There is a story behind the newspaper itself. In India, recycling is perfected to an art form, designed with a 4-layer industry. First we have the purchaser of the original newspapers. Then that person saves and stacks the papers for the used newspaper buyer, a very essential middleman. When he arrives, they settle on a price, the newspaper stack is weighed, and then he is on his way. He then sells the newspapers to the paper bag manufacturer, who makes the paper bags that are in turn bought by the vendors of the onion ring fritters.

I make these fritters like onion rings to make them fun for my kids. They also make a great appetizer to pair with drinks.

Prep Time: 20 minutes | **Cook Time:** 25 minutes | **Makes:** 6 servings

INGREDIENTS
4 medium onions, tops removed and peeled
¾ cup chickpea flour
¾ teaspoon nigella seeds
½ teaspoon cayenne pepper powder
1 teaspoon black salt
Oil for frying
Cilantro to garnish (optional)

PREPARATION
Cut the onions into ½-inch-thick rounds and separate the rounds.

Mix the chickpea flour and ½ cup of water into a thick batter (the consistency should coat easily). Stir in the nigella seeds, cayenne pepper powder, and black salt and mix well.

Heat some oil in a wok or deep skillet until hot enough for frying. Dip each onion ring in the batter and fry until crisp. You may fry 3 or 4 or more rings at a time, depending on the size of the wok or skillet. It is important not to have the rings touch each other while cooking. Remove rings from the oil and drain on paper towels before serving.

OVEN-CRISPED WINTER SQUASH
Kumro Bhaja

The closest equivalent to pumpkin in Bengali is *kumro*. There are not too many varieties of an orange squash available in winter. Though it would normally be fried, I discovered that roasting the squash in the oven with some mustard oil does something wonderful to it. I usually use delicata winter squash for this recipe, but it can be made with any other pumpkin or squash variety.

Prep Time: 10 minutes | **Cook Time:** 25 to 30 minutes (mostly unattended)
Makes: 4 servings

INGREDIENTS
2 medium delicata squashes or 1 butternut squash, peeled and cut into cubes
    (about 3 cups)
2 tablespoons mustard oil
½ teaspoon nigella seeds
1 teaspoon fresh ginger paste (page 13)
½ teaspoon salt
Juice of ½ lime

PREPARATION
Pre-heat the oven to 375 degrees F. Toss the squash in the mustard oil, nigella seeds, ginger paste, and salt to coat evenly. Spread the squash evenly onto a baking sheet and bake in the oven for about 25 to 30 minutes, until the squash is roasted, fragrant, and lightly crisp. Check the squash while it is baking since it has a high sugar content and can burn easily. Remove from the oven, sprinkle with some lime juice, and serve with rice and lentils or pair with a drier dish.

GREEN PLANTAIN AND TARO CAKES
Kachkolar Cutlet

These small, rather delectable vegetarian cakes are usually made with green (unripe) bananas. The recipe also works well with green plantains, which I find more readily available in my neck of the woods. The first time I cooked them, I was very disappointed and threw them away. The next time, I used a pressure cooker until they were very soft, and lo and behold, it worked beautifully. An extra batch of these cutlets can be made and kept in the refrigerator for at least a week to cook as a curry.

I should also take a minute to mention the importance of the banana plant in the Bengali culinary repertoire. The banana plant fits beautifully into the sustainable nature of Bengali cuisine since all parts of the plant can be used—the fruits, flowers, and stems for eating, and the leaves as serving plates.

Prep Time: 15 to 45 minutes | **Cook Time:** 25 to 30 minutes
Makes: 4 to 6 servings

INGREDIENTS

2 plantains or green unripe bananas
3 taros (sold in most Indian grocery stores, if you cannot find them you can use 1 large Idaho potato)
1 small red onion, finely chopped
3 or 4 green chilies, finely chopped
2 tablespoons finely chopped cilantro (optional)
1 teaspoon salt
½ teaspoon cayenne pepper powder
1½ tablespoons chickpea flour
Oil for shallow frying

PREPARATION

Peel the plantains and cut into 3 pieces each. Place these and 2 cups of water in a pressure cooker and pressure cook for 5 minutes. (Alternately, place plantains and water in a pot and cook on medium heat until soft.)

Peel the skin off the taros and place with the plantains in a bowl and mash with a fork. Add the onion, green chilies, cilantro (if using), salt, cayenne pepper powder, and chickpea flour and mix well. Shape into small 2-inch cakes.

Heat some oil in a deep skillet and cooking in batches, fry cakes for about 3 minutes on each side.

POPPY SEED AND GREEN CHILI FRITTERS
Posto Bora

These small, delicate creations contain a very treasured ingredient that you will see featured throughout this cookbook. Unlike other regions of India, the Bengali kitchen is not partial to nuts, so the preferred seed to achieve creaminess in a lot of recipes is the white poppy seed. It is like a balancing counterpart to the fiery mustard seed. In this recipe, poppy seeds are crushed with green chilies and onions into a paste, shaped into small balls, and fried till very delicately crisp.

Prep Time: 4 hours (to soak poppy seeds) | **Cook Time:** 15 to 20 minutes
Makes: about 10

INGREDIENTS

4 tablespoons white poppy seeds
½ cup warm water
2 green chilies
¾ teaspoon salt
1 teaspoon grated fresh ginger
1 tablespoon rice flour
3 tablespoons finely chopped onion
Oil for shallow frying

Soak the poppy seeds in the warm water for 4 hours. Place the poppy seeds, water, green chilies, salt, and grated ginger in a blender and blend until smooth and creamy. Stir in the rice flour and chopped onion.

Heat some oil in a wok or skillet. Working in batches, drop teaspoonfuls of the paste into the hot oil and fry until very lightly golden on both sides. Remove with a slotted spoon and drain on paper towels.

CRISPY EGG FRITTERS
Dim Bhaja or Mamlet

On a cold rainy night, I resurrected this recipe from the vestiges of my childhood memories. I had informed my husband earlier that evening that I would be cooking something comforting with eggs. He looked at me like I was crazy and said that an egg was an egg, and he was not sure why I thought it was comforting no matter how it was cooked. I proceeded nonetheless. After I made these fritters, I went to take a shower. When I returned I found that my husband had happily finished most of them—so much for an egg being just an egg.

Prep Time: 15 minutes | **Cook Time:** 25 minutes | **Makes:** 10 pieces

INGREDIENTS
2 eggs
¼ cup chickpea flour (besan)
2 green chilies, finely chopped
2 tablespoons ginger-cumin-coriander paste (page 14)
1 teaspoon salt
2 tablespoons finely chopped cilantro
Oil for shallow frying
Paprika or chili powder for dusting

PREPARATION
Beat the eggs with the chickpea flour until all the lumps have dissolved. Stir in the green chilies, ginger-cumin-coriander paste, and salt and beat again. Mix in the cilantro.

Heat some oil in a wok or skillet. Working in batches, drop teaspoonfuls of the batter into the oil and fry till lightly golden on both sides, about 7 to 8 minutes. Remove with a slotted spoon and drain on paper towels. Sprinkle with paprika or chili powder prior to serving.

FRIED SQUASH BLOSSOMS
Kumro Phul Bhaja

Even in India's bustling cities, freshness is a way of life, especially with fish and produce. I have already mentioned how much I love pumpkin or squash blossoms. The last time I visited Kolkata, I accompanied my mother to the market and asked her why we never got any pumpkin blossoms. It turned out that to accommodate my late-rising habits she would not get to the market until after ten in the morning. This was too late for the blossoms she informed me. I still did not quite understand, but was happy when she had them fetched for me the next day.

Later I persuaded my husband to grow the blossoms, and he would pick them for me but by the time I woke up, the blossoms were closed. So one day he actually photographed the open blossoms for me. The next day I did wake up early enough and saw the beauty of the open blossoms and also realized how very fresh the produce back in India was.

In this recipe, I use the traditional batter, but mix it with seltzer or club soda. I love the lightness the bubbles impart to the batter.

Prep Time: 20 minutes | **Cook Time:** 20 minutes | **Makes:** 4 servings

INGREDIENTS
¾ cup chickpea flour
2 tablespoons finely chopped red onion
2 or 3 green chilies, finely chopped
1 teaspoon salt
1 tablespoon finely chopped cilantro
½ teaspoon turmeric
½ teaspoon nigella seeds
1 cup club soda or water
8 to 10 zucchini blossoms
Oil for frying

PREPARATION
Place the chickpea flour in a bowl and beat until there are no more lumps. Add in the red onion, green chilies, salt, cilantro, turmeric, and nigella seeds. Mix in the club soda and beat to a light batter.

Heat some oil in a large skillet. Working quickly, dip some of the blossoms in the batter and place in the hot oil. Fry for about 4 minutes on each side, drain thoroughly. Repeat with remaining blossoms. Serve hot.

FISH ROE FRITTERS
Macher Dimer Bora

These fritters can be an acquired taste, but most people tend to love them when they do not realize what they are eating. The first time I cooked these in the U.S. was with shad roe. I was pregnant and my husband had brought home a pair of roe hoping to appease my palate. Shad roe is not that easy to find these days, but I have made these with flounder roe as well. In India, my mother usually makes this with the bhetki fish roe.

Prep Time: 20 minutes | **Cook Time:** 25 minutes | **Makes:** 4 servings

INGREDIENTS
1 pound fish roe
3 tablespoons chickpea flour
2 to 3 tablespoons chopped onion
½ teaspoon cayenne pepper powder
2 green chilies, finely chopped
1 teaspoon salt
Oil for frying

PREPARATION
Place the fish roe in a mixing bowl and mash with a fork or your hands to break the roe. Mix with the flour, onions, cayenne pepper powder, green chilies, and salt. Heat some oil in a wok or skillet. Working in batches, drop teaspoonfuls of the roe mixture into the hot oil and fry until crisp. Remove with a slotted spoon and drain on paper towels.

FRIED TILAPIA WITH GINGER AND GREEN CHILI SEASONING
Fish Fry

This recipe is an adaptation of Anglo-Indian-style breaded fried fish. The coating is more along the lines of the Indo-Chinese coating. Most people I know find the combination of tender, moist, lightly spiced fish encased in a crisp light coating quite irresistible and this is usually a welcome addition to most dinner tables. The fish can be marinated for several hours in the refrigerator if desired and I often do this the night before for an afternoon meal. This recipe is best accompanied by *Kasundi* (Fiery Mustard and Lemon Relish, page 226) for the adventurous, or ketchup and tartar sauce for a more anglicized effect.

Prep Time: 1½ hours (mostly to marinate) | **Cook Time:** 25 minutes
Makes: 4 servings

INGREDIENTS
Tilapia
2-inch piece fresh ginger. peeled
Juice of 1 lime
3 or 4 green chilies
1 tablespoon coriander seeds
½ teaspoon cumin seeds
½ teaspoon black peppercorns
⅓ cup chopped fresh cilantro
1 small red onion, peeled and quartered
1 teaspoon salt
1½ pounds tilapia fillets (or other white fish such as haddock, bhetki, or sole)

Batter
½ cup all-purpose white flour
⅓ cup cornstarch
1 teaspoon salt
1 egg

Oil for frying

Garnish
Extra green chilies

PREPARATION
Marinate tilapia fillets:
Place the ginger in the base of a blender. Squeeze in the lime juice and add 2 tablespoons of water, the chilies, coriander seeds, cumin seeds, black pepper-corns, cilantro, red onion, and salt. Blend to a smooth paste. Marinate the fish in this mixture for at least 1 hour. (This can be done outside the refrigerator in temperatures up to 65 to 70 degrees F. This usually results in a better flavor, but during warmer days it is best to keep the fish in the refrigerator.)

Prepare batter:
Sift the flour, cornstarch, and salt into a mixing bowl. Add the egg and enough water to form a batter that is the consistency of pancake batter, about ¾ cup. It should be thick enough to coat the fish easily but not too thick.

Heat some oil on medium heat in a heavy-bottomed skillet. Dip 2 or 3 pieces of the fish into the batter and add to the hot oil and fry for about 4 minutes on each side, until the fish is nice and crisp and cooked through. Drain well on paper towels. Repeat with remaining fillets. Serve garnished with the extra chilies.

Spice Two: Nigella Seeds

Tiny black nigella seeds, called *kalo jire* in Bengali, are the second of the five spices that form the Five Spice Blend (*panch phoron*, page 5). The ayurvedic taste associated with this spice is astringent, and it is said to have a cooling, lightening effect on the body. Nigella seeds have a very vivid black appearance. They are used extensively for seasoning vegetables, and are also used for lighter curries, most prominently fish curries cooked during the summer months or for sick or convalescing patients.

Much like other regions in India, the Bengali table does not usually feature salads as part of a menu. There are, however, a series of vegetables cooked in a lighter style that fill this void. These uniquely cooked dishes showcase the ingenuity, frugality, and sustainable nature of Bengali cooking. They are always made with vegetables in season. For a light stir-fry, the tempering is often done with just nigella seeds and maybe a hint of ginger.

Nigella seeds for me are synonymous with very simple homestyle fare and nostalgia. They bring back memories of my paternal grandmother's house in the outskirts of Kolkata in a region called Belur. Her house was self-contained and she had a couple of cows, an adequate garden where she grew greens and basic vegetables, and a pond in which people could catch fish and swim.

My grandmother loved feeding people and she did this wholeheartedly. I would like to think I have inherited the joy of feeding people from her. Special occasions such as weddings used to be held against the backdrop of this family house, and it was remarkable to see how much action would take place. It was also quite fascinating to see the amount of cooking that occurred, discrete and distinct for each meal: breakfast, snacks, and sweets, followed by the lunchtime meals, and of course, teatime and dinner. However, my favorite dish of hers was her simple fish curry seasoned with ginger and nigella seeds and made with thinly sliced potatoes.

Chapter Six:
Vegetarian First Courses
Sheddo, Pora ar Chorchori

The food in this category falls into the following classifications: *bhate*, in which vegetables, usually tied in a piece of cloth, are boiled with the rice; *sheddo*, which are boiled or steamed vegetables (without rice); *pora*, which literally means "burnt," but refers to the process of smoking and cooking the vegetables to the point that the outer skin is charred; and finally vegetable medleys called *chorchoris*. Greens presented by themselves are usually called *shaag*, and also adorn the beginning of the Bengali meal.

When making *bhate*, the vegetable and rice are put in the pot together and then the water is added and the rice is cooked the usual way. If for some reason you do not want to do that (it is an unusual concept if you have not gotten used to boiled vegetables being fished out from the rice growing up), they can be boiled separately. But the concept of boiling or steaming things along with the rice does offer both energy and time savings.

The *pora* or smoked vegetables also emerged in this manner, since the traditional cooking mechanism was a coal stove that retained its heat long after the food was cooked, so vegetables such as eggplants were then placed over the hot embers and charred. This smoking process is now done over any open flame, such as a gas stove or grill.

The *chorchori* is a creative way to use up small amounts of vegetables and form a creative healthy and nutritious dish.

Lentil nuggets called *boris* fortify the vegetarian dishes. These tiny drops of dried lentil paste are spread on clean muslin cloth with great care to allow them to sun-dry.

MASHED POTATOES AND BITTER MELON
Alu Korola Sheddo

The most popular starter, the bitter melon (*korola*) is well loved by the Bengalis. It is usually mashed together with potatoes to cut the bitterness. Most Bengali children grow up eating this medley several times a week for lunch.

Prep Time: 5 minutes | **Cook Time:** 15 to 20 minutes (unattended)
Makes: 4 servings

INGREDIENTS
2 potatoes, scrubbed
1 medium bitter melon
1 teaspoon salt
1 tablespoon mustard oil

PREPARATION
Cut the potatoes and bitter melon in half and place in a pot. Add water to cover and boil until vegetables are soft. Remove the vegetables, peel the potatoes and place in a mixing bowl. Remove the seeds from the bitter melon and scoop pulp into the mixing bowl. Add the salt and mustard oil and mash the vegetables together to make a fairly smooth mixture. Shape into small rounds and serve with rice and lentils.

SPICY MASHED POTATOES OR TARO
Alu ba Kochu Sheddo

A simple essential that many Bengalis consider a comfort food. It is something I make for myself when my husband is traveling and then savor its simple tasting flavors. It is best accompanied by a simple lentil dish.

Prep Time: 10 minutes | **Cook Time:** 20 minutes | **Makes:** 4 servings

INGREDIENTS
4 medium potatoes or taro
3 green chilies, minced
1 red onion, finely chopped
½ teaspoon salt
3 tablespoons mustard oil

PREPARATION
Place the whole potatoes or taro in a heavy-bottomed pot and add water to cover and boil until soft but not mushy. Cool slightly and remove the jackets. Mash the potatoes or taro with the remaining ingredients. Shape into lemon-size balls and serve with rice and lentils.

TEMPERED MASHED POTATOES WITH EGGS
Alu Dimer Bhortha

My mother often sends me care packages with family friends and their children who are traveling back and forth between India and the U.S. Recently a friend's daughter, who lives a good two hours away from us, had a package for me. When I contacted her to arrange to pick it up, she invited me to lunch.

The lunch was a leisurely, homey Bengali affair with several offerings. What intrigued me most was a fish hash called *bhortha* that she made with catfish. Inspired by this creation I have made several variations of the dish with fish and other ingredients, such as the eggs and bell peppers in this recipe.

Now while I was familiar with *bhates*, the *bhortha* was a somewhat new creature in my life. I have since discovered that they are relatively common, and have found them in homestyle Bengali restaurants in Indian neighborhoods. *Bhorthas* are more popular in the East Bengali culinary repertoire and the east Bengali versions are spicier, almost like relishes. I have featured some of them in the relish section. All of this is inspired by my friend's fish *bhortha*. Clearly I picked up more than just the care package that day!

Prep Time: 10 minutes | **Cook Time:** 25 minutes | **Makes:** 4 servings

INGREDIENTS
3 red potatoes
2 eggs
1 teaspoon salt
1 teaspoon cayenne pepper powder
2 tablespoons mustard oil
½ teaspoon nigella seeds
1 onion, very finely chopped
1 red bell pepper, finely chopped
2 green chilies, finely chopped
Juice of 1 lime

PREPARATION
Cook the potatoes till soft; then peel and coarsely mash. (If you are using new red potatoes, you may actually leave the skins on if you desire as it adds an interesting dimension of taste and is more nutritious that way.)

Boil the eggs for about 6 minutes (the yolks should be somewhat moist, not runny or dry). Peel and mash the eggs with the salt and cayenne pepper powder. Mix into the potatoes.

Heat the mustard oil in a wok or skillet on medium heat for about 30 seconds and then add the nigella seeds and wait till they sizzle. Add the onion and cook on low-medium heat, stirring until the onion is turning golden. Add the bell pepper and cook for an additional 5 to 6 minutes, till the pepper is very soft. Pour over the potato mixture and add the chilies and lime juice. Mix well and enjoy as a side dish.

SMOKED GREEN MANGOES AND POTATOES
Kacha Aam Pora

The green mango is the tangy sultry siren that has captured palates across many parts of India. This is a very versatile Bengali recipe—for an adventurous table, you can serve this with a roast or broiled fish. I have proposed cooking the mangoes on a grill, which is not very far removed from the coal stoves used in West Bengal. They can alternately be cooked on the open flame of a gas stove, but this does need some attention. If none of these alternatives are workable, by all means roast them in the oven.

Prep Time: 5 to 10 minutes | **Cook Time:** 20 to 30 minutes | **Makes:** 4 servings

INGREDIENTS
2 green mangoes
2 large Idaho potatoes
2 tablespoons mustard oil
1 small red onion, chopped
2 tablespoons chopped cilantro
½ teaspoon cayenne pepper powder
1 teaspoon salt

PREPARATION
Place the mangoes and potatoes on the grill on a low flame and cook for about 10 minutes on each side. The key objective of this step is to char the outer skin and cook the inside of the mangoes and potatoes.

Cool and peel the mangoes and carefully remove the soft cooked flesh using your hands and place in a bowl. Peel the potatoes and place in the same mixing bowl as the mangoes. Mash them together. Mix in the mustard oil, onion, cilantro, cayenne pepper powder, and salt and serve with rice and lentils.

Kal Baishaski Storms

I was in Kolkata last year in April and despite the heat, I was thrilled to experience the Kal Baishaski storms again. These pre-monsoon storms are an amazing phenomenon of nature. The skies suddenly get filled with dark, puffy cumulus clouds that are etched with thick silver linings. Then there are intense winds followed by brisk tumultuous rains that bring with them cooling calm until the sun comes out again. Green mangoes are usually torn off the trees during these storms. I personally think that this phenomenon accounts for the tender tart freshness of these fruits.

MASHED SMOKED EGGPLANT
Begun Pora

This is the most common of the smoked vegetable dishes. It is best made with the wonderful summer eggplants available in the U.S. or the delicate, plump Indian eggplant. I always say that even the smallest nuances highlight the vivid differences in Indian topography and food. When we were in Kolkata, my husband was quite impressed with the delicate plump green eggplants that are readily available in West Bengal.

This dish is a winter specialty in Bengal, since that is when the best eggplants are available. It is optimal to have a gas stove or an open-fire grill to cook these eggplants. If the skin does not get nice and smoky it is hard to get the smoke-infused taste that is essential to this dish.

Prep Time: 5 minutes | **Cook Time:** 25 minutes | **Makes:** 4 servings

INGREDIENTS
2 or 3 medium eggplants
3 tablespoons oil (preferably mustard)
2 teaspoons cumin-coriander powder (page 17)
1 teaspoon salt
1 small red onion, finely chopped
2 green chilies, finely chopped
1 tablespoon chopped cilantro

PREPARATION
Place the unpeeled eggplants on the open flame of a gas stove or on a grill. Cook them till their skin is nice and charred. Cool slightly. Remove the skins and cut eggplants into cubes.

Heat the oil in a large wok or skillet and add the cumin-coriander powder and cook for about 30 to 40 seconds. Add the eggplants and salt and mash well with the back of a spoon. Stir in the red onion, green chilies, and cilantro and cook for a few minutes to meld flavors.

MASHED SEASONED BUTTERNUT SQUASH
Kumro Sheddo

This variation of mashed vegetables is a mustard or spice lover's delight. I make this with butternut squash, which grows in the garden in fall and actually keeps well through winter. But it can be made with any other variety of orange squash, such as pumpkin or acorn squash, all of which are harbingers of cooler weather.

Prep Time: 5 minutes | **Cook Time:** 15 to 20 minutes | **Makes:** 4 servings

INGREDIENTS
1 medium butternut squash
1 teaspoon salt
1 small red onion, finely chopped
2 to 3 green chilies, finely chopped
1 tablespoon chopped cilantro
2 tablespoons mustard oil

PREPARATION
Cut the butternut squash into large chunks and scoop out the seeds. Place the squash in a large pot and add water to cover. Boil for about 10 to 12 minutes, until soft. Remove squash from the water and scoop pulp into a mixing bowl. Add the salt, red onion, green chilies, cilantro, and mustard oil and mash everything together to make a fairly smooth mixture. Shape into small rounds and serve with rice and lentils.

VEGETABLES WITH BITTER MELON SIMMERED IN MILK AND SPICES
Shukto

Shukto holds an exalted place among the vegetable medleys. This *shukto* recipe is an approximation of what my mom made with accommodations for the vegetables I like. Bitter melon is credited with being the center of the *shukto* universe. To me, however, just as important is the delicate sauce in which the vegetables are simmered. Other than the bitter melon, there are no absolutes in terms of the vegetables used but it is best to cut them into 2-inch wedges. The bitter melon does need to be chosen with care as it should be young and tender, not the tougher seedy variety.

Prep Time: 20 minutes | **Cook Time:** 30 minutes | **Makes:** 4 to 6 servings

INGREDIENTS
⅓ cup oil (preferably mustard)
10 to 12 boris (lentil nuggets, page 9)
2 small or 1 large bitter melon, cut into pieces
5 or 6 small red radishes, quartered
2 red potatoes, quartered (preferably with the peel on)
1 medium green banana, peeled and cut into wedges
½ cup chopped cauliflower
1 teaspoon salt
1 tablespoon ginger-cumin-coriander paste (page 14)
1 teaspoon mustard seed paste (page 15)
2 tablespoons poppy seed paste (page 14)
½ cup milk
2 teaspoons sugar
1 tablespoons ghee (clarified butter)
1 teaspoon panch phoron (page 5)

PREPARATION

Heat the oil in a large wok or skillet and add the boris and fry until pale golden. Remove with a slotted spoon and set aside.

Add the bitter melon and fry till somewhat crisp. Add the remaining vegetables and sauté lightly for about 2 minutes. Stir in the salt and ginger-cumin-coriander paste and cook lightly. Add the mustard seed paste, poppy seed paste, milk, sugar, and ½ cup of water and cover and simmer the vegetables until soft and a thick paste is formed, about 7 minutes.

Heat the ghee in a small skillet and add the panch phoron and wait till the spices splutter. Pour the seasoned ghee over the vegetables and serve.

CREAMED SPINACH WITH MUSTARD
Shorshe Saag

Cooking with mustard requires finding a delicate flavor balance and a little bit of effort in mellowing the taste goes a long way. I have gone through several tools and devices to find a variation of mustard that was at least close to the mustard that is freshly stone ground. In this recipe, I have substituted a quick mustard paste that is easy but still imparts a delicious mustardy taste. My husband waxed poetic to his college friend about the amazing rich taste of mustard, so when the gentleman wanted proof positive, I made this variation of Bengali spinach which is now a very popular item on our table.

Prep Time: 10 minutes | **Cook Time:** 20 minutes | **Makes:** 4 servings

INGREDIENTS
½ cup sour cream
3 cups chopped fresh spinach
1 tablespoon mustard oil
½ teaspoon cumin seeds
1 onion, finely chopped
2 tablespoons quick mustard paste (page 15)
1 teaspoon salt
⅓ cup green peas (thawed if frozen)

PREPARATION

In a blender, blend the sour cream and spinach into a puree.

Heat the mustard oil in a skillet and add the cumin seeds and wait for them to sizzle. Stir in the onion and sauté for about 5 minutes, until translucent and beginning to turn lightly golden on the edges.

Stir in the spinach mixture and cook till bubbling and cooked through, about 5 minutes. Mix in the mustard paste, salt, and peas and cook for another 3 to 4 minutes.

EAST BENGALI CREAMY VEGETABLE MEDLEY
Shapnar Shukto

This recipe was kindly shared by my friend Shapna. Her written instructions reminded me of ones my mother used to send to help me fend for myself in the early months after my arrival in the U.S. The recipe was a simple approximation in the voice of the cook, with a lot left up to the user to construct and adapt. This is essentially how the Bengali chef cooks. Like others in this book, this recipe can be adapted to accommodate the vegetables in season.

Prep Time: 15 minutes | **Cook Time:** 25 to 30 minutes | **Makes:** 4 to 6 servings

INGREDIENTS
4 tablespoons mustard oil
1 teaspoon panch phoron (page 5)
2 dried red chilies
2 green chilies, slit lengthwise
1 cup red or daikon radishes, cut into 2-inch wedges
1 cup cauliflower pieces
1 cup eggplant wedges (skin on)
1½ teaspoons salt
2 tablespoons poppy seed paste (page 14)
10 blanched almonds
1 tablespoon ghee (clarified butter)
½ teaspoon fennel seed powder
½ teaspoon red pepper flakes

PREPARATION
In a heavy-bottomed cooking pot, heat the mustard oil on medium heat for about 1 minute. Add the panch phoron and dried red chilies and heat for about 30 seconds until the spices begin to crackle and turn fragrant. Add the slit green chilies and vegetables and mix well. Cover and cook for about 3 to 4 minutes. Add ¾ cup minus 2 tablespoons of water to the vegetable mixture and bring to a simmer. Simmer on low heat for about 15 minutes, until the vegetables are tender and the water is almost evaporated.

In the meantime grind the blanched almonds with 2 tablespoons water into a paste. Add the almond paste to the vegetable mixture and stir until it coats the vegetables with a thick dry sauce.

Heat the ghee in a small skillet on medium heat and stir in the fennel seed powder and red pepper flakes. Pour the seasoned ghee over the vegetables and stir lightly before serving.

MIXED SEASONAL GREENS WITH GARLIC AND FENNEL
Rasun Phoron Diye Shaag

My husband and I like garlic, but when I was growing up it was a rather uncommon seasoning, particularly for vegetarian dishes. After I tasted a garlicky dish made with tender green beans at my cousin's house, I was inspired to create this recipe for seasonal greens. The greens used in this recipe can be anything from fresh spinach to beet greens, turnip greens, kale, chard or whatever your heart fancies.

Prep Time: 10 minutes | **Cook Time:** 15 minutes | **Makes:** 4 servings

INGREDIENTS
2 tablespoons oil
1 teaspoon fennel seeds
1 teaspoon fresh ginger paste (page 13)
3 cloves garlic, pressed
4 cups finely chopped very fresh mixed greens (spinach, beet greens, turnip greens, kale, chard, etc)
¾ teaspoon salt
½ teaspoon cayenne pepper powder

PREPARATION
Heat the oil in a large wok or skillet on medium heat for about 45 seconds. Add the fennel seeds and allow the seeds to sizzle and darken (should take less than a minute). Add the ginger paste and garlic and cook for another minute until fragrant and very lightly golden. Add the greens and salt and cayenne pepper powder. Cook, stirring frequently, for about 5 minutes, until the greens are wilted and soft. Remove from the heat and serve.

GARDEN VEGETABLES WITH LENTIL NUGGETS
Tauk Misti Chorchori

Another inspired Bengali dish, this one is made with sweet vegetables, like carrots, turnips, and yellow beets, enriched with marinated whole boris. The purpose of marinating the lentil nuggets in the lime juice and salt is to infuse them with a tartness that in turn complements the natural sweetness of the vegetables.

Prep Time: 20 minutes (plus 2 to 3 hours for marinating boris)
Cook Time: 30 minutes | **Makes:** 4 servings

INGREDIENTS
¼ cup oil
½ cup boris (lentil nuggets, page 9)
Juice of ½ lime
1 teaspoon salt
1 teaspoon chili powder

1 teaspoon ghee (clarified butter)
1 teaspoon panch phoron (page 5)
1 or 2 green chilies, slit
½ teaspoon turmeric
1 golden beet, peeled and cubed
1 or 2 small carrots, peeled and cubed
½ cup diced green beans
2 small white turnips, cubed
2 tablespoons finely chopped cilantro

PREPARATION
Heat the oil in a wok or skillet on medium heat and fry boris until crisp. Remove with a slotted spoon and place in a bowl and reserve the oil. Squeeze the lime juice on them and sprinkle with half the salt and the chili powder. Cover and marinate in a warm place for 2 to 3 hours.

Heat the reserved oil and the ghee in a large wok or skillet and add the panch phoron. When this crackles mix in the green chilies, turmeric, vegetables, and remaining ½ teaspoon salt and stir well for about 30 seconds. Stir in ½ cup of water and bring to a simmer. Cover and cook for about 20 minutes.

Mix in the marinated boris with the marinade and cook for another 5 minutes. Check seasonings and stir in the cilantro and serve.

SPRING ONIONS WITH POTATOES AND SHRIMP
Piaj-Kolir Chorchori

This is another Bengali classic that I tweaked by adding leeks to supplement the scallions. I leave it up to you to decide whether you want to do this. The term *koli* refers to a bud, in this case the buds are the green stalks of the onions. The best type of spring onions to use are a soft variety found at farmer's markets, since they have a lot of greens attached to the onion bulb. Scallions are a practical substitute.

Prep Time: 10 minutes | **Cook Time:** 25 minutes | **Makes:** 4 servings

INGREDIENTS
2 tablespoons oil
1½ tablespoons ginger-cumin-coriander paste (page 14)
1 small onion, thinly sliced
2 potatoes, peeled and cubed
1 teaspoon salt
3 bunches spring onions or scallions
½ teaspoon turmeric
Juice of 1 lime
½ pound small or medium shrimp, shelled and de-veined
1 teaspoon sugar

PREPARATION

Heat the oil in a wok or skillet on medium-low heat. Add the spice paste and cook for about 2 minutes, until it is hot and smells fragrant. Add the onion, potatoes, and half the salt and cook the mixture on low heat until the potatoes are soft.

Prepare the scallions by slicing the white parts thinly and cutting the remaining greens into 2 to 3 pieces each. Add the whites of the scallions to the potato mixture with ½ cup water and simmer till dry.

In the meantime, sprinkle the remaining ½ teaspoon salt and the turmeric and lime juice onto the shrimp. Add the shrimp, most of the scallion greens, and the sugar to the potato mixture, reserving a few scallion greens for garnish. Cook for 5 to 7 more minutes, till the greens are wilted and the shrimp is cooked. Finely chop the reserved scallion greens and scatter on the vegetables as a garnish before serving.

MALABAR SPINACH WITH VEGETABLES AND SHRIMP
Pui Chingri Chorchori

One of my husband's contributions to the cuisine of our household is that he grows a lot of the seasonal vegetables. Malabar spinach (*pui shaag*), however, was my addition to our garden. I bought some from the Indian store and then rooted it in a pot. It was eventually transplanted outside to yield a delicate, clinging green vine. The plant is a climber, so needs very little room to grow. The vine looked so pretty that I did not want to use it; until I realized that it was a case of use it or lose it as it would never survive the New York winter. Malabar spinach is similar to regular spinach, but has fleshy and more succulent leaves. It is available in Indian stores, but regular spinach can be substituted in this recipe.

Prep Time: 7 minutes | **Cook Time:** 25 minutes | **Makes:** 4 servings

INGREDIENTS
2 tablespoons mustard oil
¾ teaspoon panch phoron (page 5)
3 or 4 dried red chilies
1 cup cubed white daikon radishes or red radishes
1 small potato, peeled and cubed
⅓ medium head cauliflower, chopped
1 small eggplant, cut into small pieces
1-inch piece fresh ginger, peeled
1 teaspoon fennel seeds
½ teaspoon cumin seeds
1 teaspoon coriander seeds
3 cups chopped malabar spinach (pui shaag) or regular spinach
½ cup green peas (can be frozen)

1½ teaspoons salt
¼ pound shrimp, shelled and de-veined
½ teaspoon turmeric
½ teaspoon sugar

PREPARATION

Heat all but 1 teaspoon of the oil in a large wok or skillet. Add the panch phoron and cook till the spices crackle. Add the chilies, radishes, potato, cauliflower, and eggplant and mix well. Reduce the heat to low and cover the pot and cook for about 7 to 10 minutes.

In the meantime, grind the ginger, fennel seeds, cumin seeds, and coriander seeds into a paste. Remove the cover from the vegetables and stir well, the vegetables should be fairly soft at this point and should have released some moisture. Stir in the spice paste and add the spinach slowly, letting it wilt. You can add a little water if the mixture appears too dry, but you do not want this to get too wet. Add the peas and 1 teaspoon salt and cover the mixture.

Smear the shrimp with the remaining teaspoon of oil, the remaining salt and the turmeric. Place in the microwave and cook for 1 minute. Stir the spinach and vegetables well; the spinach should be nice and soft as should the eggplant. Mix in the shrimp and sugar and cook for another 5 minutes before serving.

MIXED GREENS AND VEGETABLE MEDLEY WITH POPPY SEEDS
Posto Chorchori

If you have read this chapter closely, by now it should be clear that a *chorchori* is essentially a good way to turn whatever vegetables you have in your refrigerator into a wonderfully balanced meal. This recipe highlights the technique of adding poppy seed paste to a basic assortment of vegetables to create a tasty, satisfying dish.

Prep Time: 10 minutes | **Cook Time:** 20 minutes | **Makes:** 4 servings

INGREDIENTS

1 tablespoon mustard oil
1 teaspoon panch phoron (page 5)
2 dried red chilies
1 medium eggplant, cut into small pieces
½ teaspoon turmeric
1 teaspoon cumin-coriander powder (page 17)
2 cups peeled and cubed pumpkin
5 small radishes, thinly sliced
2½ cups finely chopped mixed greens
1 tablespoon mustard seed paste (page 15)
1 teaspoon poppy seed paste (page 14)

PREPARATION

Heat the mustard oil in a wok or skillet and add the panch phoron and dried red chilies. When this begins to crackle, add the eggplant and cover and cook on low for 7 minutes. (The eggplant takes a little longer to cook than the other vegetables and it needs to be completely soft and smooth for the purposes of this dish.)

Add the remaining spices and vegetables and stir well. Add about ½ cup water and cook covered for 10 minutes. Remove the cover (the vegetables should be cooked and fairly dry). Stir in the mustard paste and poppy seed paste and mix well. Cook for another 1 to 2 minutes, until the flavors are absorbed and the spices are cooked through.

FIDDLEHEAD FERNS WITH POTATOES AND NIGELLA SEEDS
Dheki Shaager Chorchori

Fiddlehead ferns are the earliest harbinger of spring in New York. These ferns are also quite the delicacy in Canadian cuisine, and I learned to enjoy them as a seasonal Western vegetable. Imagine my surprise then when my friend Swapna informed me that fiddlehead ferns are a traditional vegetable in Eastern Indian cuisine too. As she stated on my facebook page, "Fiddleheads, also called *dheki saag,* is a staple in the hill regions of Northeast India, often paired with *panta bhaat* (fermented rice). My husband who is from … Chittagong introduced me to it when we were living in Montreal. Every spring we foraged for it in the Laurentian Mountains with our children."

Fiddlehead ferns are available for only a short period of time each year, but an alternate spring vegetable that works well for this recipe is asparagus. The asparagus needs to be cut into small 1-inch pieces and the cooking time needs to be shorter to make the substitution work.

Prep Time: 5 to 7 minutes | **Cook Time:** 25 minutes | **Makes:** 4 servings

INGREDIENTS
1 cup fiddlehead ferns (about ½ pound), trimmed
2 teaspoons salt
1½ tablespoons mustard oil
½ teaspoon nigella seeds
2 medium russet or Idaho potatoes, peeled and chopped
½ teaspoon turmeric
½ teaspoon cayenne pepper powder
1 or 2 green chilies
1 dried red chili
1 teaspoon fresh ginger paste (page 13)
1 tablespoon ghee (clarified butter)

PREPARATION

Put the fiddlehead ferns, 1 teaspoon of salt, and 3 cups of water in a saucepan. Bring to a boil on medium heat. Simmer for about 10 minutes. Place in a colander to drain.

Heat the mustard oil in a wok or skillet on medium-high heat for about 1 minute. Add the nigella seeds and wait for them to sizzle. Add the potatoes, turmeric, and cayenne pepper powder and cook, stirring frequently, for about 5 minutes, until the potatoes are golden and crisp.

Once the potatoes are crisp and a nice golden brown color, add the remaining teaspoon of salt, the green chilies, red chili, and ginger paste and sauté for another minute. Add the drained fiddlehead ferns and the ghee and cook for another 2 minutes.

CURRIED VEGETABLE PEEL MEDLEY
Khosha Chorchori

"*Aami jonmo neye chilaam shekele Kolkatai na chilo bus, na chilo tram na chilo motor gari.* (I was born in olden Calcutta prior to the emergence of auto transportation.)"

—Rabindranath Tagore in *Amar Chelebela*

In his memoir, the poet reminisces about the city of his childhood and how different the city felt to him as a grown up, almost like a different world. Having left Kolkata, the city of my birth, about two decades ago, I sometimes feel the same way about it. When I visit these days, there are still some vestiges of the old, simpler world it once was, but a lot has changed. The touches of Anglo charm in street names have disappeared. Everyone is talking on their mobile phones, and roadside vendors have been replaced by malls like City Center, which is a wonderful place to visit but a different world from the city of my girlhood.

One memorable figure from my childhood was Bharati, who worked in our home when my family lived on Ballygunge Circular Road. She helped us in the kitchen and also tended to me as a little girl, so I spent time with her in the kitchen, and I was completely fascinated by the preparation she made of *khosha chorchori*, using the bits and pieces of vegetables that one would normally throw into the garbage. *Khosha* refers to peels and *chorchori* is a mishmash of vegetables. It is an essential part of a meal, usually the first course served with dal. My mother also uses tender bottle gourd or zucchini peels in lentils, adding them in as they simmer.

I have re-created Bharati's *khosha chorchori* in this recipe with an assortment of cauliflower stalks and potato and zucchini peels.

Prep Time: 15 minutes | **Cook Time:** 25 minutes | **Makes:** 4 servings

INGREDIENTS

2 tablespoons oil
½ teaspoon panch phoron (page 5)
1 medium red onion, thinly sliced
1 teaspoon grated fresh ginger
½ teaspoon cumin-coriander powder (page 17)
½ teaspoon turmeric
1 teaspoon salt or to taste
2 green chilies, slit
¾ cup assorted vegetable peels (potato, zucchini, squash)
¾ cup tender green cauliflower stalks
1 potato, thinly sliced

PREPARATION

Heat the oil in a large wok or skillet. Add the panch phoron and when it splutters add the onion and ginger and cook for 5 to 7 minutes. Add the cumin-coriander powder, turmeric, salt, green chilies, vegetable peels, cauliflower stalks, and potatoes and cook, stirring frequently, for 5 minutes. Add ½ cup water, if needed, and cover and cook for 10 minutes. Serve hot.

STIR-FRIED MIXED VEGETABLES
Labra

This is yet another *chorchori*, so why give it a distinct name? That, my friend, is the essence of Bengali cuisine, where nuances—sometimes no more that the shape into which a vegetable is cut, or maybe just a change in one ingredient to ever so slightly alter the flavor—are celebrated. Bengali cuisine at its best is really an ode to subtlety. The uniqueness of the *labra* is that it is on the drier side and features a more colorful melange (read pumpkin) of vegetables.

Prep Time: 20 minutes | **Cook Time:** 30 minutes | **Makes:** 4 servings

INGREDIENTS

2 tablespoons mustard oil
1 teaspoon panch phoron (page 5)
⅛ teaspoon asafetida
2 teaspoons fresh ginger paste (page 13)
1 or 2 dried red chilies
½ pound pumpkin, peeled and cut into chunks
1 large zucchini, cut into chunks
1 small ridge gourd, peeled and cut into chunks
1 green banana, peeled and cut into chunks
1 or 2 potatoes, peeled and quartered (optional)
¾ teaspoon turmeric
1 teaspoon salt
1 teaspoon sugar

PREPARATION

Heat the oil in a wok or skillet on medium heat for about 1 minute. Add the panch phoron and when this begins to crackle add the asafetida, ginger paste, and chilies and sauté lightly. Add the pumpkin, mix well, cover, and steam cook for 5 minutes.

Add the zucchini, ridge gourd, banana, and potatoes and mix well. Mix in the turmeric, salt, and sugar. Add about ½ cup water and bring to a simmer. Cover and cook the vegetables for 10 minutes, until soft. Remove the cover and cook on high till all the water is evaporated. Check for seasonings and serve with ruti or rice.

RADISH AND CABBAGE (WITH OR WITHOUT FISH HEADS)
Mulor Chechra

In today's world we cater to an assortment of palates and tastes. To this end, I realized that even with Bengali palates there is no "one size fits all." The last time I prepared this recipe, I made his and her versions. Let me explain. The cast of characters was just four: my friend Jaba, a hardcore fish-and-rice-eating Bengali; her Bengali husband raised in Mumbai, who will not touch fish with a ten-foot pole; my husband, who is very fond of fish but draws the line at eating fish heads; and myself. The men stuck to a purely vegetarian version, while Jaba and I relished our fish heads alongside the radish and cabbage.

Daikon radish is the white radish traditionally used in Bengali cooking, but I offer an option with the milder red radish, that is local and more readily available.

Prep Time: 15 minutes | **Cook Time:** 25 minutes | **Makes:** 4 to 6 servings

INGREDIENTS
2 tablespoons mustard oil
1 tablespoon ginger-cumin-coriander paste (page 14)
½ teaspoon turmeric
½ teaspoon cayenne pepper powder
1 cup cubed daikons (white radishes) or red radishes
1 cup thinly sliced cabbage
1 cup peeled and cubed pumpkin or squash
1 cup finely chopped spinach or Swiss chard
1 teaspoon sugar
1 teaspoon salt
1 teaspoon ghee (clarified butter)
A few bay leaves

Fish head (optional)
1 small fish head
1 teaspoon turmeric
1 teaspoon salt
1 teaspoon bhaja masala (page 16)

PREPARATION

Heat the mustard oil in a large wok or skillet and add the ginger-cumin-coriander paste and cook for about 1 to 2 minutes until the paste is lightly fried. Add the turmeric, cayenne pepper powder, radish, cabbage, pumpkin or squash, and spinach or Swiss chard and stir well for 5 minutes. Mix in the sugar and salt and ½ cup water and cover and cook on low for 15 minutes. The vegetables should be very soft and partly mashed.

Heat the ghee in a small skillet and fry the bay leaves for a minute and pour over the vegetables. If not adding the fish head, you can serve at this point.

If adding the fish head, rub the fish head with the turmeric and salt. Heat some oil in a small skillet and fry the head until it is browned. Break the fish head into pieces and mix into the vegetables and cook for 5 minutes. Sprinkle with the bhaja masala and serve hot.

Spice Three: Fenugreek (Methi)

The third spice in the Five Spice Blend called *panch phoron* (page 5) is the bright yellow spice called fenugreek. It is slightly bitter-tasting, but lacks the pungency or sharpness of mustard seeds. However, much like mustard seeds when the fenugreek seeds are toasted in oil the bitterness mellows and takes on a nutty flavor. Fenugreek, like coriander, is used both in the seed form and plant form. Its soft, clover-like, fragrant green leaves are incorporated into green vegetable medleys or sometimes added to flavor the sauce when cooking chicken.

Fenugreek is also used in powdered form for some recipes. I personally find this spice pairs beautifully with black pepper—there is something about the sharp heat of black pepper that nicely balances out the gentle, fragrant bitterness of fenugreek. Its distinct and complex taste makes it a spice used in rather particular dishes, in keeping with the Bengali concept of balance. It is, however, the distinct taste and almost maple-like smell of fenugreek that provide commercial curry powder mixes their curry flavor. In its most basic form, the spice is heated and sizzled in oil which mellows its taste and transforms it into a nutty flavor.

Fenugreek, has several health benefits ranging from high proportions of minerals and vitamins to supposed benefits of enhancing milk production in nursing mothers. In fact, I was surprised to learn this after I had my children, and even more so when I realized that you could actually buy fenugreek tablets to consume this spice in concentrated doses.

Chapter Seven:
Vegetarian Entrees
Nirammesh

Bengali vegetarian recipes fall into two categories, that of strictly vegetarian cuisine and that of vegetarian dishes that are enriched with the addition of small shrimp, and in traditional cooking this also extends to the addition of fish oils. The concept is to enrich and add flavor, much like adding chicken broth or bacon to western-style vegetable dishes. These additions can be left out if you are looking for a strictly vegetarian dish. Vegetarian cuisine is traditionally used for religious celebrations and while in mourning. This is not so much to punish people, as to adhere to the Hindu prescription for purifying the body.

INFLUENCES ON VEGETARIAN CUISINE

The Marwari community (originally businessmen from the Marwar region in Rajasthan) is growing in Kolkata, and a lot of them still adhere to a vegetarian diet. The need to cater to this affluent community is very apparent in growing fast food corners and the advent of good tea shops, but it has also fostered a general revival of creativity in the vegetarian cuisine of the area. In true Bengali style, we have the second generation of Marwaris who speak Bengali well and enjoy a lot of Bengali food, particularly the street food of Kolkata. In particular, I see a lot of interesting variations with paneer, or channa as the Indian cheese is known in Bengali. Outside of a couple of curries, previously there was not such prolific use of this vegetarian protein, but now I see all kinds of foods with paneer variations. The contemporary chain of supermarkets called Big Bazaar also carries novelty items such as baby corns, colored peppers, and an assortment of mushrooms, and Bengalis have learned to add these to their vegetarian repertoire as well.

Widowhood and
Influences on Bengali Cooking

Vegetarian entrées in Bengali cuisine were usually reserved for the multitude of Hindu rituals and festivals where tradition dictates that the meals be vegetarian. Interestingly, widows actually played an important role in the development of vegetarian culinary traditions since they were often the cooks in a family and were banned from eating meat and fish. Bengali widows are the flipside of a culture that presents women as goddesses. Reading and observing the unfair treatment of these women left me with a feeling of sad bitterness.

Families with many girls suffered intense financial and social pressures. Girls needed to be married into the right caste and social standing, which usually required an appropriate dowry. In poor families, fathers of young girls were forced to marry their children to much older men, since these men were more "affordable." Girls were often married off as young as age 8 or 9 to men who were sometimes older than their fathers. When these men died, their wives were required to don white clothes, shave their heads, and eat no meat or fish. In order to keep them busy, the tasks of cooking were often relegated to these women.

Left with a repertoire of fresh vegetables, an abundance of time, and a host of restrictions (for example, garlic was supposed to stir sexual impulses, and since these women led monastic lives, they avoided it), the widows prepared vegetarian entries that were creative and simple at once. Most of these recipes also fit into the original ayurvedic tradition, which suggests that a good diet balances all the tastes and harnesses the benefits of the assorted vegetables.

Fortunately, times change and sometimes soften traditions that did not make sense. Things are more optional now and today's Bengali society allows a widow to mourn or observe these rituals at a personal level.

INDIAN CHEESE WITH POTATOES AND PEAS IN A CREAMY SAUCE
Channar Dalna

I add a little bit of cream to round off the flavors, but the deep, rich essence of this recipe is the gentle tang of the yogurt, seasoned gently with fragrant spices and a hint of sugar. I find this recipe very comforting on a cold day and, in fact, this is a winter specialty in Bengali cuisine. My great aunt made the best variation of this recipe I have ever tasted, and I've tried to re-create it here.

Prep Time: 10 minutes | **Cook Time:** 30 to 35 minutes | **Makes:** 6 servings

INGREDIENTS
1 onion
1-inch piece fresh ginger, peeled
2 green chilies
3 tablespoons oil
2 green cardamom pods
2 cloves
1-inch cinnamon stick, broken into pieces
1 potato, peeled and cubed
1 teaspoon cumin-coriander powder (page 17)
½ teaspoon turmeric
2 small tomatoes, chopped
1 cup low-fat Greek yogurt
1 cup cubed paneer (channa, page 18)
½ cup green peas
1 teaspoon cayenne pepper powder
1 teaspoon salt
1 teaspoon sugar
½ cup cream (optional)
1 teaspoon ghee (clarified butter)
1 teaspoon garam masala (page 17)

PREPARATION
Grind the onion, ginger, and chilies into a paste.

Heat the oil in a medium wok or skillet and add the cardamom pods, cloves, and cinnamon stick and cook for about 30 seconds to let the spices darken and swell up. Add the onion-chili paste and potato and cook, stirring frequently, until the potatoes are lightly golden. Add the cumin-coriander powder, turmeric, and tomatoes and cook for another 5 minutes.

Add the yogurt and mix well and continue cooking slowly on low heat for about 3 to 4 minutes. Mix in the paneer, peas, cayenne pepper powder, salt, and sugar, and bring to a simmer and cook for 5 minutes, until the mixture reaches an even simmer. Immediately add the cream, if using. (The objective here is not to let the mixture curdle, this is actually achieved in more traditional cooking by adding more oil or ghee up front, I find it easier to add cream.)

Heat the ghee in a small skillet and add the garam masala and cook until the spices begin to sizzle. Pour over the vegetable mixture and serve.

WHOLE ROASTED CAULIFLOWER WITH MUSTARD SEASONING
Phoolkopir Roast

This recipe is one of my most popular creations with guests. A very common seasoning base of mustard and yogurt is spread on a whole cauliflower that is then baked to produce a very attractive, contemporary-looking presentation.

If you can find small fresh summer cauliflowers, it is actually a good idea to use two small cauliflowers for this recipe as they cook through more quickly.

Prep Time: 45 minutes (including time to marinate cauliflower)
Cook Time: 40 minutes | **Makes:** 6 servings

INGREDIENTS
1 whole medium head cauliflower
3 to 4 tablespoons ghee (clarified butter), melted
2 tablespoons chopped cilantro

Marinade
4 tablespoons fresh mustard seed paste (page 15)
1½ teaspoons salt
1 cup low-fat Greek yogurt
1 tablespoon freshly ground black pepper

PREPARATION
Gently mix together the mustard paste, salt, yogurt, and black pepper. Separate the green base from the whole cauliflower. Score deep grooves into the cauliflower taking care not to cut through it. Rub the mustard marinade on the cauliflower and in the grooves and set the cauliflower aside for about 30 minutes. Pre-heat the oven to 375 degrees F.

Place the cauliflower on a large piece of foil and drizzle with the melted ghee. Wrap into a neat package and bake the cauliflower for about 20 minutes.

Unwrap the cauliflower and increase the oven temperature to 400 degrees F and bake the cauliflower for about 20 minutes. Remove from oven, garnish with the cilantro and serve.

PEPPER-SPICED BENGALI VEGETABLE STEW
Doi Morich Diye Sobji Ishtew

"*Stew*" or "*ishtew*" are words that have crept into Bengali culinary parlance from the British vocabulary. An *ishtew* is essentially a well-spiced stew. This recipe also has a chicken-based counterpart where whole chicken pieces are added to the vegetables and simmered.

Prep Time: 10 minutes | **Cook Time:** 20 minutes | **Makes:** 4 servings

INGREDIENTS
1 tablespoon oil
1 teaspoon minced fresh ginger
1 teaspoon salt
1 teaspoon sugar
⅛ teaspoon turmeric
⅛ teaspoon asafetida
2 potatoes, peeled and cubed
1 zucchini, cut into small wedges
1 tablespoon crushed black peppercorns
⅓ cup buttermilk
1 teaspoon ghee (clarified butter)

PREPARATION
Heat the oil in a wok or skillet and add the ginger, salt, sugar, turmeric, and asafetida and cook for about 30 seconds, till the seasonings begin to simmer. Add the potatoes and zucchini and sauté for 5 minutes. Add the black peppercorns and ⅓ cup water, cover and cook for 5 to 6 minutes. Stir in the buttermilk and cook through. Stir in the ghee before serving.

POTATOES WITH POPPY SEEDS
Alu Posto

This delicately seasoned recipe is an heirloom in the Bengali collection of classics. It is a comforting, beloved way to savor new potatoes. It's funny—this variation was taught to me by a gentleman who I met courtesy of my parents when they were trying to get me a "suitable boy." Well, things didn't work out on the matrimonial front, but I still enjoy this recipe!

Prep Time: 15 minutes | **Cook Time:** 20 minutes | **Makes:** 4 servings

INGREDIENTS
3 or 4 russet potatoes
2 tablespoons mustard oil
½ teaspoon panch phoron (page 5)
1 small onion, chopped
2 or 3 green chilies, slit

1 teaspoon cumin-coriander powder (page 17)
1 teaspoon salt
½ teaspoon sugar
½ cup poppy seed paste (page 14)

PREPARATION
Place the potatoes in a pot with water to cover and boil for about 6 to 7 minutes (the potatoes should be parboiled but not completely cooked through). Cool the potatoes, peel them, and cut into wedges and set aside.

Heat the mustard oil in a wok or skillet on medium heat for about 1 minute and add the panch phoron and wait till it crackles. Add the onion and sauté lightly for about 3 to 4 minutes, till the onion is soft and translucent. Add the green chilies and cumin-coriander powder. Add the salt and the potato wedges and mix well. Cook, stirring well, till the potatoes are coated with the spices and begin to turn golden.

Add the sugar, poppy seed paste, and ½ cup water and cook till the mixture is fairly dry (the moisture should dry out leaving a soft coating of the poppy seed paste over the potatoes).

GRATED CARROTS WITH LIME AND POPPY SEED PASTE
Gajar Posto Dalna

Our garden, or "farm" as my husband likes to call it, is all of a quarter acre. It is amazing how prolific this tiny little spot is. We grow so many interesting vegetables, including amazingly fragrant, sweet-tasting carrots. The carrots come in dark and muddy and then after a scrubbing are moist, shiny, and orange. This recipe is best with fresh tender carrots. Do not use baby carrots though as they do not have the depth of sweetness needed to create the right balance in this recipe. As the saying in my house goes, "when life gives you many carrots, make *gajar posto.*"

Prep Time: 15 minutes | **Cook Time:** 25 minutes | **Makes:** 4 servings

INGREDIENTS
2 teaspoons ghee (clarified butter)
1 teaspoon nigella seeds
1 onion, chopped
1 teaspoon fresh ginger paste (page 13)
½ teaspoon cumin-coriander powder (page 17)
1 or 2 dried red chilies
1 or 2 green chilies, slit
6 medium carrots, peeled and grated
⅓ cup poppy seed paste (page 14)
2 tablespoons chopped cilantro
Juice of 1 lime

PREPARATION

Heat the ghee in a wok or skillet and add in the nigella seeds and wait for them to sizzle lightly. Add the onion and ginger paste and cook for 1 to 2 minutes, until the onion is soft and translucent. Add the cumin-coriander powder, red chilies, and green chilies and stir well.

Add the grated carrots and cook, stirring frequently, until the mixture is aromatic, about 8 to 10 minutes.

Add the poppy seed paste and ½ cup water. Cook for 5 minutes, till carrots are fairly soft and dry. Add the cilantro and squeeze in the lime juice and serve.

CURRIED CABBAGE WITH POTATOES AND GREEN PEAS
Badha Kopir Ghanto

The first time my mother visited me after I had moved to the U.S. was when I was graduating from business school. Mom stayed with my lovely host family—the first Americans who made me feel like family. She wanted to thank them for their hospitality by cooking for them one evening, and one of the items she made was this cabbage. Noticing they liked coleslaw, my mother felt that this would be a good transition. She was spot on.

Prep Time: 20 minutes | **Cook Time:** 25 minutes | **Makes:** 4 servings

INGREDIENTS
3 tablespoons oil
1 red onion, thinly sliced
1 medium potato, peeled and cubed
1 teaspoon salt
1 teaspoon turmeric
2 teaspoons ginger-cumin-coriander paste (page 14)
1 or 2 bay leaves, broken into pieces
2 green cardamom pods, lightly bruised
1 teaspoon cayenne pepper powder
1 teaspoon sugar
1 tomato, finely chopped
3 cups finely shredded green cabbage
½ cup fresh green peas (try to avoid frozen)

PREPARATION
Heat the oil in a medium wok or skillet on medium heat for about 1 minute until very hot. Add the onion slices and sauté, stirring well, until they wilt and turn a very pale gold. Add the potato, salt, and turmeric and lower the heat and cook for about 2 to 3 minutes. Cover and cook for another 5 minutes, until the potatoes are almost done and a nice golden yellow color.

Add the ginger-cumin-coriander paste and cook for another 2 minutes. Add the bay leaves, cardamom pods, and cayenne pepper powder and mix well. Add the sugar and tomato and stir well.

Add the cabbage and peas and mix well. Cover and cook for about 7 minutes, until the cabbage is fairly soft. Mix well and cook till dry. Check for seasonings and serve.

GOLDEN CAULIFLOWER IN ORANGE MUSTARD SAUCE
Kamala Shorshe Phulkopi

The first time I had this simple yet elegant cauliflower dish at the home of one of my music teachers, I found the flavors remarkable and different from anything that I had eaten before. Oranges are used quite extensively in Bengali cooking, and the Indian orange is closer to what is known as the clementine in the U.S. The essence of the dish is in the marriage of the sweet, citrusy orange with the spicy, pungent mustard. The orange sections do not need to be symmetrical, just cleaned and chopped into small pieces. I found that prepared mustard works quite well in this recipe.

Prep Time: 7 to 8 minutes | **Cook Time:** 25 minutes | **Makes:** 4 to 6 servings

INGREDIENTS
1 large head cauliflower (about 2 pounds), cut into medium to small pieces
1 teaspoon turmeric
1 teaspoon cayenne pepper powder
Lots of freshly ground black pepper
1 teaspoon salt
⅓ cup oil
2 tablespoons mild mustard (such as Grey Poupon)
1 orange, peeled and cut into sections
Cilantro to garnish (optional)

PREPARATION
Rub the cauliflower with the turmeric, cayenne pepper powder, black pepper, and salt. Heat the oil in a wide skillet or pan. Add the seasoned cauliflower (in two batches if necessary) and cook until the cauliflower is cooked through and golden brown at spots.

Return all the cauliflower to the cooking pan and add the mustard and ⅓ cup water and cook until the water is completely absorbed. Mix in the orange sections and cook for 1 minute. Garnish with cilantro, if using and serve.

EGGPLANT IN LIGHT YOGURT SAUCE
Doi Begun

Eggplant is the other darling (the first being cauliflower) of vegetarian entrees on the Bengali table. Traditionally the eggplants were deep-fried and then cooked in the light yogurt sauce. As a healthier option, I shallow-fry the eggplants. To make this work, however, the eggplants have to be very tender. I prefer fresh eggplants of the Japanese variety. Also soaking the eggplants with salt releases some of their water and makes them easier to cook.

Prep Time: 1 hour (including time to soak eggplants)
Cook Time: 25 minutes | **Makes:** 4 servings

INGREDIENTS
6 small to medium eggplants
1 teaspoon kosher salt
1 teaspoon turmeric
⅓ cup mustard oil
3 or 4 green chilies, slit lengthwise
1 teaspoon grated fresh ginger
2 teaspoons salt
1 teaspoon cayenne pepper powder
1 teaspoon cumin-coriander powder (page 17)
1 cup low-fat Greek yogurt
2 teaspoons ghee (clarified butter)
2 or 3 bay leaves
1 teaspoon bhaja masala (page 16)

PREPARATION
Cut the eggplants into circles about ⅓ inch thick. Soak the eggplant slices in 2 cups water mixed with the kosher salt for 30 minutes or a little longer. Drain and dry the eggplants. Rub with half the turmeric.

Reserve about 2 tablespoons of the mustard oil. Add half the remaining mustard oil to a flat heavy-bottomed skillet and heat on medium heat for about 2 minutes. Add some of the eggplant slices and cook for 2 to 3 minutes (the eggplants should puff up and get nice and succulently soft and brown). Turn and cook on the other side. Remove the eggplant slices with a slotted spoon and place on paper towels to drain. Continue cooking all the eggplant slices in this manner, adding additional mustard oil as needed. Place the drained eggplant slices on a flat shallow serving platter.

Heat the reserved 2 tablespoons mustard oil in a wok on medium heat. Add the green chilies and ginger and stir lightly. Add the salt, remaining ½ teaspoon turmeric, cayenne pepper powder, and cumin-coriander powder and cook lightly for 1 minute. Mix in the yogurt and cook on very low heat for 10 minutes. (It is very important to do this on very low heat to make sure that the yogurt does not separate and curdle.) Pour this sauce over the eggplants.

Heat the ghee in a small skillet and add the bay leaves and cook for 15 to 20 seconds. Pour over the eggplants and sprinkle with the bhaja masala and serve for any festive occasion.

DRIED POTATO CURRY WITH GARLIC
Shantipur Barir Aamish Alur Dom

"*Aamish*" in Bengali means non-vegetarian, and the opposite "*niraamish*" means vegetarian. My Dadu (maternal grandfather) hails from Shantipur in West Bengal. One year when we visited his ancestral home, the chef informed me that he was making *aamish alur dom*. This is a dry, spicy potato dish traditionally eaten with *luchis* (Bengali puffed bread, page 57), so I could not quite understand why he called it non-vegetarian. Upon some examination, I discovered that the *aamish* designation was because of the use of garlic in the potatoes. As mentioned before, garlic is relatively uncommon in Bengali vegetarian cooking, especially when cooked in the Hindu tradition. Some vegetables like garlic, onions, and turnips are taboo to orthodox Hindus, so the chef considered the meal "*aamish.*"

The dish was made with new potatoes which were not peeled, but rather scraped to leave some of the delicate skin on the potato. I have tried to replicate this dish using wonderful red new potatoes with their skin on. Small baby white potatoes can also be used for this recipe.

Prep Time: 10 minutes | **Cook Time:** 30 minutes | **Makes:** 6 servings

INGREDIENTS
1 pound small red or white potatoes, halved
½ cup oil
1 teaspoon salt
1 teaspoon turmeric
1 small onion, peeled
1 tablespoon cumin-coriander powder (page 17)
3 or 4 green chilies
1 teaspoon black peppercorns
3 or 4 cloves garlic
1-inch piece fresh ginger, peeled
3 green cardamom pods
3 cloves
2-inch cinnamon stick, broken into pieces
1 tomato, chopped
2 tablespoons tamarind paste
1 teaspoon sugar
2 tablespoons chopped cilantro (optional)

PREPARATION
In a pot, heat some water until it is boiling. Add the potatoes and parboil them for about 6 to 7 minutes. Drain the potatoes and if using white potatoes, remove the peel.

Heat half the oil in a wok or skillet on medium heat for about 1 minute. Rub the potatoes with the salt and turmeric and fry till browned, about 5 minutes. Remove from pan, drain and set aside, reserving oil in pan.

Put the onion, cumin-coriander powder, green chilies, black peppercorns, garlic, ginger, and ¼ cup water in a blender and blend to make a paste. Gently bruise the cardamom pods, cloves, and cinnamon stick to release some of their flavor.

Add the remaining oil to the oil leftover from cooking the potatoes and add the bruised whole spices and cook for a few seconds. Add the onion-spice paste. Reduce the heat to low and then, stirring frequently, cook the mixture until it begins to brown. (This process does need a little patience and attention.)

Add the potatoes, tomato, tamarind paste, and sugar and cook the potatoes, stirring frequently, for 5 minutes. Cover and cook on very low heat till the potatoes are soft and the spices are rather dry. Remove from heat and serve garnished with cilantro (if using).

CREMINI MUSHROOMS IN TOMATO COCONUT GRAVY
Tomato Diye Maashroomer Malai Kari

Button mushrooms made their appearance a while back in the New Market, a Kolkata landmark and quite a fascinating place to shop. Baubles, flowers, cloths, trinkets, foods, and novelty items, this century-old "new" market has it all. Fancy boutiques, shopping arcades, and malls have emerged and happily harnessed the retail potential of the area, but none have quite taken the place of New Market. In any case, mushrooms are now popular on Bengali tables and offer a good vegetarian option for a lot of recipes.

Prep Time: 15 minutes | **Cook Time:** 35 to 40 minutes | **Makes:** 6 servings

INGREDIENTS
2 medium red onions, peeled and quartered
2-inch piece fresh ginger, peeled
5 tablespoons oil
1 teaspoon caraway seeds (shahjeera)
2 or 3 bay leaves, broken into pieces
3 green cardamom pods
3 tomatoes, grated
1 teaspoon salt
1 teaspoon dried fenugreek leaves (methi)
3 or 4 green chilies, finely chopped
1 cup light coconut milk
1 teaspoon sugar
2 cups halved cremini mushrooms (baby bella)
3 tablespoons minced cilantro

PREPARATION

Place the onions and ginger in a food processor and finely chop. Heat the oil in a wok or skillet on medium heat for about 1 minute. Add the caraway seeds and wait for them to sizzle. Add the chopped onion and ginger and cook on medium-low heat, stirring patiently and carefully, until the mixture softens and turns fragrantly golden, about 10 minutes.

Add the bay leaves. Gently bruise the cardamom pods and add them to the mixture. Add the tomatoes and salt and continue cooking slowly until the mixture is smooth and the oil begins to gently surface along the sides.

Add the dried fenugreek leaves, green chilies, and coconut milk and bring the mixture to a simmer. Add the sugar and mix well. Add the mushrooms and cook for about 7 minutes. Stir in the cilantro. Serve with rice.

GREEN PLANTAIN CAKES IN A CREAMY SAUCE
Kach Kolar Kopta

I am thrilled to see how much my students love this very simple and delicate recipe. Other than making the green plaintain cakes, this recipe takes little to no time. Since I do not use fresh coconut milk, I add some walnuts to replicate its rich creaminess. This recipes is made with the green plantain cakes featured in the *bhaja* chapter. Those cutlets can be made ahead.

Prep Time: 10 minutes (plus time for making cakes) | **Cook Time:** 15 minutes
Makes: 4 servings

INGREDIENTS
2 cups light coconut milk
½ cup walnuts
½-inch piece fresh ginger, peeled
1 teaspoon salt
1 teaspoon sugar
3 or 4 green chilies, slit lengthwise
10 prepared Green Plantain and Taro Cakes (page 90)
Juice of 1 lime or lemon
1 teaspoon cumin seeds

PREPARATION
Place the coconut milk, walnuts, and ginger in a blender and blend until smooth. Put mixture in a saucepan, add the salt and sugar and bring to a simmer. Add the chilies and plantain cakes. Add the lemon or lime juice and simmer the mixture for about 5 to 7 minutes, until sauce is thick and the plantain cakes are heated through.

Dry roast the cumin seeds in a small skillet and grind to a powder. Sprinkle over the plantain cakes and serve immediately.

BANANA BLOSSOM CURRY WITH CHICKPEAS AND COCONUT

Mochar Ghanto

This is another recipe from my mother's collection. I am very glad that she made this the last time I visited India. My mother does not often have the energy these days to make elaborate preparations, however, this last time I watched her carefully to observe and document this recipe. These recipes are a dying art, mostly due to knowledge constraints.

Prep Time: 30 minutes (plus overnight soaking of blossom)
Cook Time: 45 minutes | **Makes:** 4 to 6 servings

INGREDIENTS
1 banana blossom
½ cup cooked chickpeas
1½ teaspoons salt
1¼ teaspoons cayenne pepper powder
1 tablespoon oil
1 tablespoon ginger-cumin-coriander paste (page 14)
½ cup plus 2 tablespoons grated fresh or frozen coconut
⅓ cup milk
1 teaspoon sugar
2 teaspoons ghee (clarified butter)
1 or 2 bay leaves
2 cardamom pods
2 cloves
2-inch cinnamon stick, broken into pieces

PREPARATION
Day before, prepare banana blossom as directed in sidebar on opposite page.

Soak the chickpeas in water to cover for at least 20 minutes. Drain most of the water from the chickpeas, leaving about 2 to 3 tablespoons. Place them with the remaining water in a blender with half the salt and ½ teaspoon cayenne pepper powder and blend to a thick paste.

Heat the oil in a medium non-stick frying pan. Add the chickpea mixture and spread to about ½ inch thick. Cook on low heat for about 7 to 8 minutes on each side. You should get a large chickpea pancake that is crisp and pale brown on the outside and soft not raw on the inside. Cut or break into small pieces.

Heat the oil in the frying pan and add the ginger-cumin-coriander paste and fry lightly. Add the cooked chopped banana blossom and the remaining ¾ teaspoon salt, remaining ¾ teaspoon cayenne pepper powder, and grated coconut and cook on high for 4 minutes, stirring constantly. Add the milk, sugar, and chopped chickpea pancakes and cook for 5 minutes.

Heat the ghee in a separate small skillet and add the bay leaves, cardamom pods, cloves, and cinnamon stick and cook for 5 minutes. Line a dish with the reserved purple leaves of the banana blossom and place the curry on the plate for a pretty presentation.

Preparing Banana Blossoms

Although I observed my mom's preparation closely, when I tried her recipe on the opposite page, I was still at a loss on how to cut the tiny little unripe flowers. You see, my mother had someone to do this for her. The *mocha* is the flower of the banana plant, and at our house usually the gardener brought them in for us.

Mochas are a vivid purple and available in a good Chinese market, at least I can find them in mine. To make sure that I got the process of preparing the banana blossoms right, I made my mother clean two of these for me as I jotted notes and took pictures.

Pick medium-size banana blossom(s), very small ones or large ones are best avoided. Remove the banana blossom leaves* and carefully remove the small bunches of immature bananas. Lightly grease your hands and with a sharp knife, cut the tip off the banana blossom(s) and remove the stylus in the middle of the petals. Then place blossom(s) in the bowl of a food processor and pulse coarsely. Soak the banana blossom(s) overnight in water with some salt and turmeric added. The next day boil the blossom(s) for 15 minutes. Drain and they are ready to be used in a recipe.

*Note: I like to reserve some of the brightly colored purple leaves for serving, since they make for an attractive presentation, but this is purely optional.

GREEN BOTTLE SQUASH OR ZUCCHINI WITH POPPY SEEDS AND LENTIL NUGGETS
Bori Diye Lau Posto

In keeping with the general obsession with small details, the right *bori* or lentil nuggets are a very big deal. The interesting thing is that while my mother often sends and sometimes brings an assortment of food-related items from India, these lentil nuggets do not feature in her care packages. This is mostly because the *bori* is considered an unlucky travel item. It is difficult to fathom what gave *bori* this unfortunate distinction.

However, the good thing is that her sister, my *mashi*, does not quite prescribe to these beliefs, so she recently brought me a small packet of *boris*. Thus I discovered that there is not a huge difference between the *boris* she brought and the small ones I find in the local Indian grocery. And now my son is addicted to fried *boris*, which he has pronounced the best thing he has eaten.

This recipe is made with the pale green bottle squash sold as *lau* or *lauki* in the Indian grocery. If this is not available, you can use tender green zucchini. I do not peel the zucchini when using it.

Prep Time: 45 minutes (including time to drain squash)
Cook Time: 25 minutes | **Makes:** 6 servings

INGREDIENTS
2 small to medium green bottle squash (lau) or zucchini
2 teaspoons kosher salt
3 tablespoons mustard oil
1 teaspoon panch phoron (page 5)
1 small onion, chopped
1 teaspoon fresh ginger paste (page 13)
4 to 6 green chilies, slit
1 teaspoon sugar
⅓ cup fresh green peas (optional)
4 tablespoons poppy seed paste (page 14)
Oil for frying
15 to 20 boris (lentil nuggets, page 9)
2 tablespoons chopped cilantro

PREPARATION
Peel the squash (if you are a truly frugal Bengali chef, you will save the peels for a *chorchori*, page 111), and remove some of the center seedy section. Chop very finely (this can be done in a food processor, although purists might find this texture a little too fine). Place the squash in a colander and sprinkle with the kosher salt and set aside to drain for about 30 minutes.

Squeeze out any excess water from the squash. Heat the mustard oil in a wok or skillet and add the panch phoron and wait till the spices begin to crackle. Add the onion and ginger paste and sauté the mixture for about 5 minutes. (The onion should be wilted and soft and translucent.)

Add the squash, green chilies, sugar, and green peas, if using, and cover and cook for 5 to 7 minutes, until the vegetables are tender and soft. Stir in the poppy seed paste and continue cooking on low heat for about 3 minutes, until the mixture is fairly dry and coated with the poppy seed paste.

Heat the oil in a wok or skillet and fry the boris until crisp. Crush the boris and sprinkle over the cooked squash. Sprinkle with the cilantro and serve.

CRISP LENTIL CAKES IN LIGHT CURRIED GRAVY
Dhokar Dalna

I almost left this recipe out of this book as it is not something I make that often. Sometimes, to truly represent and do justice to a cuisine it is good to revisit its roots. I write this recipe as I sit in Kolkata where my memory is refreshed as I watch my mother making the *dhoka* as part of a festive menu and realize that a chapter on Bengali vegetarian recipes is incomplete without this classic. I have added tomatoes to the gravy for a variation, but my mother makes this recipe without tomatoes, for a more typical onion and garam masala based gravy. I also simplified the recipe by baking the basic paste.

Prep Time: 1 hour (plus 6 hours to soak lentils) | **Cook Time:** 60 minutes
Makes: 6 servings

INGREDIENTS
Lentil cakes
1 cup dried yellow Bengali gram lentils (cholar dal)
½ cup dried yellow split lentils (moong dal)
1 teaspoon salt
2 green chilies
2 tablespoons fresh ginger paste (page 13)
⅛ teaspoon asafetida
¾ teaspoon turmeric
1 teaspoon bhaja masala (page 16)
6 tablespoons oil plus additional for deep frying

Gravy
3 tablespoons oil
2 red onions, finely chopped
1 teaspoon ginger-cumin-coriander paste (page 14)
2 or 3 green cardamom pods
2 bay leaves, broken into pieces
3 tomatoes, chopped
1 teaspoon salt
1 teaspoon sugar
½ cup low-fat Greek yogurt, beaten until smooth
2 tablespoons chopped cilantro (optional)

PREPARATION
Prepare lentil cakes:
Place the lentils in 6 cups water and soak for at least 6 hours. Heat the oven to 350 degrees F. Drain the lentils and place in a blender with the salt, green chilies, ginger paste, asafetida, turmeric, and bhaja masala. Pulse a few times and then add a few tablespoons water to form a smooth but very thick paste. The objective is to use as little water as possible.

Grease a shallow 9-inch square baking dish with 6 tablespoons oil and spread in the batter. Bake the batter for about 20 minutes, until the excess moisture has evaporated, but do not over cook this (it should be moist and still sticky at this point, you just want to remove any excess moisture). Remove from the oven and cool slightly. Cut into even 2-inch squares. Remove the squares from the pan.

Heat the oil for frying in a frying pan or wok for about 5 minutes. Gently add the lentil squares and fry for about 4 minutes on each side, until the cakes are nice and crisp outside and somewhat fleshy inside. Remove with a slotted spoon and drain on paper towels.

Prepare gravy:
Heat the oil in a wok or skillet on medium heat for about 1 minute. Add the onions and sauté for about 4 minutes, until soft and beginning to turn golden. Add the ginger-cumin-coriander paste and cook for another minute. Add the cardamom pods and bay leaves and cook for 1 minute. Add the tomatoes and cook till nice and soft. Add the salt and sugar. Mix in the yogurt and cook for 3 minutes, until the sauce reaches a simmer. Add the fried lentil cakes and cook for 5 minutes in the sauce. Stir in the cilantro, if using.

QUICK SPICED POTATOES AND CAULIFLOWER WITH BABY SHRIMP
Alu Kopir Dalna

This recipe probably planted the first seeds of writing this book. Years ago I took a Greyhound bus to visit my uncle and aunt in the tiny town of Ironton, Ohio. The trip in itself was an adventure—quite amazing to cut across the country and see the reality of peoples lives between bus stops and terminals. It is not a side of life that is evident in the privacy of one's car or the quick antiseptic travel of the airplane. The tiny town was fascinating, a part of the country that I could not have imagined. Simple, quiet, and peaceful, away from the hustle and bustle of the big cities that I have lived in; I loved this visit and the few subsequent ones that I made there.

I offered to cook this simple recipe for them. I was surprised to see my aunt following me around with a notepad. She is English and years of learning recipes from her Bengali in-laws made her realize that the only way to do this was to watch and take notes. In fact, that is how I have learned a lot of cooking myself. But this was the first time I realized that people might be interested in learning and understanding Indian regional cooking.

Prep Time: 10 minutes | **Cook Time:** 20 minutes | **Makes:** 4 servings

INGREDIENTS

1 tablespoon oil
1 teaspoon panch phoron (page 5)
1 teaspoon fresh ginger paste (page 13)
3 green chilies, slit lengthwise
1 cup chopped cauliflower
1 large potato, peeled and cut into wedges
½ teaspoon turmeric
2 red tomatoes, chopped
1 teaspoon salt
½ cup medium shelled and de-veined shrimp
½ cup low-fat sour cream
2 tablespoons chopped cilantro

PREPARATION

Heat the oil in a wok or skillet and add the panch phoron and wait for the spices to begin crackling. Add the ginger paste and slit green chilies. Stir in the cauliflower and potato. Mix in the turmeric, tomatoes, and salt. Cover and cook the mixture on low heat for about 10 minutes.

Remove the cover, the vegetables should be nice and soft at this point. Stir in the shrimp and sour cream and bring the mixture to a simmer. Cook for about 5 minutes. Stir in the cilantro and serve.

FRESH SAUTEED OKRA WITH MUSTARD
Shorshe Bhindi

My husband and children love okra, so I keep trying to find ways to cook this simple green vegetable. It is such a nutritious powerhouse that it is difficult to go wrong with it. This recipe is a simple creation with the ever-favorite mustard. I love to have this every time I visit Kolkata—tender, green okra contrasts beautifully with the soft spiciness of hand-ground mustard. I prefer the quick-cook variation of mustard for this recipe.

Prep Time: 20 minutes | **Cook Time:** 15 to 20 minutes | **Makes:** 4 servings

INGREDIENTS

3 tablespoons oil (preferably mustard)
1 teaspoon nigella seeds
1 teaspoon fresh ginger paste (page 13)
1 pound fresh okra, cut into 1-inch pieces
1 teaspoon turmeric
1 teaspoon salt
2 tablespoons quick prepared mustard I (page 15) or regular
    mustard seed paste (page 15)

PREPARATION

Heat the oil in a wok or skillet on medium heat for 1 minute. Add the nigella seeds and wait for them to start sizzling. Add the ginger paste and cook for about 30 seconds. Add the chopped okra, turmeric, and salt and cook for about 10 minutes, stirring frequently. Stir in the mustard paste and cook for another 2 minutes before serving.

WINTER SQUASH IN A SPICY COCONUT AND MUSTARD SAUCE
Shorshe Kumror Korma

This is another interesting medley of seasonings. The addition of garlic and curry leaves adds a touch that people typically don't associate with this palate of flavors. If desired, this recipe can also be made with either eggplant or cauliflower.

Prep Time: 15 minutes | **Cook Time:** 30 minutes | **Makes:** 4 to 6 servings

INGREDIENTS

4 tablespoons mustard oil
¾ teaspoon mustard seeds
½ teaspoon caraway seeds
3 cloves garlic, pressed
1 tablespoon fresh ginger paste (page 13)
3 cups peeled and cubed winter squash (pumpkin or delicata)
1 teaspoon salt
½ teaspoon sugar
4 to 6 curry leaves
4 green chilies, slit lengthwise
4 tablespoons Greek yogurt
1 tablespoon fresh mustard seed paste (page 15)
2 cups coconut milk
1 teaspoon garam masala (page 17)

PREPARATION

Heat the oil in a wok or skillet on medium heat for about 1 minute. Add the mustard seeds and caraway seeds and saute for about 1 minute. Add the garlic and ginger paste and cook for another minute. Add the squash and stir well. Add the salt, sugar, curry leaves, and green chilies and cook for about 5 minutes, until the squash is turning golden in spots.

Add the yogurt and mix well and cook until the yogurt is absorbed. Stir in the mustard paste and coconut milk and bring the mixture to a simmer. Simmer for 15 minutes, until the gravy thickens and the squash is soft. Sprinkle with the garam masala and mix in.

SPICED PUMPKIN WITH CHICKPEAS
Kumro Chokka

I once came home from music class with a large wedge of fresh pumpkin that had been grown and presented to me by my music teacher. This amused my husband and brother-in-law to no end, since the pumpkin, or for that matter any squash, is hardly an object for gifting or admiration. I had planned to make *luchi* and chickpeas that evening so they were not expecting the pumpkin to be transformed to a *chokka* (dried pumpkin curry with chickpeas). A traditional *chokka* actually uses *potol* (pointed gourds) instead of the green bell pepper that I used in this recipe. Once they sampled this dish, it was one more that my husband declared was his all-time favorite.

This is the second time in this book where bell peppers are a substitution for the pointed gourd. It is important to note that this substitution works because of the texture—the taste is different—but they are more readily available.

Prep Time: 30 minutes | **Cook Time:** 30 minutes | **Makes:** 6 servings

INGREDIENTS
2 tablespoons oil
1 small red onion, chopped
1 tablespoon ginger-cumin-coriander paste (page 14)
2 teaspoons salt
1 teaspoon sugar
1 teaspoon turmeric
4 cups peeled and cubed pumpkin
2 green bell peppers, cut into wedges
½ cup cooked chickpeas
1 teaspoon garam masala (page 17)
½ cup yogurt
1 tablespoon ghee (clarified butter)
1 or 2 bay leaves
2 green cardamom pods
2 cloves
3-inch cinnamon stick, broken into pieces

PREPARATION
Heat the oil in a wok or skillet. Add the onion and ginger-cumin-coriander paste and cook for about 1 to 2 minutes. Add the salt, sugar, turmeric, pumpkin, and green bell peppers and mix well. Cook the mixture on high for about 3 to 4 minutes, letting the spices coat the pumpkin.

Add the chickpeas, garam masala, and yogurt and mix well. Cover and cook for about 15 minutes. Remove the cover and stir well.

Heat the ghee in a small skillet and lightly cook the bay leaves, green cardamom pods, cloves, and cinnamon stick for about 45 seconds. Pour the seasoned ghee over the cooked pumpkin before serving.

DRY SPICED KOHLRABI WITH SHRIMP
Chingri Maach Diye Olkopir Ghanto

Cooking a recipe such as this, using a homey vegetable with rather complex seasoning and a lot of texture, would convince my mother that I fussed over eating Bengali food when I was young simply to give her a hard time. For most people, the simple, home-cooked delicacies they grew up eating did not always seem especially great. It is only when I moved away that I realized how wonderful some of these recipes were.

Prep Time: 15 minutes | **Cook Time:** 45 minutes | **Makes:** 4 servings

INGREDIENTS
2 kohlrabis with leaves
2 tablespoons mustard oil
1 teaspoon panch phoron (page 5)
1 red onion, finely chopped
1½ teaspoons fresh ginger paste (page 13)
½ teaspoon turmeric
2 green chilies
1 teaspoon salt
1 tomato, finely chopped
2 tablespoons grated coconut
2 tablespoons beaten Greek yogurt
½ cup large shelled and de-veined shrimp
1 teaspoon ghee (clarified butter)
2 green cardamom pods
2 cloves
1-inch cinnamon stick, broken into pieces

PREPARATION
Remove the leaves and small stems from the kohlrabi and finely chop them. Cut the kohlrabi into small cubes.

Heat the oil in a wok or skillet on medium heat for about 1 minute. Add the panch phoron and when this begins to crackle, add the onion and ginger paste. Sauté, stirring gently, for about 7 minutes, until the mixture is turning nicely golden.

Add the diced kohlrabi and chopped stems and leaves and mix well. Stir in the turmeric and green chilies. Cover and cook the mixture for 5 minutes. Remove the cover and stir well. Add the salt, tomato, and coconut and stir well. Mix in the yogurt and cook on low heat for about 25 minutes, until the vegetables are soft and there is a thick sauce. Stir in the shrimp, cover, and cook for another 5 minutes on low heat. Check the seasonings.

Heat the ghee in a small skillet and add the green cardamom pods, cloves, and cinnamon stick and cook for a minute. Pour the seasoned ghee over the kohlrabi and stir in.

TURNIPS AND GREEN PEAS IN COCONUT SAUCE
Salgam Monoroma

This recipe is loosely adapted from a Bengali cooking show I saw when I was in Kolkata. It is very interesting to see the growing popularity of cooking programs in India. These shows are also an eye-opener into the modern Bengali kitchen, where a lot of the traditional bell metal cookware has been replaced by hard anodized contemporary pots and pans.

As I do with most other recipes, I simplified this down to the basics. If you want you can actually cook it in a slow cooker which gives the best effect once you have browned the turnips and cooked it through.

Prep Time: 25 to 30 minutes | **Cook Time:** 45 minutes | **Makes:** 6 servings

INGREDIENTS
3 tablespoons oil
1 teaspoon mustard seeds
⅛ teaspoon asafetida
1 teaspoon fresh ginger paste (page 13)
1 red onion, thinly sliced (optional)
6 to 8 small turnips (with purple tops), scraped and cut into eighths
1½ teaspoons salt
¾ cup fresh or frozen green peas
1½ cups light coconut milk
1 tablespoon chopped cilantro
1 tablespoon crushed red pepper flakes

PREPARATION
Heat the oil in a wok or skillet and add the mustard seeds and wait for them to crackle. Add the asafetida and ginger paste and wait for it to sizzle lightly. If using the onion add it at this point and cook until it softens and begins to turn lightly golden. Add the turnips and salt and cook for about 3 to 4 minutes.

Add the green peas and coconut milk. Simmer on low heat for about 25 to 30 minutes (the vegetables should be very soft at this point). (If you wish to use the slow cooker, the mixture can be transferred to a slow cooker after adding the coconut milk and cooked on low for 1½ hours undisturbed.)

Stir in the cilantro and sprinkle with the red pepper flakes before serving.

TOFU WITH TOMATOES AND BELL PEPPERS IN CASHEW NUT GRAVY
Moghlai Tofu

I think tofu makes a nice addition to the Indian table, especially when served in a rich gravy such as this. Gravies with fancy Moghlai-sounding names are now popular items on catering menus in Bengal. Their exotic names signifying something beyond the run-of-the-mill everyday menu. Here the creamy cashew nut gravy works beautifully with the lighter flavor of the tofu.

Prep Time: 1 hour (mostly for soaking seeds and nuts)
Cook Time: 30 minutes | **Makes:** 4 servings

INGREDIENTS
1 tablespoon poppy seeds
8 cashew nuts
1 cup warm whole milk
3 tablespoons oil
1 red onion, finely chopped
1 tablespoon grated fresh ginger
1 teaspoon cumin-coriander powder (page 17)
2 tomatoes, pureed
1 green chili, finely chopped
1 teaspoon salt
1 teaspoon sugar
¼ teaspoon saffron strands
1 green bell pepper, cut into small pieces
8 ounces extra-firm tofu, cubed

PREPARATION
Soak the poppy seeds and cashew nuts in the warm milk for 45 to 60 minutes.

Heat the oil in a wok or skillet on medium heat. Add the onion and sauté for about 5 minutes, until it wilts and begins to turn pale gold. Add the ginger and cumin-coriander powder and mix well. Add the tomatoes, green chili, salt, and sugar. Continue simmering the mixture on low heat for about 7 minutes, until the mixture is thick and bubbly.

In the meantime place the cashew mixture in the blender and add the saffron and blend until smooth.

Add the bell pepper to the tomato mixture and cook for 3 minutes. Gently stir in the tofu and sauté lightly for 3 minutes. Stir in the cashew mixture and cook for 6 minutes, stirring occasionally. Serve hot with your choice of bread or rice.

CHILI BASIL PANEER
Lanka Tulsi Diye Channar Dalna

This recipe is an adaptation of an Indo-Thai creation that is rather popular in India. I am not surprised that the food of Thailand is popular on the Bengali table, since there is a lot of commonality in the flavors. Sometimes, instead of using paneer, I make this recipe with extra-firm tofu that has been pressed and drained.

Prep Time: 10 minutes | **Cook Time:** 20 minutes | **Makes:** 4 servings

INGREDIENTS
Paneer
2 tablespoons cornstarch
1 teaspoon salt
1 pound paneer (channa, page 18), cut into 2-inch pieces
Oil for light browning

Chili basil sauce
2 tablespoons oil
1 tablespoon grated fresh ginger
½ teaspoon sesame oil
4 tablespoons light soy sauce
⅓ cup tomato ketchup
¼ cup cooking wine
1 tablespoon cornstarch
10 to 15 Thai basil leaves
5 green chilies, sliced lengthwise into slivers
2 tablespoons finely chopped cilantro

PREPARATION
Prepare the paneer:
In a small bowl, mix the cornstarch and salt with 3 tablespoons of water. Lightly dip the paneer pieces into the mixture. Heat the oil in a medium wok or skillet and add the paneer pieces and cook lightly for 1 to 2 minutes on each side. Drain and set aside.

Prepare chili basil sauce:
Heat the oil in a wok or skillet. Add the ginger and sauté lightly for about 1 minute. Add the sesame oil. Mix together the soy sauce, ketchup, cooking wine, and cornstarch and add to the ginger mixture. Bring the mixture to a simmer. Add the basil leaves and cook for about 1 minute.

Add the paneer and green chilies to the sauce and cook for about 1 minute. Stir in the cilantro and serve.

WINTER SQUASH AND RED CHARD CURRY
Kumro Diye Lal Shager Ghanto

This particular creation is what I like to call the "zero mile curry." It is made with red chard and the delicate squash from our backyard, hence the ingredients travel zero miles to the table. It can be made with any combination of orange squash and red greens, but to get the right appearance do not substitute the red greens with green ones. I sometimes put a little crumbled Indian cheese (paneer) in it to add some protein.

Prep Time: 15 minutes | **Cook Time:** 25 minutes | **Makes:** 4 servings

INGREDIENTS
1 small red onion
½-inch piece fresh ginger, peeled
2 green chilies
⅓ cup mustard oil
2 bay leaves, broken into pieces
1 teaspoon black cumin seeds (called shahi jeera; smaller than regular variety)
1 medium winter squash, peeled and cut into small cubes (about 2 cups)
¼ cup Greek yogurt, beaten
½ teaspoon salt
1 teaspoon sugar
1 cup finely chopped red or rainbow chard (include some of the tender red stems)
1 teaspoon ghee (clarified butter)
1 teaspoon garam masala (page 17)

PREPARATION
Place the onion, ginger, and green chilies in a blender and blend to a paste.

Heat the mustard oil in a wok on medium heat for about 1 minute. Add the bay leaves and black cumin seeds and cook for about 30 seconds. Add the onion-chili paste and cook on medium heat, stirring frequently, for about 3 minutes (the paste should lose its wet appearance and separate into blotches in the oil).

Add the squash and mix well. Cook for about 5 minutes, until the squash releases some moisture, is well coated with the onion mixture, and begins to turn pale golden in spots.

Add the yogurt, salt, and sugar and cover and cook for 4 minutes, until the squash is soft and the yogurt is almost absorbed. Add the red chard and mix well till it is wilted.

Heat the ghee in a small skillet and lightly cook the garam masala for about 15 seconds. Pour this over the squash and mix well before serving.

SWEET AND SPICY CURRIED CABBAGE
Badhakopir Misti Dalna

This light recipe is directly inspired by Meenakshie DasGupta's book. It is also very inspiring that she was one of the first chefs to open a full-fledged Bengali restaurant in Kolkata. I realize that this might sound strange, but as I have mentioned before, Bengalis typically do not eat homestyle food at restaurants.

I vary the recipe by using coconut milk instead of coconut and by adding carrots to complement the sweetness imparted in the recipe.

Prep Time: 15 minutes | **Cook Time:** 25 minutes | **Makes:** 4 servings

INGREDIENTS
2 tablespoons oil
1 teaspoon mustard seeds
1 red onion, thinly sliced
3 or 4 green chilies, slit lengthwise
1 medium head green cabbage, shredded (about 3 cups)
½ cup grated fresh carrots
1 teaspoon cumin powder
1 cup coconut milk
1½ teaspoons sugar
1 teaspoon salt

PREPARATION
Heat the oil in a wok or skillet and add the mustard seeds and cook until they sizzle. Add the onion and cook until nice and soft, about 4 minutes. Add the green chilies, cabbage, and carrots and mix well. Add the cumin powder, coconut milk, sugar, and salt. Simmer the mixture until the coconut milk is absorbed.

Chapter Eight:
Eggs
Dim

There are meat-and-potatoes families, and then there are egg-and-potatoes families, like mine. My dad and I both love eggs! And he made a mean egg curry. I was thrilled to see how popular my father's egg curry recipe was when I posted it on my blog. There has to be a correlation between genetics and food tastes, since this year my seven-year-old son presented me with a unique valentine card. It pictured a bear with a speech box that said, "Be my Valentine." Below this he had written in by himself "Mom, you make the best eggs!"

THE WELL-TRAVELED EGG

Most Bengalis keep eggs handy to use as a quick fix—like the simple trick of adding a boiled egg to a meal of spicy mashed potatoes and rice, which is still my idea of ultimate comfort food. Others spend hours on egg curries with many ingredients. It is also common to cook eggs with potatoes. In India, eggs, like most fresh foods, are usually bought and used when needed. But I often pick up an extra carton with my weekly groceries, just in case. In this chapter, I use this compact and convenient powerhouse of nutrition to showcase some foreign influences on Bengali food. These recipes give us a good picture of how seasonings have developed over the course of Bengal's history.

MY FATHER'S DRY EGG CURRY
Bapir Dimer Dalna

This recipe was one of my dad's specialties—something he made when we traveled and went on our version of a picnic. Group picnics are very much a part of the Bengali lifestyle, combining two favorite pastimes—socializing and travel. The family picnic is a little different. Typical foods would be dried curried potatoes, or potatoes and eggs, as in this case, and the puffed breads called *luchis*, all diligently packed in the all-purpose tiffin carrier. Dry curries like this are always best eaten with an Indian bread such as *luchis* (page 57) or any of the flatbreads presented in Chapter Three.

Prep Time: 15 minutes | **Cook Time:** 25 to 30 minutes | **Makes:** 6 servings

INGREDIENTS
⅓ cup oil
6 hard-boiled eggs, shelled
2 teaspoons salt
¾ teaspoon turmeric
1 teaspoon cayenne pepper powder
1 red onion, finely chopped
2 cloves garlic, finely chopped
1 teaspoon freshly ground black pepper
2 teaspoons cumin-coriander powder (page 17)
2 tomatoes, chopped
10 small baby potatoes, peeled (can use regular potatoes cut evenly)
½ cup fresh or frozen peas

PREPARATION
Heat half the oil on low-heat in a non-stick wok or skillet. While the oil is heating, rub the eggs with half the salt and ¼ teaspoon of the turmeric. Place the eggs in the oil and fry, stirring constantly, till well browned, keeping heat low to prevent the eggs from blistering. (You want them to brown evenly.) Remove the eggs with a slotted spoon and set aside.

Add the remaining oil to the wok. Add the cayenne pepper powder, onion, and garlic and cook the mixture on low heat. In a separate small bowl, stir together 3 tablespoons water, the black pepper, and cumin-coriander powder. Add to the wok along with the tomatoes and potatoes and cook for about 3 to 4 minutes. Stir in ½ cup water, cover, and cook on low for 10 minutes, until the potatoes are soft.

Add the eggs, peas, and remaining 1 teaspoon salt and ½ teaspoon turmeric and cook for 5 more minutes. Make sure that the potatoes are very soft and covered in a thick gravy.

EGGS COOKED WITH BLACK PEPPER AND FENUGREEK
Dim Morich

The combination of black pepper and fenugreek is a common spice mixture used in some Bengali homes. I have seen it typically used for fish dishes, but I liked the combination and have adapted it well for eggs in this recipe.

This recipe can be made with whole hard-boiled eggs or halved hard-boiled eggs, depending on your preference. Cutting the eggs makes them more appealing and allows them to absorb more of the flavorful sauce. The challenge is to make sure that the halved eggs are handled delicately so the yolk and whites don't separate. I carefully prepare the sauce first and then add the eggs. For the ease of availability I use lemon in this recipe instead of the traditional tamarind.

Prep Time: 10 minutes | **Cook Time:** 25 minutes | **Makes:** 4 to 6 servings

INGREDIENTS
6 hard-boiled eggs
1 teaspoon fenugreek seeds
1 tablespoon black peppercorns
3 tablespoons oil
1 onion, finely chopped
2 teaspoons fresh ginger paste (page 13)
1 tablespoon garlic paste (page 14)
Juice of 1 lemon
3 tablespoons Greek yogurt
1 teaspoon salt
1 small bell pepper, slivered (optional, this is for appearance more than taste)
2 tablespoons chopped cilantro

PREPARATION
Shell the eggs and carefully cut them in half lengthwise and set aside. Place the fenugreek seeds and the black peppercorns in a spice or coffee grinder and grind into a powder.

Heat the oil in a wok or skillet. Add the onion and cook for about 5 minutes, until wilted and beginning to turn lightly golden. Add the ginger paste, garlic paste, and lemon juice and cook for 3 to 4 minutes.

Reduce the heat to low. Add the yogurt and salt and bring to a simmer. Gently add the eggs, yolk side up and cook for 2 to 3 minutes, spooning the sauce over the eggs. Add the red bell pepper, if using. Remove the eggs carefully onto a serving dish and garnish with cilantro before serving.

SPICY OMELET CURRY
Omelet Dalna

I use the long Italian bell peppers in this recipe, because I want a combination of high flavor with mild heat.

Prep Time: 10 minutes | **Cook Time:** 30 minutes | **Makes:** 6 servings

INGREDIENTS
⅓ cup oil
6 large eggs
4 to 6 tablespoons chopped cilantro
3 green chilies, finely chopped
2 teaspoons salt
1 cup finely chopped onions
8 to 10 baby fingerling potatoes, peeled
½ teaspoon turmeric
1 teaspoon fresh ginger paste (page 13)
2 tomatoes, chopped
3 or 4 mild green chilies (such as Italian long peppers), slit lengthwise
1 teaspoon cumin-coriander powder (page 17)
2 teaspoons coarsely ground black peppercorns
1 tablespoon chopped cilantro (optional)

PREPARATION
Heat half the oil in a frying pan. Beat the eggs with the cilantro, green chilies, 1 teaspoon salt, and 2 to 3 tablespoons chopped onions. Pour the eggs into the frying pan and cook on low till set, about 7 to 8 minutes (this is done like a thin frittata). Carefully remove from the pan.

Add the remaining oil to the frying pan and heat. Add the potatoes and quickly brown on all sides. Add the remaining onions, remaining 1 teaspoon salt, turmeric, and ginger paste and turn the heat to low and cover and cook for about 5 minutes, till the potatoes are halfway done. Add in the tomatoes, green chilies, and cumin-coriander powder and mix well and cook for 2 to 3 minutes until the tomatoes soften.

Cut the cooked eggs into cubes and gently stir into the spice mixture. Add the black pepper (several generous grinds actually works well for this purpose). Garnish with the cilantro.

EGGS WITH ONIONS AND BELL PEPPERS
Dimer Jhal Ferazi

It is hard to discern the origins of this Anglo-Indian inspired recipe. We had something called *jhal ferazi* every so often when I was in school, and I was quite surprised to see that it is a common item on Indian restaurant menus abroad. Potatoes can be added to this dish if desired.

Prep Time: 20 minutes | **Cook Time:** 15 minutes | **Makes:** 6 servings

INGREDIENTS
3 tablespoons butter
2 tablespoons oil
1 teaspoon cumin-coriander powder (page 17)
1 teaspoon fresh ginger paste (page 13)
2 cloves garlic, pressed
2 small onions, quartered and layers separated
2 bell peppers, seeded and quartered
2 tomatoes, cut into wedges
6 hard-boiled eggs, shelled
4 green chilies, finely chopped
1½ teaspoons salt
2 tablespoons chopped cilantro

PREPARATION
Heat the butter and oil in a frying pan. Add the cumin-coriander powder and cook for about 30 seconds. Add the ginger paste and garlic and cook for about 1 minute. Add the onions and bell peppers and cook for about 5 minutes.

Add the tomatoes, eggs, green chilies, and salt. Cook the mixture, stirring occasionally, for about 5 minutes, until the tomatoes start softening and the juices start flowing. Mix well and garnish with the cilantro and serve.

EGGS WITH CHEESE AND WHITE SAUCE
Egg Mornay

There is an entire branch of cooking in India, still served in clubs and other multi-cuisine restaurants, that labels itself "Continental." The cuisine is influenced by western flavors, but has its own distinct specialties, such as this white sauce and cheese creation. One of the first exercises in the cooking lab when I studied "home science" in school was learning how to make a good white sauce without lumps. Continental cuisine is still a bonafide branch of Indian cooking. If you grew up with the rather established club culture in India, chances are you had your fill of continental cuisine as a child and are nostalgic about some of the specialties just like I am.

Prep Time: 10 minutes | **Cook Time:** 30 minutes | **Makes:** 6 servings

INGREDIENTS
6 hard-boiled eggs, shelled
3 tablespoons butter
1 tablespoon oil
2 garlic cloves, pressed
1 cup chopped scallions
2 tablespoons all-purpose white flour
2 cups whole milk
1 teaspoon salt
1 teaspoon freshly ground pepper
1 cup grated mild white cheese (such as a jack cheese)
2 tablespoons chopped parsley

PREPARATION
Heat the oven to 375 degrees F. Carefully cut the eggs in half lengthwise and place them in a flat square casserole.

Heat the butter and oil in a saucepan until the butter has melted. Add the garlic and scallions and cook for about 5 minutes. Add the white flour and stir for about 30 seconds, mixing well to prevent lumps. Slowly pour in the milk, stirring constantly (you can use a whisk), and stir over low heat until the sauce has thickened (should coat the back of a spoon). Stir in the salt and pepper.

Pour the sauce over the eggs and cover with the cheese. Bake for 20 minutes. Garnish with the parsley and serve hot.

EGG CURRY WITH COCONUT MILK AND CURRY LEAVES
Dhakhini Dimer Malaikari

This is a simple creation that I usually make with leftover mustard. I like to enrich the base of the sauce with coconut milk to add body. This recipe can be adapted for fish or cubed chicken or mushrooms, if desired. The curry leaves used in this rather delicate sauce are a South Indian influence.

Prep Time: 10 minutes | **Cook Time:** 25 minutes | **Makes:** 6 servings

INGREDIENTS
2 tablespoons mustard oil
1 teaspoon nigella seeds
1 teaspoon whole cumin seeds
10 green curry leaves
1 tablespoon prepared mustard (optional)
1 green bell pepper, cut into very thin strips
1 teaspoon salt
1 cup coconut milk
6 hard-boiled eggs, shelled

PREPARATION

Heat the mustard oil in a saucepan. Add the nigella seeds, cumin seeds, and curry leaves and wait till they begin to sizzle. Add the mustard and bell pepper and stir well. Stir in the salt, coconut milk, and ½ cup water and simmer the sauce for 5 minutes.

Cut slits in the sides of the eggs (to allow the gravy to penetrate) and lower them into the sauce. Cook for about 5 minutes on medium heat before serving. This dish can be served over white rice or with roti.

EGGS IN A CARAMELIZED ONION SAUCE
Dimer Do Piazza

My husband and I have often debated the origins of this recipe, which came into Bengali cuisine through the influences of Mughal reign. Some legends say that Akbar's minister Birbal created this when he had two onions on hand, since "*do*" means "two" and "*piazza*" means "onion." But some variations say that this refers to twice the amount of onions than regular dishes have. And my scientist husband expounds that it literally means "two varieties of onions."

   Well, we have yet to come to a conclusion, but I can tell you that this is a pretty good rendition of eggs.

Prep Time: 15 minutes | **Cook Time:** 50 minutes | **Makes:** 4 servings

INGREDIENTS
4 hard-boiled eggs
¾ teaspoon turmeric
¾ teaspoon chili powder
2 teaspoons salt
6 tablespoons oil
2 bay leaves
3 green cardamom pods
3 cloves
2-inch cinnamon stick, broken into pieces
1 onion, finely chopped
1 teaspoon ginger paste (page 13)
1 teaspoon garlic paste (page 14)
3 green chilies, finely chopped
4 tomatoes, chopped
3 or 4 small potatoes, peeled
½ cup Greek yogurt
6 shallots or small onions, halved
1 tablespoon bruised black peppercorns (whole peppercorns hit with
   a mortar to release their flavor)
2 tablespoons chopped cilantro

PREPARATION

Peel the eggs and coat with half the turmeric, half the chili powder, and half the salt. Heat half the oil in a non-stick skillet and cook the eggs on low, stirring frequently, till browned. Place in a large casserole (I use a 9-inch square casserole). Heat oven to 350 degrees F.

Heat the remaining oil in a wok or skillet on medium heat for 1 minute. Add the bay leaves, cardamom pods, cloves, and cinnamon stick and cook for a few seconds. Add the onion, ginger paste, and garlic paste and cook for 5 minutes, until the mixture is aromatic and lightly browned. Add the chilies, tomatoes, and potatoes and cook for 5 to 7 minutes. Remove from heat and add the yogurt, shallots, and peppercorns.

Pour the potato mixture over the eggs in the casserole and stir gently. Cover with foil or the casserole lid and bake for 20 minutes. Remove the cover and bake for another 10 minutes, until the shallots are browned. Remove from the oven, garnish with cilantro and serve.

EGGS IN A SPICY VINEGAR SAUCE
Dimer Vindaloo

The influence of the Portuguese in Kolkata was mostly due to the spice trade. The use of vinegar and garlic in this recipe is an example of some of the culinary influences that the Portuguese inspired in Indian cuisine.

Prep Time: 20 minutes | **Cook Time:** 25 minutes | **Makes:** 6 servings

INGREDIENTS
⅓ cup cider vinegar
1 teaspoon mustard seeds
1 teaspoon coriander seeds
3 dried red chilies
3 cloves garlic
1-inch piece fresh ginger, peeled
1 teaspoon salt
1 teaspoon sugar
4 tablespoons oil
1 onion, thinly sliced
2-inch cinnamon stick, broken into pieces
2 or 3 cardamom pods
4 to 6 green chilies, slit lengthwise
6 hard-boiled eggs, peeled
2 tablespoons chopped cilantro

PREPARATION

Pour the vinegar in a bowl and add the mustard seeds, coriander seeds, dried red chilies, garlic, and ginger and soak for about 10 minutes. Grind or blend this mixture to a paste. Stir in the salt and sugar. Heat the oven to 375 degrees F.

Heat the oil in a small skillet. Add the onion and cook for 5 minutes, until they softened and beginning to turn golden at the edges. Add the cinnamon stick, cardamom pods, green chilies, and vinegar-spice paste and cook for about 7 to 8 minutes.

Slice the eggs carefully in half lengthwise. Place the egg halves in a casserole dish in a single layer with the yolk sides up and pour the sauce over them. Bake for about 10 minutes. Remove from the oven and garnish with the cilantro and serve.

Spice Four: Fennel Seeds

Sweet fennel seeds are the fourth spice in the Five Spice Blend (*Panch Phoron*, page 5). Fennel is called *mouri* in Bengali and yields an anise-like sweet flavor. It is the only spice in the Five Spice Blend that is also eaten uncooked, usually as a mouth freshener after the meal.

Seeds highlight an interesting characteristic of the Five Spice Blend, in that depending on what it is combined with, different nuances dominate. When the recipe is inherently sweet, such as in a chutney, the fragrance and sweetness of fennel dominates.

Fennel seeds are used for tempering dishes, and fennel seed powder is added to fillings, such as the green peas that are stuffed into Bengali breads called *kachori* (page 59).

Fish market in Bengal

The Bengali Five Spice Chronicles

Chapter Nine:

Fish
Maach

Fish, cultivated in ponds and fished with nets in the freshwater rivers of the Ganges Delta, is the dominant "meat" in Bengali cooking. Almost every part of the fish is eaten (except fins and innards); the head and other parts are usually used to flavor curries.

Buying fish in Bengal is quite a ritual. In fact this is the task of the man of the household, who purchases the fish early in the morning before he leaves for work when the freshest fish can be found in the markets. A friend once told me that his father was passionate about two things after his retirement, his Sunday golf and morning fish shopping.

Like rice, fish is a food of great importance to Bengalis because good fish is available in infinite bounty in the region. In fact, fish is among the gifts that a bride's family sends to the groom's family, and the prized fish head is reserved for the groom during the wedding feast.

A lot of people love fish but are daunted by the prospect of cooking it. We tend to eat fish often because of its versatility. I've included both simple recipes and more complex ones in this chapter. The most classic Bengali fish recipe (*macher patla jhol,* page 169) is a thin nigella-seasoned curry that is a combination of fish and vegetables. It is to Bengali cuisine what bouillabaisse is to French cooking—the signature seafood stew.

The flavors of mustard paste, poppy seed paste, and coconut reign supreme in this chapter. Most of the recipes use fish that I find more commonly available in the local fish markets around me, such as salmon, rainbow trout, brook trout, and, of course, the ever-popular shrimp. Typical Bengali fish such as the rui (carp), papda, and parshe (mullet) can sometimes be found outside of India in ethnic specialty stores, but it is up to you whether you want to take the extra time to procure these.

NAVIGATING THE BENGALI FISH MARKET

More than forty types of mostly freshwater fish are common in the Bengali culinary repertoire. Some of these include carp (called *rui*), koi (climbing perch), the wriggling catfish family of tangra, magur, and shingi, the pink-bellied Indian butter fish (*pabda*), and shrimp (*chingri*). The challenge for me, however, was to find the local relatives of these Bengali fishes in my U.S. fish market. For the purpose of practicality, I use substitutes that are more readily available in the U.S., and prefer fish in the filleted form rather than the fish steaks that are usually used in Bengali cuisine.

FRYING FISH FOR BENGALI FISH CURRIES

For everyday purposes, I usually skip the typical Bengali step of frying the fish before simmering it in gravy. I haven't really missed the calories that come with this extra step. In Bengal's hot climate, frying fish before further cooking it in a sauce was a way to increase its shelf life. If you have the time and do not mind some additional calories, you can deep-fry the fish first for most of the curries in this chapter.

The key is to fry the fish till fairly crisp and then keep it intact when cooking it in the sauce. It takes quite a bit of time and needs a delicate touch. The oil should be heated well prior to lowering the fish into it to make sure that the fish gets done quickly without much splattering. A large flat skillet, preferably with anodized coating, works better for this purpose that the traditional wok. It creates less of a mess and the fish gets cooked more quickly. The fish, even heavier fishes such as salmon, should be rubbed with turmeric and salt prior to frying.

Some of the recipes in this chapter provide directions for broiling fish instead of flash frying it. And of course, fresh fish can also be simmered directly in the sauces without pre-cooking—it is not typical, but it does not significantly alter the taste.

Fishing for Love

My husband and I did not bump into each other
in the middle of the road and begin singing our
way into each other's hearts, the way people do
in Bollywood films. In fact, I received an answering machine message
from him one evening. He had gotten my number from a mutual
well-wisher who thought since Anshul was new to town it might be
good for us to connect. In those days, I had gotten quite proficient at
dodging the various suitors my extended family set up for me and so
waited until about 11 p.m. to return the call, thinking I could leave a
message back and then go my merry way. Well, Anshul like me is also
a late night homebody. He was at home and wide awake and we got
to talking and realized that getting to know each other better was not
such a bad idea after all. It took us practically no time to realize that
we both loved food and that, in particular, he was passionate about
fish and seafood along with fresh vegetables.

Interestingly enough, back then I did not really know the first thing
about cooking fish, which was quite a surprise to my husband who
thought that a Bengali girl would be far more skilled in handling the
nuances of cooking fish. The first fish that I cooked was salmon
(actually a fish that can be used well for some of the recipes calling
for the amazing *hilsa*—the crown jewel in the crown of fish cooking
in Bengal) and it met with his approval.

SALMON WITH MUSTARD LEMON CHIVE BUTTER
Salmon Maacher Roast

This is a delicate and simple preparation of roasted fish (usually *hilsa*). This was actually one of the first recipes that I cooked for my husband, once I got the hang of cooking fish in the U.S. Wrapping the fish in foil instead of banana leaves and baking it in the oven yields very good results. The recipe on page 165, "Mustard-Coated Fish Wrapped in Banana Leaves," provides instructions for wrapping fish in the traditional banana leaves if you want to try it.

Prep Time: 10 minutes | **Cook Time:** 20 minutes | **Makes:** 4 servings

INGREDIENTS
1 tablespoons fresh mustard seed paste (page 15)
3 tablespoons butter, melted
2 tablespoons chopped chives
Salt to taste
1 teaspoon fresh ginger paste (page 13)
Juice of 1 lemon
4 salmon steaks (about 2 pounds)

PREPARATION
Pre-heat over to 450 degrees F.

Mix the mustard seed paste, butter, chives, salt, ginger paste, and lemon juice together.

Cut pieces of foil to fit the salmon steaks comfortably and place a salmon steak on each piece. Place about 2 to 3 tablespoons of the mustard mixture on each salmon steak and spread evenly. Wrap each steak in the aluminum foil and place on a baking sheet.

Bake for 15 to 20 minutes. Enjoy with rice or mashed potatoes.

CARP OR RAINBOW TROUT WITH CILANTRO, TOMATO AND MUSTARD SAUCE
Tomato Sohorshe Rui

I made this recipe when my dear friends Dr. and Mrs. Brush were visiting. I met Dr. Brush, a professor of colonial history, at a faculty picnic at my university. An amazing gentleman who spent his boyhood in pre-independent India, Dr. Brush told me tales of West Bengal as he knew it, before the hustle and bustle when the Anglo-Indian culture dominated. I sometimes wonder what my life would have been like had I not met the Brushes. They not only welcomed me into their hearts and lives, but they helped slowly ease me into New York culture in such a subtle manner that I barely noticed it at the time. I will be forever grateful for their friendship and Dr. Brush's wonderful foreword to this book.

The Brushes enjoyed this fish recipe, which I usually try to make with carp, something that is close to the all-purpose Bengali fish *rui*. Because of the mild-tasting firm flesh of the fish, it is used for the more vibrant sauces—but of course if you are a Bengali, mustard sauce is never a problem.

This recipe can also be made with mahi mahi, tilapia, or rainbow trout (which is what I tend to use) with good results.

Prep Time: 15 minutes | **Cook Time:** 45 minutes | **Makes:** 4 servings

INGREDIENTS
2 pounds carp steaks, rainbow trout, or other white fish,
    cut into 2-inch pieces
1 teaspoon turmeric
1 teaspoon salt
4 tablespoons oil, plus additional for drizzling
½ teaspoon nigella seeds
1 onion, finely chopped
1 tomato, chopped
2 tablespoons mustard seed paste (page 15)
2 tablespoons low-fat Greek yogurt
3 tablespoons finely chopped cilantro

PREPARATION
Place the fish on a flat cooking sheet and sprinkle with the turmeric and half the salt. Drizzle with some oil and broil on low till lightly browned on both sides, about 3 to 4 minutes on each side.

Heat the 4 tablespoons oil in a wok or skillet on medium heat for about 1 minute. Add the nigella seeds and let them sizzle lightly. Add the onion and cook for about 6 minutes, stirring frequently, until it reaches a soft pale golden consistency.

Add the tomato and continue cooking for another 5 minutes, until the mixture is thick and pulpy. Stir in the remaining ½ teaspoon salt, the mustard seed paste, and yogurt and cook the sauce on low heat, stirring frequently, for about 15 minutes. (The key is to get a nice smooth creamy-textured sauce, without letting the yogurt curdle.)

Carefully add the fish to the sauce and simmer for another 7 to 8 minutes, stirring the fish very gently and occasionally to mix the fish in but not let the fish break up. Stir in the cilantro before serving.

CARP IN A RICH ONION GRAVY
Rui Macher Kalia

A *kalia* is usually made with a heavy white fish such as the carp, but I have made it successfully with halibut as well. This is a formal recipe, cooked for occasions such as weddings and dinner parties. If carp or halibut are not available, this recipe can also be made with red snapper steaks.

Prep Time: 40 minutes (including 30 minutes to marinate fish)
Cook Time: 45 minutes | **Makes:** 4 servings

INGREDIENTS
2 pounds carp or halibut steaks
1½ teaspoons turmeric
2 teaspoons salt
Juice of 1 lime
⅓ cup oil
2 bay leaves
3 green cardamom pods
½-inch cinnamon stick, broken into pieces
2 or 3 cloves
2 or 3 medium red onions, thinly sliced
1 tablespoon ginger-cumin-coriander paste (page 14)
1 teaspoon cayenne pepper powder
1 cup Greek yogurt
1 teaspoon sugar
1 teaspoon garam masala (page 17)

PREPARATION
Rub the fish with 1 teaspoon turmeric, 1 teaspoon salt, and the juice of the lime and let sit for 20 to 30 minutes.

Rub the fish with 1 to 2 teaspoons oil and broil on low, turning once, till some-what golden on both sides, about 4 minutes on each side.

Heat the remaining oil in a wok or skillet on medium heat. Add the bay leaves, cardamom pods, cinnamon stick, and cloves. When the spices darken (after a few seconds) add the onions and remaining ½ teaspoon turmeric and cook on low heat, stirring frequently, till golden brown, about 15 minutes.

Add the ginger-cumin-coriander paste and cayenne pepper powder and cook on low for another 10 minutes until the mixture is thick and fairly dry. Add the Greek yogurt and sugar and heat through to a slow simmer, trying not to break the yogurt.

Gently stir in the fish and the remaining 1 teaspoon salt and cook for about 5 minutes. Stir in the garam masala and cook for 1 to 2 more minutes.

FISH IN A LIGHT GINGER GRAVY
Halka Pabda Macher Jhol

A simple gravy like this is reserved for the smaller whole fish that most Bengali cooks feel are too fresh to be tainted with heavier flavors. Recipes like this are also prepared during the summer when it is too hot for heavier fare. I love to make this with fresh summer tomatoes, while my grandmother would use something more traditional like green bananas. The whole whiting used in this recipe is a close cousin to the Bengali fish called *pabda* and I often use it as a substitute.

Prep Time: 10 minutes | **Cook Time:** 35 minutes | **Makes:** 4 servings

INGREDIENTS
6 to 8 whole medium whiting (about 2 pounds total)
1 teaspoon salt
2 teaspoons turmeric
Oil for frying

Ginger gravy
2 tomatoes
1-inch piece fresh ginger, peeled
¼ cup cilantro leaves
2 green chilies
2 tablespoons mustard oil
¼ teaspoon fenugreek seeds
½ teaspoon nigella seeds
1 teaspoon cumin-coriander powder (page 17)
1 teaspoon salt
Juice of 1 lime (optional)

PREPARATION
Rub the fish with salt and turmeric. Heat some oil in a skillet and fry the fish gently till crisp on one side, about 6 minutes; turn and cook for another 5 minutes and then drain on paper towels.

Make the ginger gravy:
Place the tomatoes, ginger, cilantro, and chilies in a blender with a little water and grind to a paste. Heat the mustard oil in a saucepan on medium. Add the fenugreek seeds and nigella seeds and cook until fragrant. Add the seasoned tomato paste and cook stirring well for about 10 minutes. Add the cumin-coriander powder, salt, and 1 cup water. Bring the gravy to a simmer. Squeeze in the lime juice if using.

Add the fish to the gravy and simmer for about 10 minutes. Garnish the fish with some cilantro leaves before serving.

MUSTARD-COATED FISH WRAPPED IN BANANA LEAVES
Macher Paturi

For this recipe, the fresh green leaves of the banana plant are converted into a package for mustard-coated fish and placed over a steaming pot of rice, allowing the rice and fish to cook together.

Banana leaves can be found in Mexican grocery stores. But if you cannot find the leaves, you can wrap the fish in foil. These packages can also be placed over a grill and cooked to char the leaves and infuse a smoky taste.

This recipe is usually made with *hilsa* when it is in season and the *bhetki* fish at other times. I have found that red snapper works well if they are not available.

Prep Time: 10 to 15 minutes | **Cook Time:** 20 minutes | **Makes:** 4 servings

INGREDIENTS
2 tablespoons poppy seed paste (page 14)
2 tablespoons fresh or quick mustard seed paste (pages 15-16)
1 teaspoon salt
1 to 2 tablespoons oil (preferably mustard)
2 pounds hilsa or red snapper, cut into 4 or 5 serving pieces
Banana leaves for wrapping and string for tying
Juice of 1 lime (optional)

PREPARATION
Mix the poppy seed paste and mustard paste with the salt and oil. Add the fish and toss until coated.

Cut pieces of the banana leaves to comfortably fit a piece of fish and place a portion of the fish with some of the marinade on the center of each leaf. Bring the edges of the banana wrapper together and tie the package.

Place the fish packets in a steamer and steam the fish for about 20 minutes.

Remove fish carefully from the wrapper and squeeze some lime juice over the fish and serve.

BAKED FISH IN A GREEN POPPY SEED PASTE
Dhone Posto Diye Bhapa Maach

The process of steaming fish is very popular in Bengali cooking. A lot of steamed (*bhapa*) recipes work wonderfully in a lower temperature oven with the casserole sitting in another baking dish filled with some hot water. I find this method of cooking extremely useful and practical.

Using sour cream is a relatively newer phenomenon in Bengali cuisine, introduced by caterers who cook for a lot of special events these days. The sour cream ensures a smoother sauce, since yogurt might break and curdle if the heat is not gentle and even. A recipe such as this is usually made with a firm white-fleshed fish called *bhetki* in India; in the U.S., I usually make it with whiting fillets. Whiting fillets are delicate and need to be cooked with care. For a more robust option, firm fish steaks such as salmon or catfish can be used.

If you have the time, you can bake this fish in banana leaves (like for the *paturi* recipe on page 165), this will add an extra layer of flavor to the steamed fish.

Prep Time: 20 minutes | **Cook Time:** 20 to 25 minutes (unattended)
Makes: 4 servings

INGREDIENTS
3 tablespoons poppy seed paste (page 14)
⅓ teaspoon chopped cilantro, plus extra to garnish
3 tablespoons low-fat sour cream
1 teaspoon salt
6 or 7 green chilies
4 tablespoons oil
1½ pounds fresh whiting fillets
1 or 2 dried red chilies

PREPARATION
Pre-heat the oven to 300 degrees F. and place a large baking pan half filled with hot water in the oven. (The baking pan should be large enough to comfortably accommodate the casserole containing the fish.)

Put the poppy seed paste, cilantro, sour cream, salt, and 3 green chilies in a blender and blend into a paste. It should be a smooth and creamy pale green paste.

Put the oil in a flat casserole or baking dish (large enough to hold the fish fillets in a single layer). Put the green spice paste in the casserole and then place the fish in a single layer on top and mix lightly so that the fillets are well-coated with the paste. Slit the remaining green chilies and toss over the fish and add the dried red chilies. Place the casserole in the baking dish with water in the oven and bake for about 20 minutes, until fish is cooked through and flakey. Serve immediately with rice.

BAKED CURRIED TAMARIND SWORDFISH OR HILSA
Tetul Diye Ilish Maach

The search for a substitute for the legendary *hilsa* or *ilish* fish can take you far and wide, often without a result. Everyone had a different suggestion—some say salmon, some say swordfish, and others, like me, say the shad fish, which is native to the Hudson River in New York. The quest, however, has resulted in a fair amount of experimentation and in turn I have learned to appreciate other fish for their own merit. This recipe is something that I like to make with swordfish and, of course, it would work well with *hilsa*. In India one would use fresh tamarind, but the jarred tamarind concentrate available in the U.S. lacks the same flavor, so I punch it up with a little lime juice.

Prep Time: 15 to 20 minutes | **Cook Time:** 30 minutes | **Makes:** 4 servings

INGREDIENTS
1 tablespoon oil
1 teaspoon panch phoron (page 5)
1½ tablespoons tamarind paste
2 tomatoes, chopped
1 teaspoon salt
½ teaspoon turmeric
4 tablespoons fresh lime juice
¼ cup mustard oil
1 red onion, peeled, cut in eighths and layers separated
3 green chilies, slit halfway lengthwise
1½ pounds swordfish, cut into 2-inch cubes
2 tablespoons chopped cilantro

PREPARATION
Heat the oven to 350 degrees F.

Heat the oil in a wok or skillet on medium heat for about 1 minute. Add the panch phoron and wait till the spices crackle. Then add the tamarind paste (this also splutters and coagulates in clumps almost immediately). Cook for about 1 minute and then turn off the heat.

Add the tomatoes to the pan and stir lightly. Mix the salt and turmeric with the lime juice and then add the mustard oil. Mix into the tomato-tamarind mixture.

Place the swordfish in a single layer in a casserole. Add the onion and green chilies. Pour the tomato mixture over the fish. Bake for about 25 minutes. Add the chopped cilantro and serve.

SALMON WITH YOGURT AND FRESH HERBS
Methi Dhone Pata Diye Doi Maach

Cooking fish and yogurt together is a subtle and much appreciated Bengali pairing. This dish is usually delicately seasoned with caramelized onions, but this variation that I developed uses fresh summer fenugreek. If fresh fenugreek is not available, dried fenugreek sold as *kasuri methi* works fine. I like to make this with wild salmon since the flavors temper the full-bodied, natural taste of the fish effectively. Since the base is prepared in the food processor, I get a rich, complex sauce without much fuss.

Prep Time: 15 minutes | **Cook Time:** 30 minutes | **Makes:** 6 servings

INGREDIENTS
1½ pounds salmon steaks, cut into cubes
1 teaspoon salt
1 teaspoon turmeric
2 or 3 cloves garlic
1-inch piece fresh ginger, peeled
1 onion
2 or 3 green chilies
2 tomatoes
2 to 3 tablespoons oil
1 teaspoon cumin seeds
4 green cardamom pods
2 cloves
2-inch cinnamon stick, broken into pieces
1 teaspoon sugar
½ cup strained or Greek yogurt
½ cup fresh fenugreek leaves
2 tablespoons chopped cilantro

PREPARATION
Rub the salmon with the salt and turmeric and set aside. Finely chop the garlic, ginger, onion, chilies, and tomatoes in a food processor.

Heat the oil in a wok or skillet on medium heat. Add the cumin seeds, cardamom pods, cloves, and cinnamon stick and cook for 30 seconds, until the spices darken. Add the tomato mixture and cook on medium heat, stirring frequently, till the liquid evaporates and the oil shimmers through the spice mixture, about 15 minutes.

Gently add the seasoned salmon to the tomato mixture along with about ½ cup water. Simmer the salmon for 10 minutes.

In a small bowl, beat the sugar with the yogurt until smooth and then stir in the fenugreek and cilantro. Gently add this to the fish curry and cook on very low heat for about 5 to 6 minutes. It is important not to let the curry boil at this point otherwise the yogurt will break.

FISH STEW WITH VEGETABLES IN A LIGHT BROTH
Macher Patla Jhol

This simple classic is probably as good as everyday Bengali cooking gets. Nothing beats this homey stew of vegetables and fresh white fish. Good types of fish for this dish are catfish, haddock, trout, or any other mild, fresh-tasting fish. While you can use any vegetables of your choice, the best choices are cauliflower, long eggplants, potatoes, and sweet potatoes. Every Bengali home has its version of this dish, and the children grow up being nourished by it.

Prep Time: 15 minutes | **Cook Time:** 35 minutes | **Makes:** 4 servings

INGREDIENTS
2 pounds catfish or halibut, cut into cubes
2 teaspoons turmeric
2 teaspoons salt
2 tablespoons oil, plus oil for frying the boris
1 teaspoon panch phoron (page 5)
2 dried red chilies
2 tablespoons ginger-cumin-coriander paste (page 14)
1 onion, ground into a paste
2 or 3 green chilies, slit lengthwise
2 long thin eggplants, quartered (these are the long thin eggplants usually available in an Indian store, but Japanese eggplants work as a substitute)
¼ head cauliflower, cut into florets
1 potato, peeled and cut into 16 thin slices
15 to 20 boris (lentil nuggets, page 9)

PREPARATION
Place the fish in a mixing bowl. Rub with 1 teaspoon turmeric and sprinkle generously with 1 teaspoon salt. Place the fish under the broiler and broil for about 3 to 4 minutes on each side. Set the fish aside.

Heat the oil in a wok or skillet on medium heat. Add the panch phoron and red chilies. When this splutters, add the ginger-cumin-coriander paste, onion paste, green chilies, and remaining 1 teaspoon salt.

Rub the remaining 1 teaspoon turmeric on the eggplant, cauliflower and potatoes. Add to the pan and fry on medium-high heat for about 5 minutes, until the mixture is fragrant and the vegetables are beginning to brown.

Heat the oil for frying the boris in a separate pan and add the boris and fry till pale golden. Add the crisp boris and 1 cup water to the vegetable mixture and cover and simmer the vegetables for an additional 10 minutes until very soft.

Lightly stir in the fish and simmer for 2 to 3 minutes. Check the seasonings and serve hot.

HILSA OR SHAD WITH CILANTRO AND MUSTARD
Dhone-Shorshe Diye Illish Maach

The *hilsa* is one of the most coveted fish in the Bengali fish universe. In fact, when this dish was served to the vegetarian Indian Prime Minister Manmohan Singh on a state visit to Bangladesh, the dignitary agreed to sample the delicacy to acknowledge the honor. The bony exquisite-tasting fish is extremely pricey, but a must-have for special occasions. It is available frozen in Bengali grocery stores.

There is a gentleman in the New York area who hails from Bangladesh and seems to have cornered the Bengali home catering business. He made this fish for my *shaad*, which my aunt hosted in New York. A *shaad*, which literally means taste, is the Bengali version of a baby shower. Nowadays we've merged the concepts of a baby shower and the *shaad*, but the latter is a little different since it focuses more on the expectant mother than the baby and the food is usually carefully chosen with her in mind. Typically, gifts at a Bengali *shaad* also focus on the mother since often people feel it is unlucky or inauspicious to bring gifts for the unborn baby. In fact, my mother could hardly get over her discomfort when I mentioned the concept of a baby registry.

One of the most amazing preparations that I enjoyed at my *shaad* was this *ilish maach* (*hilsa*). After some effort, I've been able to approximate it. My recipe is a little lighter, but still close to what the caterer had prepared. The interesting technique in this dish is straining the mustard paste to mute its flavor.

Prep Time: 20 minutes | **Cook Time:** 45 to 50 minutes | **Makes:** 4 to 6 servings

INGREDIENTS
Basic curry base
¼ cup mustard oil
½ teaspoon turmeric
½ teaspoon cayenne pepper powder
3 tablespoons ginger-cumin-coriander paste (page 14)
1 teaspoon salt
1 onion, very finely chopped (the food processor works pretty well for this)

Fish
1 tablespoon mustard oil
½ teaspoon mustard seeds
1 teaspoon sweet paprika (if you can handle the heat, you can use chili powder)
3 or 4 fresh green chilies, slit lengthwise
8 tablespoons freshly ground mustard seed paste (page 15), diluted
    with ¾ cup warm water
1 pound hilsa or shad steaks (about 10 pieces)
1 teaspoon salt
1 teaspoon turmeric
2 tablespoons chopped green cilantro

PREPARATION
Prepare curry base:

Heat the mustard oil in a wok or skillet and add the turmeric and cayenne pepper powder. After a few seconds add the ginger-cumin-coriander paste and cook the mixture for about 2 to 3 minutes, stirring frequently. Add the salt and onion and cook, stirring frequently, for 10 to 15 minutes, until the onions are very lightly browned. (The mixture should be fragrant and the oil should shimmer through the spices at this point.)

Prepare fish:

Heat the mustard oil in a separate wok or skillet and add the mustard seeds. When they crackle add the paprika, green chilies,1 cup water, and the curry base. Let this simmer for 5 to 7 minutes. Strain the mustard seed paste into the sauce using a metal tea strainer to get in as much as possible. Let the sauce simmer for 15 minutes until it begins to thicken.

Rub the fish with the salt and turmeric and let sit while the sauce is simmering. When sauce is ready, gently add in the fish (since the fish is not fried it needs to be handled gently so as not to break up). Simmer the fish for 7 minutes. Check seasonings and add the cilantro and serve with rice. (This dish keeps well for a couple of days in the refrigerator and the flavors actually settle in after a couple of hours.)

SPICY CURRIED POMPANO
Pomfret Macher Jhol

I cannot cook pomfret or the pompano fish without using cilantro. There are several variations to the way my mother makes this fish, but it is usually never without tomato and cilantro, two items she rarely uses or combines otherwise.

Prep Time: 10 minutes | **Cook Time:** 40 minutes | **Makes:** 4 to 6 servings

INGREDIENTS
2 pounds pomfret or pompano steaks
1 teaspoon turmeric
2 teaspoons salt
1 teaspoon cayenne pepper powder
½ cup oil
1 onion, thinly sliced, plus 1 small onion, peeled
1-inch piece fresh ginger, peeled
2 or 3 green chilies
½ cup loosely packed chopped cilantro plus additional for garnish
2 tomatoes
3 green cardamom pods
3 cloves
1-inch cinnamon stick, broken into pieces
1 teaspoon cumin-coriander powder (page 17)
1 potato, peeled and cut into slices
1 teaspoon sugar

PREPARATION

Place the fish steaks in a mixing bowl and rub with the turmeric, 1 teaspoon salt, and cayenne pepper powder. Heat the oil in a wok or skillet on medium-high heat for a few minutes. Add the fish and fry till lightly crisp on one side, about 3 to 4 minutes; turn and cook for about 3 to 4 minutes on the other side. Remove the fish to a paper towel-lined plate.

In the oil remaining in pan, lightly fry the sliced onion for about 6 to 7 minutes, until softened and beginning to turn golden brown. In a blender, blend the whole small onion, ginger, green chilies, cilantro, tomatoes, and remaining 1 teaspoon salt to a paste and add to the sliced onions. Mix in the cardamom pods, cloves, and cinnamon stick and cook for about 5 to 6 minutes, stirring the mixture well. Add the cumin-coriander powder, potato slices, and I cup water and stir well. Cover and cook for 10 minutes, until the potato slices are soft.

Stir in the sugar and then add the fried fish to the sauce and cook for 7 minutes. Garnish with cilantro and serve.

RED SNAPPER IN A COCONUT TAMARIND SAUCE
Bhetki Macher Roast

The firm-fleshed *bhetki* fish is much loved for frying. Smaller versions of this fish are less coveted, but still liked and sold as baby *bhetki*. I find the taste of red snapper close to this baby *bhetki*.

The fish is cooked with the beloved mustard and an assortment of other sauces. The crowning glory of cooking these fish is that they are usually available filled with roe. In general, fish with roe are well-liked by Bengalis. I use red snapper either whole or in fillets to cook this recipe. I either stuff or rub the fish with an herb paste, broil or fry it until crisp, and then toss it with the coconut tamarind reduction.

Prep Time: 20 minutes | **Cook Time:** 35 to 40 minutes | **Makes:** 6 servings

INGREDIENTS
Herb stuffing
½ cup fresh cilantro
3 green chilies
⅓ cup grated or shredded coconut
1 teaspoon salt
2 tablespoons milk

Fish
6 whole red snappers, cleaned, or red snapper fillets
2 teaspoons salt
1½ teaspoons turmeric
1 tablespoon fresh ginger paste (page 13)
1 teaspoon cayenne pepper powder

oil for frying or broiling

Coconut tamarind sauce
2 tablespoons oil
½ teaspoon whole cumin seeds
½ teaspoon mustard seeds
1½ teaspoons ginger-cumin-coriander paste (page 14)
1 teaspoon salt
3 tablespoons tamarind paste
2 cups coconut milk
1 teaspoon sugar

Garnish
Brown onions (page 42)
Chopped cilantro

PREPARATION
Prepare herb stuffing:
Place all the ingredients for the herb stuffing in a blender and blend into a paste.

Prepare fish:
Cut about 2 or 3 gashes across the body of each whole fish. Rub the fish evenly with the salt, turmeric, ginger paste, and cayenne pepper powder. Stuff each fish with the prepared herb stuffing. (If using fillets, rub the fish evenly with the herb mixture.) Heat some oil in a large frying pan and carefully fry the fish on each side for about 7 minutes, until the fish is crisp and well done. (Alternately place in the oven and broil on low until crisp and cooked through.)

Prepare coconut tamarind sauce:
Heat the oil on medium heat for about 1 minute in a small skillet and add the whole cumin seeds and mustard seeds and heat until they begin to crackle. Stir in the ginger-cumin-coriander paste and cook for 2 to 3 minutes, until the mixture smells aromatic and toasty. Add the salt and tamarind paste and cook for about 1 to 2 minutes. Add the coconut milk and sugar and bring to a simmer. Cook for about 5 minutes.

To serve, place a whole fish on each plate, pour a small amount of the coconut tamarind sauce on each fish. Garnish with the brown onions and cilantro prior to serving.

SEARED COD WITH A RED AND WHITE SAUCE
Doodhe-Alta Maach

The combination of cooking fish in two different sauces—one light and one dark, usually with mustard and tamarind—is called *ganga jamuna*. In an attempt to stick with this dual-colored concept but try some different flavors, I make this dual-colored fish recipe with a white poppy seed and almond paste and a red pepper and fennel paste. The name is from a classic term referring to a pink complexion (something that is considered very desirable), the combination of milk (*doodh*) and the red dye for feet (*alta*).

Prep Time: 25 minutes | **Cook Time:** 40 minutes | **Makes:** 4 servings

INGREDIENTS
Red Sauce
2 red bell peppers, cut into strips
2 to 3 tablespoons oil
1 teaspoon fennel seeds
2 green chilies
1 teaspoon salt
1 teaspoon sugar

White Sauce
4 tablespoons poppy seed paste (page 14)
½ cup blanched almonds
½ cup milk
2 tablespoons oil
1 teaspoon fresh ginger paste (page 13)
1 teaspoon salt

Fish
4 cod steaks or fillets
1 teaspoon turmeric
1 teaspoon cayenne pepper powder
1 teaspoon salt
⅓ cup oil
Juice of 1 lemon
Lots of ground black pepper

PREPARATION
Prepare red sauce:
Heat the oven to 350 degrees F. Place the red bell peppers on a baking dish and drizzle with half the oil. Bake the peppers for 20 minutes. When the peppers are ready, heat the remaining oil in a skillet and add the fennel seeds. When they sizzle, add the green chilies, salt, sugar, and roasted red bell peppers and toss lightly. Place mixture in a blender and blend until smooth. Set aside.

Prepare white sauce:
Place the poppy seed paste, almonds, and milk in a blender and blend into a smooth paste. Heat the oil in a small saucepan. Add the ginger paste and sauté lightly for 2 minutes. Add the milk mixture and salt and simmer for 5 minutes. Set aside.

Prepare fish:
Rub the fish with the turmeric, cayenne pepper powder, and salt. Heat the oil in a skillet until smoking. Place the fish pieces in a single layer in the pan and cook until crisp on both sides. Squeeze in the lemon juice.

To assemble, place a fish steak or fillet on each serving plate and top each piece with a little of each sauce. Sprinkle with lots of black pepper and serve.

SUPER-QUICK MUSTARD COCONUT SHRIMP
Sorshe Narkol Chingri

I am skeptical of using the microwave for practical cooking, but this recipe is an exception. I make this frequently because of its quick turn-around time and reasonably authentic taste.

Prep Time: 15 minutes | **Cook Time:** 10 minutes | **Makes:** 4 servings

INGREDIENTS
3 tablespoon mustard oil
1 tablespoon mustard seed paste (page 15)
1½ tablespoons sweet coconut flakes
½ teaspoon salt
½ teaspoon turmeric
6 green chilies, slit halfway lengthwise
1½ pounds large shrimp, shelled and de-veined

PREPARATION
Mix the mustard oil, mustard paste, coconut, salt, and turmeric well in a bowl. Add the green chilies and shrimp and toss to coat. Let rest for 10 minutes.

Microwave the mixture on high for 4 minutes. Stir well and microwave on high for another 4 minutes. Serve immediately.

QUICK AND ZESTY PINEAPPLE SHRIMP
Chot Pot Anarosh Chingri

The Kolkata Chinese community, still centered around the tangra region of the city, is a contained migrant community that has not made a huge impact on Bengali society in some aspects. The culinary impact of Indo-Chinese food, however, is difficult to ignore. There are so many popular restaurants with this variety of food and most delivery and catering restaurants feature the Indo-Chinese chili chicken or fish on their menu. Home cooks usually have soy sauce and vinegar ready to add a novel touch to their otherwise Bengali recipes. This recipe, great for a quick meal in a hurry, was created in the spirit of Indo-Chinese cuisine.

Prep Time: 10 minutes | **Cook Time:** 25 minutes | **Makes:** 4 servings

INGREDIENTS
1 pound large shrimp, peeled and de-veined
1 tablespoon soy sauce
1 teaspoon vinegar
4 tablespoons oil
1 teaspoon cumin seeds
2 or 3 dried red chilies, lightly crushed
1 bunch scallions, cut into 1-inch long pieces
2 or 3 green chilies, finely chopped
1 tablespoon grated fresh ginger
1 tomato, coarsely chopped
1 cup pineapple juice
1½ teaspoons cornstarch
1 teaspoon salt
2 tablespoons chopped parsley or cilantro

PREPARATION
Place the shrimp in a bowl and sprinkle with the soy sauce and vinegar. Heat the oil in a wok or skillet and add the cumin seeds and red chilies and cook for about 30 to 40 seconds, until the cumin seeds begin to sizzle and the red chilies darken. Add the scallions, green chilies, ginger, and tomato and cook for about 5 minutes. Add the seasoned shrimp and cook for 5 to 7 minutes and then turn off the heat.

In the meantime, bring the pineapple juice to a boil in a small saucepan. Dissolve the cornstarch in 2 tablespoons water and mix into the juice. Cook the pineapple juice until thick and reduced to about half its original volume. Pour this sauce over the shrimp and gently stir together and cook through for about 2 minutes. Sprinkle with the chopped parsley or cilantro.

CREAMY SHRIMP CURRY
Chingri Macher Korma

Try to get the large shrimp, often sold in the supermarkets as colossal shrimp, for this recipe. As always, it is better to try to buy wild-caught varieties of fish and seafood.

Prep Time: 15 minutes | **Cook Time:** 25 minutes | **Makes:** 4 servings

INGREDIENTS
2 tablespoons oil
2 medium onions, finely chopped
1 tablespoon fresh ginger paste (page 13)
1 teaspoon garlic paste (page 14)
2 green chilies, finely chopped
1 or 2 green cardamom pods
½ cup sour cream
1 pound large shrimp, shelled and de-veined
½ teaspoon turmeric
1 teaspoon salt
1 tablespoon chopped cilantro

PREPARATION
Heat the oil in a wok or skillet and add the onions and cook on medium-low heat for at least 6 to 7 minutes, stirring occasionally. (The objective is to let these sweat and turn into a pale golden saucy state.) Add the ginger paste, garlic paste, and chilies and cook for 2 to 3 minutes, until the mixture is cooked and aromatic.

Increase the heat to medium and add the cardamom pods, sour cream, shrimp, turmeric, and salt and cook for 2 to 3 minutes, until the mixture begins to bubble. Add ½ cup water and cook for 6 minutes, until the mixture is nice and thick and the shrimp are cooked through. Stir in the cilantro. Enjoy over white rice.

SHRIMP IN A SPICY CARAMELIZED ONION AND TOMATO SAUCE
Chingri Bhuna

A *bhuna* is a preparation of fish or meat in a dry thick tomato-based sauce. This style of cooking, particularly using shrimp, is a Bangladeshi or East Bengali tradition. As with other foods, in this style of cooking the generous use of green chilies is essential. This recipe is for my cousin Sharmila, who likes this dish a lot and has often asked me for it.

Prep Time: 15 minutes | **Cook Time:** 25 minutes | **Makes:** 4 to 6 servings

INGREDIENTS
1½ pounds shrimp, shelled and de-veined
½ teaspoon turmeric
1½ teaspoons salt
3 tablespoons oil
1 large red onion or 2 medium red onions, thinly sliced
1 teaspoon fresh ginger paste (page 13)
3 cloves garlic, finely chopped
2 or 3 bay leaves
1-inch cinnamon stick, broken into pieces
2 green cardamom pods
2 cloves
½ teaspoon sugar
2 tomatoes, cut into eighths
1 tablespoon Greek yogurt
4 green chilies, coarsely chopped (about ½ cm pieces)
1 tablespoon chopped cilantro

PREPARATION
In a bowl, mix the shrimp with the turmeric and 1 teaspoon of salt and set aside.

Heat the oil in a wok or skillet on medium heat for about 30 seconds. Add the onions and cook for 3 to 4 minutes until softened and pale golden at the edges. Add the ginger paste and garlic and cook for 2 minutes. Add the bay leaves, cinnamon stick, cardamom pods, and cloves and stir and cook for 2 minutes. Add the sugar and remaining ½ teaspoon salt and mix well. Add the tomatoes and cook for 4 minutes, until they soften and begin to turn pulpy.

Add the seasoned shrimp and continue to simmer until the sauce dries out and the oil resurfaces on the sides. Stir in the yogurt and cook for 2 minutes. Stir in the green chilies and cook for 1 minutes. Serve garnished with cilantro.

STEAMED MUSSELS IN A CREAMY COCONUT CURRY
Mussels Malaikari

My mother usually made this recipe, which pairs a coconut sauce with fish, with whole large lobster-size prawns. It is difficult to find such spectacular whole prawns in the U.S. markets. I also make this recipe with mussels and think that this works well. Large fresh mussels certainly do justice to this lovely sauce and offer a beautiful presentation. Mussels are, however, an improvisation to the Bengali palate, whose general preference rests with freshwater fish.

Prep Time: 20 minutes | **Cook Time:** 30 minutes | **Makes:** 4 to 6 servings

INGREDIENTS
3 tablespoons oil
1 onion, thinly sliced
1 teaspoon fresh ginger paste (page 13)
2 tomatoes, chopped
1 teaspoon cayenne pepper powder
4 green cardamom pods
4 cloves
3-inch cinnamon stick, broken into pieces
1 teaspoon salt
1½ teaspoons sugar
2 cups coconut milk
2 pounds fresh mussels, scrubbed and debearded
3 green onions, finely chopped

PREPARATION
Heat the oil in a wok or skillet. Add the onion and cook for about 5 to 7 minutes, until soft and beginning to turn golden. Add the ginger paste, tomatoes, and cayenne pepper powder and cook until the tomatoes begin to turn soft. Add the green cardamom pods, cloves, and cinnamon stick and cook for 2 minutes. Add the salt, sugar, and coconut milk and simmer for 10 minutes.

Add the mussels to the sauce and cook for about 5 minutes, till the mussels all open, and then simmer for 2 more minutes. Discard any mussels that didn't open. Garnish with the green onions.

Spice Five: Cumin Seeds

The last spice in the Five Spice Blend (*panch phoron*, page 5) is cumin seeds (*jire*). They are a brown, savory, slender seed that is used not only in the *panch phoron* blend, but also on their own in both whole and powdered forms. Cumin is a versatile and transcultural spice, enjoyed in cuisines from the Middle East to South America, and is probably one of the most commonly used spices in all Indian cuisine.

In Bengal, small fineness is defined by the cumin seed. For example, finely chopping onions to achieve soft, smooth gravies is essential in Bengali cuisine, so home chefs are admonished to chop their onions "as finely as cumin seeds."

Chapter Ten:

Poultry
Moorgi

CHICKEN ON THE BENGALI PLATE

For some unknown reason, Bengalis embraced chicken a little later in the game then those in other parts of India. Although with the advent of frozen food markets, it is quite common to see chicken on the regular home menu.

Chicken sold in India has two classifications: *desi* and broiler. The *desi moorgi* is really the free range variety and while it takes longer to cook, it tastes better. I recommend the free range variety or Cornish hens for the recipes in this book. Indian chickens are still not doused with as many steroids as their American counterparts and therefore tend to be much smaller in size, but though the size is important it really is more about texture.

The chicken has been comfortably adapted to several interesting recipes, including some light, saucy recipes which are quite flavorful.

Bhai Phota

All the men in my life have been instrumental in my culinary development, and my brother is no exception. He is a decade or so younger than me and came into my life as a very pleasant surprise. I consider it a huge joy in life to have a sibling to call your own. My first forays into cooking chicken were during the Bengali festival of Bhai Phota—which is a sort of brother's day. It is one of the festivals at the tail end of the long season of Hindu festivals commencing with the Durga Puja.

The Bhai Phota is a day when sisters and brothers fast, and sisters pray to ensure their brother's well being. Brothers usually travel to their sisters (if the sister is married) for a visit. The sister usually anoints her brother with a dot of sandalwood paste on the forehead (called the *phota*). Then she says, "*Bhaer kopale dilam phota, jomer dore porlo kata*" (essentially the sister says that she is warding off death by placing the dot on the brother's forehead). The sandalwood paste is an obstruction for Jom (the God of Death). Once the solemnities are over, the feasting begins. The feast foods are usually the brother's favorites. When my brother was young, he loved eating chicken. Over the years a lot of the chicken recipes I developed have been for him, either for Bhai Phota or on other occasions.

Bhai Phota is fortunately one of the festivals that has translated well into a transplanted lifestyle and we celebrate it annually even though we are no longer in India. In my home, I am fortunate to be able to continue the tradition with my brother and my two children, since I have a boy and a girl who have grown to expect this festival in our house once a year. From my young son's perspective, this seems to be the only festival that is dedicated to him, so he calls it "the boy festival." And of course since he likes my version of lightly spiced fried chicken, he wants it made for him every year to celebrate.

CHICKEN IN A CARAMELIZED ONION COMPOTE
Murgir Makha Jhol

I am not a winter person. Like some woodland creatures, I go into the human version of hibernation during the winter months. The only thing that I do like about winter is cooking and watching the beauty of the soft snow falling.

Several recipes, including this one, have been created in the cool silence of my winter kitchen. There is something wonderfully therapeutic watching a creation like this come together in complex perfection. The tempting scents of the warm spices and caramelized onions help keep the cold at bay.

Prep Time: 15 minutes | **Cook Time:** 35 minutes | **Makes:** 4 to 6 servings

INGREDIENTS
4 to 5 tablespoons oil
2 red onions, finely chopped
2 pounds chicken on the bone, cut into small pieces
1 tablespoon fresh ginger paste (page 13)
1 teaspoon cayenne pepper powder
1 teaspoon turmeric
1 teaspoon salt
2 teaspoons cumin-coriander powder (page 17)
1 green bell pepper, thinly sliced (optional)
2 green chilies, finely chopped
2 medium tomatoes, chopped
3 green cardamom pods
3 cloves
2-inch cinnamon stick, broken into small pieces
2 tablespoons finely chopped cilantro

PREPARATION
Heat the oil in a wok or skillet and add the onions and sauté for 2 to 3 minutes. Add the chicken, ginger paste, cayenne pepper powder, turmeric, salt, and cumin-coriander powder and cook on medium-high heat, stirring occasionally, for 15 minutes. (The chicken gradually browns and the onions soften, melt, and turn into a beautiful caramelized mush.)

Add the green bell pepper and green chilies and cook for another 10 minutes. The chicken should be coated in a rich, soft thick brown sauce.

Add the tomatoes, cardamom pods, cloves, and cinnamon stick and cook for 5 to 7 minutes, until the tomatoes are soft and well mixed. Stir in the cilantro and enjoy!

CURRIED TURKEY MEATBALLS
Koftar Jhol

My parents traveled quite extensively due to my father's work. We lived in different parts of the world and one of those places was Tanzania in Africa, when I was age seven to ten. There I took after-school cooking classes, an activity that I enjoyed immensely. I was thrilled when the teacher taught the class how to make meatballs (*koftas*) in a curry sauce. The traditional recipe for such a dish would include ground goat meat, but I adapted it for more readily available ground chicken or turkey.

Koftas are traditional festive Anglo-Indian fare. When Anglo-Indians are ready to celebrate, it's time for the *burra peg* (large shot of whiskey), yellow rice, dal, and ball curry (a slang or colloquial name for *koftas*).

Prep Time: 25 minutes | **Cook Time:** 30 minutes | **Makes:** 6 servings

INGREDIENTS
Meatballs
1 pound ground turkey
3 green chilies, finely chopped
1 tablespoon grated fresh ginger
1 teaspoon garam masala (page 17)
1 teaspoon cayenne pepper powder
2 tablespoons lime juice
⅓ cup chopped cilantro
2 tablespoons ghee (clarified butter)

Curry sauce
2 tablespoons ghee (clarified butter)
3 cardamom pods
3 cloves
1-inch cinnamon stick, broken into pieces
1 red onion, finely chopped
2 cloves garlic, finely chopped
1 large tomato, chopped
3 green chilies, finely chopped
2 teaspoons commercial curry powder
2 teaspoons salt
1 teaspoon sugar
⅓ cup light cream

PREPARATION
Make the meatballs:
Heat the oven to 375 degrees F. Mix the turkey, chilies, ginger, garam masala, cayenne pepper powder, lime juice, cilantro, and ghee. Grease a baking pan. Shape the meat into walnut-size balls and place in a single layer on the pan. Bake the meatballs for 15 minutes turning them once.

Make the curry sauce:

In the meantime, heat the ghee in a wok or skillet. Add the cardamom pods, cloves, and cinnamon stick and cook for 1 to 2 minutes. Add the onion and garlic and cook, stirring well, for about 10 minutes, till the onions are lightly browned. Add the tomato, chilies, curry powder, salt, and sugar and cook till the tomatoes are soft.

Mix in 2 cups water or broth and bring to a simmer. Add the cooked meatballs to the sauce and cook for 10 minutes. Stir in the light cream and heat through.

CHICKEN IN A CREAMY YOGURT SAUCE
Moorgir Rezala

The true Bengali *rezala* lover might be rather disappointed that I have shaved off a lot of the grease from the traditional recipe. However, if you give this recipe a shot you might not even miss those calories.

Prep Time: 45 minutes (including 30 minutes to marinate chicken)
Cook Time: 60 minutes | **Makes:** 6 servings

INGREDIENTS
2 pounds chicken pieces (on the bone), skinned
1 tablespoon fresh ginger paste (page 13)
1 tablespoon garlic paste (page 14)
1½ teaspoons salt
1 teaspoon cumin-coriander powder (page 17)
1 teaspoon cayenne pepper powder
⅓ cup cashews
1 cup strained or Greek yogurt
A few bay leaves
1 tablespoon whole garam masala (page 17)
1 tablespoon black peppercorns
3 green chilies, slit lengthwise
3 or 4 whole dried red chilies

Garnish
¾ cup chopped onions
½ teaspoon saffron strands

PREPARATION
Rub the ginger paste, garlic paste, salt, cumin-coriander powder, and cayenne pepper powder onto the chicken and set aside for 30 minutes. Heat oven to 300 degrees F.

Grind the cashews into a smooth paste with 3 tablespoons of the yogurt. Beat the remaining yogurt until smooth. Mix the yogurt with the chicken and add the cashew nut paste, bay leaves, whole garam masala, and black peppercorns.

Place the mixture in an ovenproof casserole. Scatter the red and green chilies on top. Cover the casserole tightly with foil and bake in oven for 1 hour.

Remove the chicken from the oven, stir in the chopped onions with a light hand. Scatter the saffron over top and enjoy for a delicious treat.

The Muslim Cuisine of Bengal

There are two layers to Muslim cuisine's influence on Bengali food. The first is the effect on the cuisine of the country called Bangladesh, as it shares a strong cultural heritage with West Bengal; and the second is the historic influence of the Muslim rule of India as well as the adaptation and shared heritage of the Muslims in West Bengal.

Bengal (before its partition into eastern and western parts) has been under Muslim rule since the Delihi Sultanate in the early 12th century. For over five hundred years, however, the center of Muslim rule in Bengal was centered in Dhaka (now the capital city of Bangladesh). West Bengal came under Muslim influence only when Murshid Quli Khan became the governor of Bengal and moved the capital from Dhaka to the newly founded city of Murshidabad in the late 17th century.

From the culinary point of view, a key influence on the food came much later, when Wajid Ali Shaj, the last Nawab of Awadh, was exiled to Metiabruz in the outskirts of Kolkata. He is said to have brought with him hundreds of cooks and *masalchis* (spice mixers), who on his death dissipated into the population, starting restaurants and food carts all over Bengal. Syed Mustaque Murshid, a descendant of the 1,000-year-old Syed clan of Murshidabad and chef de cuisine of the Suryaa Hotel in Delhi, was recently featured in a food festival in Delhi promoting this brand of cuisine. He attributes this variety and style of cuisine to certain historical facets, such as catering to the Mughal rulers during their visits to Murshidabad. This city is a wonderful place to visit to get a glimpse of the historical heritage of India and, of course, buy the famous Murshidabad silks.

Popular recipes that have developed from the Muslim heritage, including the *rezalas* and *handi kababs*, are peppered throughout this book, but are most prominent in the chapters on poultry and meat dishes.

WHOLE POTATOES COOKED WITH GROUND CHICKEN
Keema Diye alur Dom

Sometimes my husband brings his interns to our home for short sojourns, usually when they are going through the homeless phase between doctoral studies and work. While I enjoy having them over, the marked difference between their lifestyles and mine increasingly highlights the fact that I am getting older.

One of these students was Anju. He stayed for two summers in the area while doing his summer work with my husband. He often dropped by in the evenings and joined us for dinner, spending time chatting with me and helping me in the kitchen. One weeknight I realized that it was a milestone birthday for him. None of us knew until that evening. Once it was brought to my attention, I realized I had to do something to mark the occasion—so much for my pre-planned simple soup and toast dinner! I finally decided on *alur dom* and *luchi*, then figuring he needed a little meat to mark the occasion, I added *keema* (ground chicken) to my *alur dom* and the results were well appreciated.

Prep Time: 10 minutes | **Cook Time:** 45 minutes | **Makes:** 4 servings

INGREDIENTS
⅓ cup oil
1 tablespoon cumin-coriander powder (page 17)
1 teaspoon cayenne pepper powder
½ teaspoon turmeric
1 onion, thinly sliced
1 teaspoon fresh ginger paste (page 13)
10 whole baby potatoes, peeled
2 teaspoons salt
1 cup green peas (can be frozen)
1 pound ground chicken
2 tomatoes, chopped
1 teaspoon sugar
1 teaspoon freshly ground peppercorns
Juice of ½ lime

PREPARATION
Heat the oil in a wok or skillet. Add the cumin-coriander powder, cayenne pepper powder, and turmeric, followed almost immediately by the onion and ginger paste and cook for 5 to 7 minutes. Add the baby potatoes and salt and cook in the onion mixture for 10 minutes, till well-coated with the spices.

Add the peas and ground chicken and stir well. Cook, gradually adding ½ cup water and stirring till the mixture gets fairly dry. Add the tomatoes and sugar and cover and cook on low heat for 15 minutes, till the potatoes are very soft but intact. Garnish with ground pepper and lime juice and serve with *luchis* (page 57).

RICH YOGURT AND TOMATO CHICKEN
Kaasha Doi Tomato Murgi

This recipe is also one of the recipes I developed the last time my father was visiting. It was inspired by a local cooking marathon, and I was especially thrilled when the newspaper actually picked up this recipe, which nicely showcases summer tomatoes and fresh green chilies.

Prep Time: 20 minutes | **Cook Time:** 40 minutes | **Makes:** 4 servings

INGREDIENTS
3 to 4 tablespoons oil
1 onion, finely chopped plus 1 whole onion
2 pounds boneless skinless chicken thighs, cut into small pieces
1-inch piece fresh ginger, peeled
3 cloves garlic
2 tomatoes
2 green chilies
1 to 2 teaspoons salt
1 teaspoon turmeric
1 teaspoon sugar
½ cup cilantro leaves
½ cup Greek yogurt
2 teaspoons cumin seeds, freshly ground

PREPARATION
Heat the oil in a wok or skillet. Add the chopped onion and cook for 5 minutes, until lightly browned on the edges. Add the chicken and cook on medium heat, stirring frequently, for about 10 minutes (the chicken should be well-browned and the onions should cling to the chicken in a soft caramelized mixture).

In the meantime, put the whole onion, ginger, garlic, tomatoes, and chilies in a food processor and blend. Add this mixture to the chicken with the salt, turmeric, and sugar and continue cooking on medium heat, stirring from time to time, until the mixture is dried and the oil resurfaces, a good 20 minutes.

Stir in the cilantro, yogurt, and cumin and heat through. Cool slightly and serve!

CHICKEN WITH BLACK PEPPER AND FENUGREEK
Methi-Morich Murgi

This chicken dish uses some classic although less common seasonings: fenugreek and black pepper. It gets its flavorful seasonings from the slow-cooking process. Black pepper is used quite a bit in Bengali cuisine. This recipe is one that I adapted from something I had at an *eiburo bhat*, the Bengali equivalent of a bridal shower. The rituals of the day focus on beautifying the bride and the food is usually prepared according to the bride's food preferences. This interesting recipe happens to be something that the bride in question, and I in turn, liked very much.

Prep Time: 40 minutes (including 30 minutes to marinate chicken)
Cook Time: 45 minutes (mostly unattended) | **Makes:** 4 to 6 servings

INGREDIENTS
1½ pounds boneless skinless chicken thighs, cut into 1½-inch pieces
1 teaspoon turmeric
2 teaspoons salt
Juice of 1 lime
2 tablespoons oil
1 onion, finely chopped
1 teaspoon grated fresh ginger
2 tomatoes, finely chopped
2 green cardamom pods
2 cloves
2-inch cinnamon stick, broken into pieces
1 tablespoon black peppercorns, coarsely crushed
½ tablespoon whole fenugreek seeds, coarsely crushed
1 teaspoon dried fenugreek leaves (kasuri methi)
2 tablespoons chopped cilantro

PREPARATION
Sprinkle the chicken with the turmeric and salt and squeeze the juice of the lime over it. Let the chicken rest for about 30 minutes.

Heat the oil in a wok or skillet. Sauté the onion and ginger for 10 minutes on low heat, stirring frequently. Add the tomatoes, cardamom pods, cloves, cinnamon stick, and seasoned chicken and mix well. Stir in the peppercorns and fenugreek seeds and cook on high for 10 minutes, stirring constantly, till the chicken appears to brown in places.

Reduce the heat to low and cook, stirring occasionally, for at least another 20 minutes. Stir in the fenugreek leaves and garnish with cilantro and serve.

MUSTARD CHICKEN STEAMED IN YOUNG COCONUTS
Dab Moorgi

Cooking shrimp in young green coconut shells is a delicious and traditional delicacy. Lately, I am thrilled to see the proliferation of young coconuts in the local markets and I have adapted this recipe using chicken. The young coconuts that are available in most markets have some of the outer skin carved off so they tend to be white rather than green, however, they turn a golden shade of brown during the cooking process resulting in a pleasant and earthy color. The tender juices of the coconut and the coconut cream soften during the cooking process to offer a rich and balanced flavor.

Prep Time: 25 minutes | **Cook Time:** 2 hours (unattended) | **Makes:** 6 servings

INGREDIENTS
1½ pounds skinless boneless chicken thighs
¼ cup mustard seed paste (page 15)
2 green chilies, finely chopped
4 tablespoons mustard oil
½ tablespoon fresh ginger paste (page 13)
1½ teaspoons salt
2 young coconuts
Juice of 2 limes or lemons
2 tablespoons chopped cilantro

PREPARATION
Pre-heat the oven to 375 degrees F.

Cut the chicken in ½-inch pieces. Mix the chicken with the mustard seed paste, green chilies, mustard oil, ginger paste, and salt.

Carefully cut a 2-inch circle out of the top of the young coconuts and drain out most of the water. Stuff the coconuts with the chicken mixture. Close the hole with the coconut circle or with aluminum foil and put the coconuts in an oven-proof casserole. Bake in the oven for 2 hours.

Remove coconuts from the oven and allow to cool slightly. Remove the top or aluminum foil and squeeze in the lime or lemon juice.

Serve the chicken spooned over steamed rice and garnished with cilantro.

HONEY GINGER CHILI CHICKEN
Misti Chili Chicken

This is a fairly simple rendition of the ever-popular Indo-Chinese chili chicken, with some honeyed notes. The honey ginger modifies this otherwise familiar dish making it slightly sweeter, actually in some ways more American-style Chinese. For me, stressful days call for really greasy fried rice—probably because it takes me back to the Chinese takeout days of grad school. The restaurant that comes to mind was within walking distance of the university and located at the base of the train tracks. I would watch the trains pass by while the cook whipped up my food in all of eight minutes. A special of Roast Pork Fried Rice and Fried Half Chicken was sold for $4.50. This recipe is inspired by those cheap but comforting and memorable meals.

Prep Time: 2½ hours (including 2 hours to marinate chicken)
Cook Time: 35 minutes | **Makes:** 6 to 8 servings

INGREDIENTS
1½ pounds chicken on the bone, cut into fairly small pieces
1-inch piece fresh ginger, peeled
3 cloves garlic
5 green chilies
⅓ cup soy sauce
3 tablespoons mild vinegar (such as cider vinegar)
⅓ cup oil
2 medium onions, cut into eighths and layers separated
1 green bell pepper, cut into thin strips
3 to 4 tablespoons honey

Garnish
2 to 3 tablespoons oil
2 tablespoons julienned fresh ginger
2 to 3 tablespoons chopped cilantro

PREPARATION
Put the chicken pieces in a bowl. Place the ginger, garlic, and green chilies in a grinder and grind to a paste. Add to the chicken along with the soy sauce and vinegar and toss to coat. Cover and marinate chicken for about 2 hours.

Heat the oil in a wok or skillet on medium heat. Add the chicken mixture and cook, stirring frequently, on medium-low heat, until the mixture is dry and begins to sizzle and turn golden, a good 20 to 25 minutes. Add the onions, bell pepper, and honey and mix well and cook for an additional 5 minutes.

In a separate small pan, heat the oil for garnish and cook the ginger till fairly crisp. Pour the seasoned oil and ginger over the chicken. Garnish with the cilantro and serve.

CHICKEN AND GREEN PAPAYA STEW
Pepe Murgir Jhol

It is interesting how many ways nutritious vegetables are thrown into essential Bengali foods. One common vegetable used in various forms is the papaya. The green, unripe version is added to curries, such as this light chicken curry. This delicate chicken stew makes a wonderful supper on a cold day with or without rice.

Prep Time: 45 minutes (includes marinating time) | **Cook Time:** 45 minutes if using pressure cooker; or 60 minutes if using saucepan | **Makes:** 4 to 6 servings

INGREDIENTS
Juice of 1 lime
1 small chicken, skinned, jointed, and cut into small pieces
2 teaspoons turmeric
2 teaspoons salt
¼ cup oil
1 onion, very finely chopped
1-inch piece fresh ginger, peeled
1 tablespoon cumin seeds
1 tablespoon coriander seeds
1 teaspoon black peppercorns
3 green cardamom pods
3 cloves
1½-inch cinnamon stick, broken into pieces
2 medium potatoes, peeled and quartered
½ small green papaya, peeled and cut into small pieces
1 large carrot, peeled and cut into pieces
½ cup peas (can be frozen)
2 tomatoes, quartered

PREPARATION
Squeeze the lime juice on the chicken and rub it with the turmeric and salt and set aside for 30 minutes.

Heat the oil in a wok or skillet. Add the onion and seasoned chicken and cook on low heat, stirring frequently, until onions caramelize and chicken turns pale golden, about 10 minutes.

Grind the ginger, cumin seeds, coriander seeds, and black peppercorns into a paste and add to the chicken with the cardamom pods, cloves, and cinnamon stick. Cook the mixture, stirring frequently, for about 15 more minutes. Add the potatoes, papaya, carrot, peas, tomatoes, and 2 cups water.

Place mixture in a pressure cooker and cook under pressure for about 15 minutes. Open the pressure cooker and you should have a light chicken stew brimming with the colorful vegetables and fragrant with the coriander and black pepper. (Alternately, if you don't have a pressure cooker, you can simmer the mixture in a saucepan until chicken is very tender.)

CHICKEN WITH POPPY SEED SAUCE
Posto Murgi

I had initially developed this recipe just to use up some extra poppy seed paste that I had, but the mellow flavors have made it quite a hit in my household.

Prep Time: 20 minutes | **Cook Time:** 30 minutes | **Makes:** 4 servings

INGREDIENTS
3 tablespoons oil
1 red onion, thinly sliced
1 tablespoon fresh ginger paste (page 13)
1 tablespoon garlic paste (page 14)
3 green cardamom pods
3 cloves
1-inch cinnamon stick, broken into pieces
1 teaspoon cumin-coriander powder (page 17)
¾ teaspoon cayenne pepper powder
1½ pounds skinless boneless chicken, cut into small pieces
½ cup poppy seed paste (page 14)
⅓ cup cashews
2 tablespoons milk

PREPARATION
Heat the oil in a wok or skillet. Add the onion and cook for 5 to 7 minutes, till turning brown. Add the ginger paste, garlic paste, cardamom pods, cloves, cinnamon stick, cumin-coriander powder, cayenne pepper powder, and chicken. Cook the chicken on high heat, stirring frequently, till well browned and the oil separates from the spice mixture.

Lower the heat and add the poppy seed paste and ½ cup water and simmer for 10 minutes. Process the cashews with the milk to make a creamy paste and mix into the chicken. Bring to a boil and remove from heat.

SILKEN SPICED CHICKEN
Reshmi Moghlai Moorgi

I have seen a lot of recipes here and there with the name *reshmi*, which means silk. I was mostly unconvinced that meat could be silky, but the good thing about the kitchen is that we live and learn.

This recipe is one of my first accidental creations that was a success. I am very nostalgically attached to it. I discovered this recipe during my grad school days. The gravy I was preparing was thinner than I would have liked, and my cooking inexperience left me unsure as to how to thicken it. Eggs were available in the refrigerator by the dozen, so I cracked one into the pot and gently stirred and watched. The egg added a gentle thickness and rich smoothness, and just the right texture to this soft chicken. This interesting texture ended up being a great hit, and I was lauded for creativity. So the lesson here is that sometimes you can save the day by improvisation.

Prep Time: Overnight (to marinate chicken) | **Cook Time:** 45 minutes
Makes: 6 servings

INGREDIENTS
1 tablespoon fresh ginger paste (page 13)
1 tablespoon garlic paste (page 14)
Juice of 2 limes
1½ teaspoons cumin-coriander powder (page 17)
1 teaspoon salt
¾ teaspoon cayenne pepper powder
2 pounds boneless skinless chicken thighs, cut into small pieces
1 whole onion, peeled plus 1 onion, thinly sliced
3 green chilies
3 to 4 tablespoons chopped cilantro
2 to 3 tablespoons butter
2 tablespoons oil
1 teaspoon cumin seeds
½ cup Greek yogurt
1 egg
4 green cardamom pods, bruised

PREPARATION
Place the ginger and garlic pastes in a bowl and stir in the lime juice. Add the cumin-coriander powder, salt, and cayenne pepper powder and mix well. Toss this with the chicken to coat in a large container and marinate in the refrigerator overnight.

Place the whole onion, green chilies, and cilantro in a food processor and process until finely chopped.

Heat the butter and oil in a wok or skillet and add the sliced onion and cumin seeds. Cook for about 5 minutes, until the onion softens and begins to turn golden. Add the chopped onion mixture and chicken with marinade. Gently cook the chicken on medium heat until the mixture is fairly dry, fragrant, and well browned, about 15 to 20 minutes.

Add the yogurt and cook on low heat until it begins to simmer. Beat the egg and mix in with the cardamom pods and cook the mixture until the egg begins to coat the chicken.

ROAST CHICKEN MARINATED WITH LEMON, CHILIES, AND MOLASSES
Moorgir Roast

There are many variations of roast chicken seasoned with Indian spices. Some of these hail back to early British times, with names such as Gypsy Chicken. This is my variation. This recipe employs a very simple spice marinade and is basted with a combination of clarified butter and mustard oil. The marinade can also be used on chicken drumsticks with good results.

Prep Time: 6½ hours (including 6 hours to marinate chicken)
Cook Time: 2 hours (mostly unattended) | **Makes:** 6 servings

INGREDIENTS
4 cloves garlic
2-inch piece fresh ginger, peeled
6 green chilies
2 dried red chilies
1 teaspoon turmeric
1½ tablespoons fennel seeds
2 tablespoons salt
1 tablespoon molasses
2 lemons, halved and seeded
2 small organic free-range chickens (usually about 2 pounds each at farmer's markets)
1 tablespoon ghee (clarified butter)
2 tablespoons mustard oil
2 small red onions, sliced

PREPARATION
Place the garlic, ginger, green chilies, dried red chilies, turmeric, fennel seeds, salt, and molasses in a blender. Squeeze in the lemon juice and blend to a paste. Rub this marinade all over the chickens and under the skin. Take care to reach the crevices. Cover the chickens and place in the refrigerator to marinate for about 6 hours.

Pre-heat the oven to 350 degrees F. Grease a baking dish large enough to hold the chickens. Place the chickens in the dish. Mix the ghee and mustard oil. Brush the chickens liberally with this mixture. Place in the oven and bake for about 1 hour, removing once to brush with the oil mixture.

Turn the chickens, brush with oil mixture again and bake for about 45 to 60 more minutes. The chicken should be well browned and tender. Turn off the oven and let the chicken rest for about 20 minutes. Cut the chickens into serving-size pieces, garnish with the onion slices before serving.

Family Weddings

When I was growing up, family weddings were a one-week affair, but at a bare minimum, the ritual of the wedding ceremony is a three-day affair. It begins with a host of preliminary ceremonies, starting with beautifying and preparing the bride for her big day. This is then followed by an *Ashirbad* (blessing ceremony), where the bride is usually blessed by her family and members of the groom's family. A corresponding ceremony is held for the groom. There is an assortment of food and constant excitement. Just a generation back there were full-time professional chefs that pretty much camped out and dealt with all the food needs. Nowadays this process is a simpler and less daunting one, particularly for the bride's family. Like all things modern, it is a tradeoff between sentiment and convenience. There is also more control of the event by the bridal couple and the general preference these days seems to err towards practicality and simplicity.

The bride is decorated with sandalwood paste in preparation for the wedding, and then the groom arrives with the groomsmen. As a child, I also insisted on being decorated for each of the weddings of my aunts. The wedding then takes place at the appointed hour. *Piris*, wooden plank chairs finished with colorful designs, are used for various traditional purposes in Bengal including weddings. The Bengali bride is seated on a *piri* and carried into the ceremony by her brothers. This tradi-tion harks back to the days when the brides were much younger and easier to carry. She comes in with her face covered with a betel leaf. She is raised to eye-level with the groom and then removes the leaf and looks up to present herself to him. This meeting of the eyes is considered auspicious and a moment of connection, and is called *Shubho Dristi* ("auspicious look").

On the third formal day of the rituals, the party moves to the groom's house. There the bride actually cooks at her in-laws house for the first time during the day, and there is usually a reception for the bride called the *Bau Bhat*.

Chapter Eleven:

Meat Dishes
Mangsho

Mutton (usually referring to goat meat) and other heavier meats are usually an important feature for festive occasions like weddings. In this chapter, I provide recipes using lamb instead of goat meat, since lamb tends to be more readily available in U.S. supermarkets. The choice of meats tend to be interesting, since most Hindu households still do not eat beef and Muslim households do not eat pork. I tend to work most frequently with lamb or goat and occasionally with pork, so the recipes here mimic my eating preferences.

But these recipes work very well, if not better, with traditional goat meat if you can find it. Since red meat is usually not an everyday choice in most Bengali households, many of these recipes require more elaborate preparation. I have, however, also included some lighter preparations to show the breadth of simplicity.

SPICY LAMB WITH MUSHROOMS AND GREEN ONIONS
Mushroom Piyaj Diye Mangsho

A few weeks ago, I had totally run out of green chilies and my husband was dispatched on the errand to procure more. When he returned, I found myself the proud owner of half a dozen brightly colored habanero peppers. I tried them in this lamb recipe with some lovely green onions and mushrooms from the farmer's market and had a new appreciation for the habenero.

Prep Time: 20 minutes | **Cook Time:** 30 minutes | **Makes:** 4 servings

INGREDIENTS
1 pound boneless leg of lamb, cut into 1-inch cubes and frozen
2 tablespoons oil
1 teaspoon minced fresh ginger
2 garlic cloves, pressed
¼ cup soy sauce
1 habanero pepper, finely chopped
½ teaspoon butter
⅔ cup chopped mushrooms
1 cup finely chopped scallions
1 tablespoon rice vinegar
1 teaspoon sugar

PREPARATION
Place the frozen lamb cubes on a cutting board and cut each cube into paper-thin slices. (It is essential that the lamb is frozen to obtain the right result.)

Heat the oil in a heavy-bottomed pan and add the ginger and garlic and saute lightly. Add the lamb and cook till the pinkness is somewhat gone, about 5 minutes. Add the soy sauce, habanero pepper, and ⅓ cup water and cover and cook for about 15 minutes.

In the meantime, heat the butter in a small skillet and sauté the mushrooms for 3 to 4 minutes.

Carefully remove the lid from the pot with the lamb and stir in the mushrooms. Cook for another 10 minutes on relatively low heat, until the mixture is fairly dry.

Meanwhile add the scallions to the small skillet and cook till wilted. Stir the scallions, rice vinegar, and sugar into the lamb mixture and mix well.

LAMB OR GOAT CURRY WITH MINT
Poodina Diye Mangshor Jhol

I often use the mint that grows so plentifully in summer in New York as it complements some of the light, subtle Bengali flavors as in this simple mutton curry. I find this dish comforting in winter too, when you can add all the lovely root vegetables to the gravy. Other than the faintly subtle, yet distinct taste of mint, this dish is much like the food of my childhood, hearty and nourishing.

Prep Time: 10 minutes | **Cook Time:** 25 to 30 minutes in pressure cooker; or 60 minutes in saucepan (mostly unattended) | **Makes:** 4 servings

INGREDIENTS
3 to 4 tablespoons oil
1 teaspoon cumin seeds
1 red onion, chopped
1 tablespoon fresh ginger paste (page 13)
1 tablespoon garlic paste (page 14)
1 teaspoon turmeric
1 tablespoon ginger-cumin-coriander paste (page 14)
1 teaspoon crushed black peppercorns
2 green chilies, very finely chopped
¾ pound boneless lamb or 1 pound goat meat on the bone, cut into 1-inch pieces
1½ teaspoons salt
1 teaspoon sugar
2 small potatoes, peeled and quartered
2 tomatoes, quartered
2 tablespoons finely chopped fresh mint
½ cup fresh or frozen green peas
4 tablespoons chopped cilantro
1 teaspoon garam masala (page 17)

PREPARATION
In a pressure cooker, heat the oil on medium heat for about 1 minute. Add the cumin seeds and when the seeds begin to sizzle, add the onion, ginger paste, and garlic paste. Cook for 5 minutes, until the mixture is nice and fragrant and the onion turns softly golden.

Add the turmeric, ginger-cumin-coriander paste, peppercorns, green chilies, and lamb and mix well. Add the salt and sugar and cook on medium-high heat for 10 minutes, stirring frequently.

Add the potatoes, tomatoes, mint, and peas (if using fresh peas, if using frozen do not add at this time). Add 2 cups water, check for salt and adjust if needed, and cook under pressure for 15 minutes. (If you are not using a pressure cooker, you can add some more water and continue cooking the meat until it is nice and soft, usually about 40 minutes.)

Cool slightly, remove the lid, stir in peas if using frozen, and mix in the cilantro and garam masala. Serve over plain white rice.

SLOW-COOKED DRY MUTTON OR LAMB WITH A TANGY SEASONING
Tauk Mangshor Kasha

The kasha-style of cooking (dry and slow-cooked) is classic in Bengali cooking. A good *mangshor* or mutton *kasha* can win over the hearts of most Bengali men. In fact, I have a friend (a very accomplished scientist) who is willing to trade handyman services for a meal of this mutton curry and some *luchi*. My recipe adds a touch of tartness (*tauk* in Bengali), which is my adaptation of the classic recipe.

Prep Time: 6 hours (mostly to marinate meat) | **Cook Time:** 90 minutes (mostly unattended) | **Makes:** 4 to 6 servings

INGREDIENTS
2 pounds goat meat or lean lamb on the bone, cubed
¼ cup vinegar
2 tablespoons cumin-coriander powder
2 teaspoons cayenne pepper powder
1 teaspoon turmeric
1½ teaspoons garam masala (see page 17)
2 teaspoons salt
1 teaspoon sugar
4 tablespoons oil
2 red onions, finely chopped
10 cloves garlic
1-inch piece fresh ginger, peeled

PREPARATION
Toss the meat with the vinegar, cumin-coriander powder, cayenne pepper powder, turmeric, garam masala, salt, and sugar and refrigerate to marinate for at least 5 hours.

Heat the oil in a wok or skillet. Add the onions and cook for 5 minutes. Chop the garlic and ginger in a food processor and add to the onions and cook for about 2 minutes. Add the meat with the marinade spices and cook for about 10 minutes on medium heat, until the spices are fragrant and the oil begins to shimmer on the surface.

Add 3 cups water and bring to a simmer; cover and cook undisturbed for about 1 hour. Remove the cover and cook on high till the liquid evaporates and the oils coat the meat in a sheen-like texture. It is important to watch and stir the meat towards the end of this process so it doesn't burn.

MUTTON OR LAMB CURRY WITH POTATOES AND BELL PEPPERS

Alu Capsicum Diye Mangsho

This recipe was developed for my brother, who likes to eat well but does not enjoy cooking. When he visits me he craves good Bengali food, the simple homey variety that is difficult to find outside the house. So whenever he visits, we have a few days of homestyle cooking: simple, lightly seasoned stews and stir-fried vegetables served with a generous dose of white rice.

Prep Time: 15 minutes | **Cook Time:** 50 minutes in pressure cooker; or 1½ hours in saucepan | **Makes:** 4 to 6 servings

INGREDIENTS
2 pounds goat meat or lamb on the bone, cubed
2 teaspoons turmeric
2 teaspoons salt
Juice of 1 lime
2 onions
2-inch piece fresh ginger, peeled
2 to 4 cloves garlic
3 green chilies
¼ cup oil
2 tablespoons cumin-coriander powder (page 17)
1 tablespoon whole black peppercorns
3 green cardamom pods
3 cloves
2-inch cinnamon stick, broken into pieces
2 small potatoes, peeled and cut into eighths
2 large tomatoes, chopped
2 green bell peppers, sliced

PREPARATION
Rub the turmeric and salt on the meat. Squeeze on the lime juice and set aside to marinate while preparing the remaining ingredients.

Place the onions, ginger, garlic, and green chilies in a food processor and process till finely chopped.

Heat the oil in a pressure cooker. Add the onion mixture and the seasoned meat. Cook on high for 10 minutes, stirring frequently. Add the cumin-coriander powder, peppercorns, cardamom pods, cloves, and cinnamon stick and stir and cook for 10 more minutes.

Add the potatoes and stir and cook for 5 minutes. Add the tomatoes and peppers and mix well. Add 1 cup water, check seasonings, and cook under pressure for 25 minutes. (If you do not have a pressure cooker, cook the meat on low heat until fork tender, about 1 hour.)

SUNDAY SLOW-COOKED LAMB SHANKS
Robibarer Makha Mangsho

I cook lamb shanks in the slow cooker. Cooking in earthenware pots on low heat is fairly traditional in a lot of regional Indian cuisine, and using the slow cooker is a modernized variation. Try to buy smaller lamb shanks so that you can offer a single shank to each person and avoid serving them an inordinate amount of meat.

Prep Time: 20 minutes | **Cook Time:** 4 hours (in slow cooker)
Makes: 6 servings

INGREDIENTS
6 small lamb shanks (about 4 pounds total)
1 tablespoon turmeric
2 teaspoons salt
1 teaspoon cayenne pepper powder
Juice of 1 lime or lemon
2 red onions, peeled
4 to 6 cloves garlic
2-inch piece fresh ginger, peeled
6 green chilies
¼ cup oil
2 teaspoons sugar
1 tablespoon ginger-cumin-coriander paste (page 14)
4 tomatoes, coarsely chopped
10 cardamom pods, bruised
2 or 3 bay leaves
10 cloves
4-inch cinnamon stick, broken into pieces
2 tablespoons finely chopped cilantro

PREPARATION
Mix the lamb shanks with the turmeric, salt, and cayenne pepper powder to coat. Squeeze in the lime juice and set this aside to marinate while the onions are browning.

Place the onions, garlic, ginger, and green chilies in a food processor and process until finely chopped. Place the oil and the chopped onion mixture in a slow cooker that is set on low. Cover and cook for about 1 hour (at this point the onions should be pale golden and the room should be very fragrant).

Add the seasoned lamb, sugar, ginger-cumin-coriander paste, tomatoes, cardamom pods, bay leaves, cloves, and cinnamon stick. Cover and cook the lamb for 3 hours on low heat, stirring every hour. At the end of the process, you should have a rich saucy curry. Remove from the cooker, garnish with the cilantro and serve.

CRISPY CUMIN CORIANDER LAMB

Jire Makha Bhaja Mansho

Since I like to pride myself in being able to develop quicker recipes, I felt that I owed one of my favorite meat dishes the distinction of developing it into a quick version. This recipe marries traditional Bengali dry seasonings with a quicker, non-traditional style of creating and preparing the meat.

Prep Time: 2 hours and 45 minutes (mostly for freezing lamb)
Cook Time: 30 minutes | **Makes:** 4 servings

INGREDIENTS
1 pound boneless leg of lamb, cut into 1-inch cubes
2 teaspoons salt
1 teaspoon cayenne pepper powder
2 tablespoons chickpea flour (besan)
1 tablespoon cornstarch
6 tablespoons oil
1 red onion, chopped
4 cloves garlic
1-inch piece fresh ginger, peeled
2 green chilies, finely chopped
1 tablespoon cumin-coriander powder (page 17)
2 tomatoes, chopped
3 tablespoons chopped cilantro

PREPARATION
Freeze the lamb cubes for at least 2 hours. Cut the lamb cubes while still frozen into thin slices. Let meat sit at room temperature for 30 minutes to thaw.

In a large mixing bowl, mix 1 teaspoon salt, the cayenne pepper powder, chickpea flour, and cornstarch. Add the lamb and lightly toss to coat the pieces thoroughly, the moisture from the lamb should allow the flour mixture to cling to the meat. Heat the oil in a large flat heavy-bottomed skillet. Add the seasoned lamb and cook on high heat for about 2 to 3 minutes on each side until nicely crisp and cooked through. Carefully remove the lamb with a slotted spoon.

In the oil remaining in pan, on medium heat, sauté the chopped onion for about 5 minutes, until translucent and beginning to turn softly golden. Place the garlic, ginger, and green chilies in a food processor and process until very finely chopped. Add this mixture to the sautéed onions and cook until nice and fragrant, about 2 to 3 minutes.

Add the cumin-coriander powder, the remaining 1 teaspoon salt, and the tomatoes and cook for about 7 to 8 minutes, until a thick sauce is formed. Gently add the crisp lamb and toss lightly for about 1 minute to coat with sauce. Stir in the chopped cilantro and serve right away.

CHILDHOOD MUTTON OR LAMB CURRY
Chelebelar Mangshor Jhol

This is a hearty stew of winter vegetables and tender goat meat. If you use lamb for this preparation, please make sure that all the fat is trimmed from the meat. During my college days, I often dropped into my grandmother's house if I could make time for lunch. She would invariably have some freshly made rice pudding and a simple, steaming hot lunch ready for me—often featuring her version of this mutton curry.

Prep Time: 20 minutes | **Cook Time:** 45 minutes in pressure cooker; or 75 minutes in saucepan | **Makes:** 4 to 6 servings

INGREDIENTS
3 to 4 tablespoons oil
1 teaspoon turmeric
1½ teaspoons cayenne pepper powder
1 tablespoon ginger-cumin-coriander paste (page 14)
1 tablespoon fresh ginger paste (page 13)
1 onion, chopped
2 cloves garlic, finely chopped
2 pounds young goat meat or lamb with some bones, cut into cubes
2 teaspoons salt
3 or 4 bay leaves
3-inch cinnamon stick, broken into pieces
2 tomatoes, quartered
1 teaspoon sugar
2 or 3 small potatoes, quartered
2 beets, quartered
2 medium carrots, cut into medium rounds
½ cup green beans, cut into pieces
½ cup green peas

PREPARATION
Heat the oil in a pressure cooker or saucepan. Add the turmeric and cayenne pepper powder and cook lightly. Add the ginger-cumin-coriander paste, fresh ginger paste, onion, and garlic and cook for 5 minutes. Add the meat, salt, bay leaves, and cinnamon stick and cook this mixture on high heat for about 15 minutes, stirring frequently to allow uniform browning.

Lower the heat and add the tomatoes and sugar and cook for another 5 minutes. Add the potatoes, beets, carrots and 2 cups water and bring to a simmer. Cook the mixture under pressure for 15 minutes. (If you are not using a pressure cooker, cover and simmer the meat on medium-low heat for about 45 minutes, adding an additional 1 cup water halfway through the process, until the meat is soft and fork tender.)

Add the beans and green peas and cook for another 5 minutes. Check the seasonings and serve.`

CREAMY SLOW-COOKED LAMB SHANKS
Hando Mangsho

This is a bone-in version of a recipe that I tasted at a non-descript Bengali restaurant in Manhattan. Other than the planning time that the recipe needs, it is rather easy to prepare, especially done in a slow cooker. The use of the poppy seeds in this recipe sets it apart from its North Indian counterparts. While I like to use lamb shanks, any good cut of bone-in meat will work.

Prep Time: overnight (to marinate meat)
Cook Time: 4 hours (mostly unattended in slow cooker) | **Makes:** 6 servings

INGREDIENTS
6 small lamb shanks (about 3 to 4 pounds total)

Marinade
1 cup Greek yogurt
1 tablespoon black peppercorns
4 cloves garlic
1-inch piece fresh ginger, peeled
2 teaspoons salt
4 blades fresh mace
1 tablespoon whole garam masala (page 17)

Cooking sauce
3 tablespoons poppy seed paste (page 14)
4 tablespoons ghee (clarified butter)
1 cup sliced browned onions

Garnish
3 tablespoons rose water
1 tablespoon minced green chilies

PREPARATION
Place all the ingredients for the marinade in a blender and blend until very smooth. Place the lamb shanks in the marinade and marinate in the refrigerator overnight.

Place the lamb and marinating sauce in a slow cooker. Add the poppy seed paste, ghee, and browned onions. Slow cook the lamb shanks for 4 hours, stirring the meat occasionally.

Cool for 10 minutes, stir in rose water and minced chilies. Serve with rice or bread.

PICKLE-SPICED LAMB CURRY
Panch Phoron Mangso

Despite its strong flavors, this is a perfect recipe to make ahead for company, since it should rest for 24 hours at room temperature for the flavors to settle in. It is also called *lamb achari*, and is cooked with a combination of the Bengali five spice blend (*panch phoron*) and mustard oil, a double combination that is the base of a lot of Indian pickles.

The intense flavors of this dish dictate that the meat be eaten in small portions. In general, this recipe also tastes good served warm or at room temperature.

Prep Time: 24 hours (mostly to let flavors mature)
Cook Time: 45 minutes (mostly unattended) | **Makes:** 10 servings

INGREDIENTS
⅓ cup mustard oil
2 teaspoons panch phoron (page 5)
2 onions, chopped
2 cloves garlic, finely chopped
2 teaspoons shredded fresh ginger
2 teaspoons salt
1 teaspoon turmeric
1½ pounds lamb chops
2 teaspoons red pepper flakes
1 cup fresh tomato puree
1½ teaspoons sugar
⅓ cup commercial lemon or mango pickle, finely chopped
3 tablespoons chopped cilantro

PREPARATION
Heat the mustard oil in a large skillet and add the panch phoron. Wait for the spices to crackle and then add the onions, garlic, and shredded ginger and sauté for 5 minutes on medium heat.

Add the salt, turmeric, and lamb chops and cook for about 5 to 7 minutes, until the lamb is well-coated with the spices.

Add the red pepper flakes, tomato puree, sugar, and 2 cups water and mix well. Mix in the lemon pickle. Cook covered on low heat for 30 minutes.

Remove the cover and cook until the liquid has evaporated. Stir in the cilantro.

Set the meat aside for 24 hours at room temperature (under 65 degrees F) to let the flavors mature before serving (or marinate in the refrigerator on warmer days).

MY AUNT'S LAMB CASSEROLE
Chotomashir Manshor Caserole

Some people are placed in this world for just a short period of time. My mother's youngest sister was one of those people in my life. My aunt was a legendary cook and one of the first experimental cooks that I encountered. She was one of the people who influenced and impacted and shaped my culinary style when I spent two summers with her in England. That time enhanced my knowledge of the diversity of the migrant Bengali lifestyle and, of course, my aunt's culinary repertoire. She made a variation of lamb curry that she finished off casserole-style—a small investment of hands-on time with incredibly delicious results. This recipe is based on my recollections of that dish.

Prep Time: 15 minutes | **Cook Time:** 75 minutes (mostly unattended)
Makes: 6 to 8 servings

INGREDIENTS
2 onions
3 cloves garlic
2-inch piece fresh ginger, peeled
4 green chilies
¼ cup oil
2 pounds lamb chops (on the bone)
1 teaspoon coriander powder
1 teaspoon turmeric
2 teaspoons salt
2 teaspoons sugar
3 bay leaves
3-inch cinnamon stick, broken into pieces
6 cardamom pods
4 cloves
1 tablespoon whole black peppercorns
1 cup sliced mushrooms
1 cup tomato ketchup
2 tomatoes, chopped
Cilantro to garnish

PREPARATION
Place the onions, garlic, ginger, and green chilies in a food processor and process until chopped. Heat the oil in a skillet and add the onion mixture and sauté for about 5 minutes. Add the lamb with the coriander powder, turmeric, salt, and sugar and mix well.

Place the bay leaves, cinnamon stick, cardamom pods, cloves, and whole pepper-corns in a mortar and bruise lightly with the pestle. Add to the lamb mixture and cook for about 15 minutes on medium heat, stirring the mixture frequently. In the meantime pre-heat the oven to 375 degrees F.

Place the lamb mixture in a casserole. Stir in the mushrooms, tomato ketchup, and tomatoes. Cover the casserole with foil and bake for 30 minutes. Increase the heat to 425 degrees F and bake uncovered for 20 to 25 minutes.

BENGALI LAMB AND DRIED PEA KABABS
Tikiya

This recipe is a Bengali variation of the North Indian lentil and mutton kebabs called *shammi kababs*. It is from the Murshidabad region of Bengal and uses whole dried peas instead of chickpeas. I have tried various tricks to shorten the cooking time, but the kababs would not hold during the frying process, a sign that there was too much moisture in the mixture, because it had not been dried out enough. Finally I learned to plan ahead and let the meat and lentils cook together to soft perfection, and the *tikiyas* held together as they were meant to. So the recipe does take a little time, but it can be made in bulk and the kababs can be frozen and then defrosted before frying.

Prep Time: 45 minutes | **Cook Time:** 3½ hours (mostly unattended)
Makes: 6 to 8 servings

INGREDIENTS
1 pound lamb (I use bone-in loin chops)
⅔ cup whole dried peas (motor) or yellow split peas (motor dal)
2½ teaspoons salt
4 green chilies
2 dried red chilies
4 cloves
2-inch cinnamon stick, broken into pieces
1 tablespoon cumin seeds
1 tablespoon coriander seeds
1 teaspoon sugar
4 cloves garlic
2-inch piece fresh ginger, peeled
2 hard-boiled eggs, peeled
1 small onion, chopped
2 tablespoons chopped cilantro
1 egg
Oil for frying

PREPARATION
Place the lamb, dried peas, 2 teaspoons salt, green chilies, dried red chilies, cloves, cinnamon stick, cumin seeds, coriander seeds, sugar, garlic, ginger, and 7 cups water in a large heavy-bottomed pot and simmer on medium-low heat for 3 hours, until the peas and meat are soft and the water is completely evaporated. (Check toward the end to make sure mixture doesn't get dry too soon and add a little water as needed.) Cool the mixture.

Mash the hard-boiled eggs and stir in the chopped onion and the remaining ½ teaspoon salt and set aside.

Remove the lamb from the pot and remove from bones. Put the lamb meat back into the pot.

Puree the lamb mixture in a food processor (working in batches if necessary) until very smooth (it should look like a thick muddy paste, that holds firm when shaped into patties). Place mixture in a bowl and stir in the cilantro and raw egg. (At this point test the mixture by forming one small cake and frying it, if the cake appears to separate, add some flour to the mixture.)

Break off a handful of the lamb mixture and form into an oval patty. Place a little hard-boiled egg mixture in the center and cover over with the lamb mixture and re-form into an oval patty. Repeat with the rest of the lamb mixture. Place the patties in the freezer and freeze for 20 minutes.

Heat some oil in a skillet and add 2 to 3 of the cakes at a time and fry on both sides until golden. Drain on paper towels and serve with a chutney or a mustard relish.

GROUND LAMB STUFFED MINI PEPPERS IN ONION CARDAMOM SAUCE
Choto Capsicumer Dolma

> *"Bajra Manik Diye Gatha Ashar Tomar Mala."* (The monsoon garland is decked with thunder gemstones.)
>
> —Rabindranath Tagore

The Bengalis love the rain enough to write poems and songs about the rainy season. I am always inspired to write or cook, and sometimes to do both, when it rains. In fact, my Facebook friends are always surprised and annoyed at my positive posts about the weather on a rainy, wet, and slushy day.

This recipe is a variation of the classic dolma, wax gourds called *potols* stuffed with fish, meat, or cottage cheese. I often make this recipe to celebrate a rain- or snow-kissed day.

Prep Time: 30 minutes | **Cook Time:** 40 minutes (mostly unattended)
Makes: 6 servings

INGREDIENTS
¼ cup oil
1 teaspoon cumin powder
1 onion, finely chopped, plus 1 onion, ground
1-inch piece fresh ginger, peeled and grated
1 cup ground lamb or goat meat

2½ teaspoons salt
½ teaspoon garam masala (page 17)
1 teaspoon cayenne pepper powder
1 tomato, chopped
20 mini bell peppers (try using a mixed color combination)
1 teaspoon fresh ginger paste (page 13)
4 green cardamom pods
4 cloves
1-inch cinnamon stick, broken into pieces
2 bay leaves
2 green chilies, finely chopped
1 cup Greek yogurt
1 teaspoon sugar
2 tablespoons chopped cilantro

PREPARATION

Heat about half the oil in a wok or skillet. Add the cumin powder, chopped onion, and ginger and cook for about 5 to 7 minutes, until the onion softens and begins to turn golden.

Add the ground meat, half the salt, the garam masala, and cayenne pepper powder. Stir in the chopped tomato and cook the mixture for about 10 minutes, until dry and well mixed.

Gently cut off the tops of the peppers and remove any ribs and seeds from the insides. Stuff the peppers with the ground meat mixture and arrange in a greased baking dish.

Pre-heat the oven to 350 degrees F.

Heat the remaining oil in a wok or skillet and cook the ground onion and ginger paste till browned. Add the green cardamom pods, cloves, cinnamon sticks, bay leaves, and green chilies and mix well. Add the yogurt in small batches, cooking until each batch is absorbed. Add the sugar and remaining 1¼ teaspoons salt. Cook the mixture stirring well for about 10 minutes, until well browned and thick.

Pour the gravy over the peppers and bake for 20 minutes. Garnish with the cilantro prior to serving.

PORK IN A SPICY VINEGAR-BASED SAUCE
Bandel Vindaloo

It took me some time to realize that there was no single recipe for *vindaloo*. After subsequent observation and understanding of Raghavan Iyer's *660 Curries* (a fascinating book offering us quite the cornucopia of recipes), I even learned that not all *vindaloos* are spicy. The *vindaloo* is a Portuguese-inspired recipe that uses a combination of garlic, chilies, and vinegar in its spicing. The variation given here is strong in its mustard-based overtones, which is not surprising since all the fusion influences are usually paired with the cuisine of the region.

Prep Time: 1 hour (including 40 minutes for marinating)
Cook Time: 30 minutes | **Makes:** 4 servings

INGREDIENTS
⅓ cup cider vinegar
2 cloves garlic
1½ teaspoons mustard seeds
1 teaspoon cumin seeds
1 teaspoon coriander seeds
2 dried red chilies
1-inch piece fresh ginger, peeled
1 green chili
1 teaspoon salt
1 teaspoon sugar
1 pound lean pork tenderloin
⅓ cup mustard oil
2-inch cinnamon stick, broken into pieces
2 bay leaves
1 red onion, chopped
2 tablespoons finely chopped cilantro

PREPARATION
Place the cider vinegar, garlic, mustard seeds, cumin seeds, coriander seeds, dried red chilies, ginger, green chili, salt, and sugar in a blender and let soak for about 15 minutes. In the meantime, cut the pork into 1-inch pieces and place in a bowl.

Blend the vinegar-spice mixture into a smooth paste and pour over the meat and toss to coat. Marinate for about 30 to 40 minutes.

Heat the mustard oil in a wok or skillet on medium heat until fairly hot. Add the cinnamon stick and bay leaves and cook for a few seconds. Add the red onion and cook the mixture, stirring well, for about 3 to 4 minutes, until beginning to turn golden. Add the meat with marinade and continue cooking the mixture for about 20 minutes, until it is dry and the meat is cooked through. Garnish with the cilantro and serve with rice.

ROASTED PORK WITH POTATOES AND ONIONS
Pork Bhuni

This recipe, that I tasted in Darjeeling, has Anglo-Indian roots. The small elevated towns in various parts of India are called hill stations, the preferred places for the British to live due to the cooler temperatures. A lot of the hill stations are now great holiday destinations and have hotels that boast several colonial-influenced dishes on the menu. On a trip to Darjeeling to peruse schools for my brother, I fell in love with some local culinary creations and other colonial cuisine that we ate, including this recipe.

Darjeeling's real gift to the world is its famous tea that most days gently nudges me on to face life. I do, however, temper the gentle caffeine of Darjeeling with coffee later in the day to handle the pace of life in New York City.

Prep Time: 2½ hours (mostly marinating) | **Cook Time:** 80 minutes
Makes: 4 servings

INGREDIENTS
⅓ cup cider vinegar
2 dried red chilies
1-inch piece fresh ginger, peeled
1 tablespoon coriander seeds
2 pounds pork tenderloin, cubed
3 teaspoons salt
2 teaspoons sugar
¼ cup oil
2 onions, sliced
2 cloves garlic, pressed
½ teaspoon turmeric
2 potatoes, peeled and cut into eighths
1 tomato, chopped
2 tablespoons tomato ketchup
1 tablespoon chopped cilantro

PREPARATION
Place the vinegar, red chilies, ginger, and coriander seeds in a blender and blend until smooth. Place the marinade in a bowl and toss in the pork, about 2 teaspoons of the salt, and the sugar. Marinate the pork for about 2 hours.

Heat the oven to 350 degrees F. Place the pork with the marinade in a casserole and bake for about 45 minutes.

When pork is done roasting, heat the oil in a wok or skillet. Add the onions and cook for 5 to 7 minutes, until soft and beginning to turn translucent and golden on the edges. Add the garlic, turmeric, potatoes, and remaining 1 teaspoon salt. Cover and cook for about 5 minutes. Add the roasted pork and mix well. Add the tomato and tomato ketchup and cook for about 15 minutes, until the potatoes are nice and soft. Stir in the cilantro and serve.

A Land of Endless Festivities

The Goddess Durga, a ten-headed and ten-handed woman with the combined strengths and blessings of all the gods, was created to overcome the demon Mahishashura since he had received a boon that he was not to die at the hands of a man. She is worshiped in various parts of India, but dominates the festive stage in Bengal. In the Autumn, the ten-day festival of Durga Puja transforms the region into an enormous carnival where religion and retail thrive hand in hand. The landscape is dotted with festival-themed billboards, and food shops announce promotions of festive foods, creating an atmosphere that is extremely difficult to resist.

While other festivals do not quite reach the prominence of Durga Puja, Bengalis love to celebrate the mother Goddess in various forms. Shortly after Durga Puja, you have Lokkhi Puja that celebrates Lokkhi or Laxmi, the Goddess of Wealth. The emphasis of Laxmi in the Bengali cultural context is as much on domestic peace as on wealth. The Goddess is welcomed into every home with ornate rice paste decorations called the *alpana*. She is considered fickle and fastidious, and therefore the homemaker is encouraged to keep a peaceful and tidy home to please her. Two weeks after Lokkhi Puja, is Kali Puja where Durga's alter-ego Kali is worshipped. Kali Puja takes place a day before Diwali, the festival of lights that is today one of the best and most popular Indian holidays. Kali is the Goddess of Night, depicted in dark colors with a garland of human heads. She has her tongue out in a very characteristic Bengali expression of shame, since she accidentally stepped on her husband Shiva.

As the seasons change from winter to spring, there is a celebration for the Goddess Saraswati or Vasantee (feminine epitomization of spring). Saraswati is also worshipped as the Goddess of Learning. Young girls usually wear yellow or white to celebrate the occasion and this festival is observed in all the learning institutions across the region, from schools to universities. In between these celebrations there are several other miscellaneous celebrations for deities such as Manasha, who wards off snakes; Kartikeya, the son of Durga; and Vishwakarma, the God of Mechanical Activities, among others. Dotted in between these Hindu festivals are Muslim holidays, such as Id, and the Christian festivals of Easter and Christmas, and then there are national and other secular holidays that collectively keep the Bengali calendar filled and the kitchens busy.

Chapter Twelve:

Chutneys, Relishes and Bhortas
Chaatney, Tauk ar Bhortas

THE ROLE OF THE BENGALI CHUTNEY

The Bengali chutney might be the parent of the popular western-ized sweet condiment sold as chutney in glass jars. The Bengali version is a palate cleanser, served toward the end of the meal, usually with crisp thin lentil wafers called *papars* in Bengali.

The chutney (pronounced *chaatney* in Bengali) like other food items has a couple of variations, such as the *ambol* and the *tauk*. At their baseline these creations are sweet and sour and made with acidic seasonal fruits such as green mango, tomato, and green papaya. The tomato is probably the most common. My guess is that tomatoes are a relative newcomer to the Bengali kitchen, and since people were not sure what to do with them, they introduced them to the table in the benign form of a chutney. The everyday chutney is a lightly spiced creation that balances sweet, salty, spicy, and tart flavors. The more elaborately flavored chutneys for weddings and festivals contain dry fruits and tend to be thicker in consistency. These condiments are, however, not made in bulk or treated as preserves. In past years, I found other fruits such as the plum and tomatillo that I think work well as chutneys. The naturally acidic consistency of these fruits satisfies the same criteria used in traditional options for the chutney.

Competing with the chutney is the creation from Bangladesh called *bhorta*. A *bhorta* is a spicy puree of almost anything. I have learned to love these creations from the assortment of Bangladeshi restaurants in New York.

TOMATO, CRANBERRY AND DATE CHUTNEY
Tomato Cranberry ar Khejurer Chaatney

The last time I visited Kolkata, I ate tomato chutney made with dates. It was an interesting change from the typical chutney made with dried mango leather called *aam shotto*. In this recipe, I added some cranberries for additional tanginess since I think that doing this gets us closer to the taste of natural tomatoes.

Prep Time: 15 minutes | **Cook Time:** 20 minutes | **Makes:** 10 servings

INGREDIENTS
2 tablespoons oil
½ tsp panch phoron (page 5)
2 or 3 dried red chilies
6 tomatoes, coarsely chopped
½ cup fresh cranberries
½ cup fresh dates, cut into thin slices
⅓ cup or more dark brown sugar or molasses

PREPARATION
Heat the oil in a wok or skillet. Add the panch phoron and red chilies and saute until the chilies darken and the panch phoron crackles, about 40 seconds. At this point add the tomatoes and cranberries and cook for about 4 minutes. Add the fresh dates and brown sugar or molasses (you can add additional brown sugar if you like a sweeter chutney) and cook the chutney until it is fairly thick, about 15 minutes. Chill the chutney before serving.

SWEET AND SOUR TOMATO AND GINGER CHUTNEY
Tomatoes Jhaal Chaatney

This is a somewhat savory variation on the classic tomato chutney. I developed this recipe for people who find the traditional tomato chutney a little too sweet.

Prep Time: 20 minutes | **Cook Time:** 7 minutes | **Makes:** 1 cup

INGREDIENTS
1½ tablespoons mustard oil
1 teaspoon nigella seeds
1 tablespoon grated fresh ginger
4 green chilies, finely chopped
4 tomatoes, chopped
1 teaspoon salt
3 tablespoons sugar
Juice of 1 lime
⅓ cup roasted peanuts, coarsely ground
2 tablespoons chopped mint
1 teaspoon bhaja masala (page 17)

PREPARATION

Heat the mustard oil in a wok or skillet on medium heat for about 1 minute. Add the nigella seeds and wait till they sizzle and then add the ginger and cook for about 30 seconds. Add the green chilies, tomatoes, salt, and sugar and mix well. Let this cook for about 2 minutes. Squeeze in the lime juice and simmer for another minute. (This relish should be cooked just enough to dissolve the salt and sugar and allow the flavors to meld together.)

Mix in the peanuts and mint and cook for about 30 seconds. Turn off the heat and stir in the bhaja masala and let the relish rest for about 1 minute. This relish keeps for about 3 weeks when stored in an airtight jar in the refrigerator.

GREEN PAPAYA CHUTNEY
Plastic Chutney

A "plastic" chutney consists of delicate, thinly sliced pieces of unripe papaya in a tangy-sweet sauce. The pieces of the papaya turn translucent and cling to each other like small chips of plastic, accounting for the name of the chutney. It was something my mother made very often while I was growing up. The traditional style of cutting the green papaya for this chutney is into razor-thin approximately 1 cm squares.

Prep Time: 10 minutes | **Cook Time:** 20 minutes | **Makes:** 8 servings

INGREDIENTS
½ cup sugar
Juice of 2 limes
½ teaspoon salt
1 cup very thinly sliced green papaya, cut into 1 cm squares
2 teaspoons raisins

PREPARATION
Place the sugar and ½ cup water in a pan. Squeeze the lime juice over the sugar. Add the salt and bring to a simmer. Stir in the pieces of green papaya. Cook on high for 15 minutes, till the liquid has almost evaporated. Add the raisins and cook for 2 to 3 more minutes. Chill the chutney prior to serving.

FRESH PINEAPPLE CHUTNEY
Anaraser Chaatney

Another classic chutney—the pineapple is a favored fruit in the Bengali kitchen. I like to add dried cranberries along with the traditional raisins to this chutney for a nice contrast of colors.

Prep Time: 15 minutes | **Cook Time:** 25 minutes | **Makes:** 15 servings

INGREDIENTS
3 tablespoons mustard oil
1 teaspoon panch phoron (page 5)
3 dried red chilies
1 fresh pineapple, pulp cut into small chunks
½ cup mild vinegar (such as cider vinegar)
2 tablespoons raisins or dried cranberries
1 cup sugar
1 teaspoon salt
1 teaspoon bhaja masala (page 16)

PREPARATION
Heat the mustard oil in a wok or skillet. Add the panch phoron and red chilies and when this begins to splutter add the pineapple and cook for 5 minutes. Add the vinegar, raisins or cranberries, sugar, salt, and 1 cup water. Cook for 15 to 20 minutes. Stir in the bhaja masala. Chill and serve.

GREEN MANGO CHUTNEY
Kancha Aamer Chaatney

Green mango chutney is a favorite in the warmer months of the year. Unlike tomato or pineapple chutneys, green mango chutney contains no other fruits but the beloved delicate green mango in its freshest form. Although green mango is available frozen (which I think works well for lentils and other recipes), it is best to work with the fresh variety for this recipe to get the right firm texture.

Prep Time: 15 minutes | **Cook Time:** 25 minutes | **Makes:** 6 to 8 servings

INGREDIENTS
2 green mangoes
½ teaspoon turmeric
½ teaspoon salt
2 tablespoons oil
1 teaspoon panch phoron (page 5)
2 or 3 dried red chilies
1 cup sugar
1 teaspoon fennel seeds
½ teaspoon bhaja masala (page 16)

PREPARATION

Peel the green mangoes and cut into small cubes. Rub with the turmeric and salt and set aside.

Heat half the oil in a wok or skillet on medium heat for about 30 seconds. Add the panch phoron and when it begins to splutter add the dried red chilies and sauté lightly. Add 2 cups water and bring to a simmer. Add the sugar and cook on medium-high heat for about 10 minutes, until it forms a light syrup.

Add the seasoned mangoes and cook for another 7 to 8 minutes, until the mango is soft and coated with a fairly thick sauce.

Heat the remaining 1 tablespoon oil in a small skillet. Add the fennel seeds and when they sizzle add the bhaja masala. Pour this over the mango chutney and gently stir in. This chutney stores well in the refrigerator for up to a month.

COCONUT MINT CHUTNEY
Narkol Pudinar Chaatney

This recipe is from the collection of a home cook, my childhood friend's older sister Sangeeta, who serves it with some nice and spicy fish cakes. In summer when mint is plentiful I make this as an accompaniment to fish cakes or to the meal in general. If you have fresh coconut around, this is one of those recipes that I think definitely benefits from its use.

Prep Time: 20 minutes | **Makes:** ½ cup

INGREDIENTS
½ cup grated coconut
3 green chilies
½ teaspoon black peppercorns
1 teaspoon salt
2 cups fresh mint leaves
⅓ cup low-fat Greek yogurt
1 teaspoon mustard oil
¼ teaspoon mustard seeds
¼ teaspoon fennel seeds

PREPARATION
Place the coconut in a blender. Add the green chilies, black peppercorns, salt, mint leaves, and yogurt and blend until smooth. Pour into a bowl.

Heat the mustard oil in a small skillet on medium heat for about 1 minute. Add the mustard seeds and fennel seeds and cook till the mustard seeds pop. Mix the oil lightly into the chutney.

LIGHT AND TANGY GREEN MANGO CURRY
Aam Jhol

This recipe is a traditional variation made with the beloved green mango. It is a cross between a chutney and a *jhol* (the light curry often served as a part of the regular meal rather than towards the end as one does with chutneys). The refreshing light gravy pairs nicely with rice if needed and is perfect for the summer when it is usually eaten. The freezer section of the Indian grocery store carries frozen green mangoes.

Prep Time: 10 minutes | **Cook Time:** 25 minutes | **Makes:** 6 servings

INGREDIENTS
2 or 3 green mangoes
2 tablespoons mustard oil
¾ teaspoon panch phoron (page 5)
½ teaspoon turmeric
3 or 4 dried red chilies
½ teaspoon salt
¾ cup sugar
1 teaspoon ghee (clarified butter)
½ teaspoon bhaja masala (page 16)
2 bay leaves, broken into pieces

PREPARATION
Cut the mangoes with their skin on into wedges, removing the seed. It is important to eliminate the seeds completely.

Heat the mustard oil in a wok or skillet. Add the panch phoron and wait till the spices crackle, and then add the green mangoes, turmeric, red chilies, and salt and cook the mixture for about 5 minutes. Add the sugar and 2 cups water and simmer the mixture for about 15 to 20 minutes, until the mangoes are soft and there is plenty of pale yellow gravy around them.

Heat the ghee in a small skillet and add the bhaja masala and bay leaves and cook for a few seconds. Pour this over the green mango curry and stir in. Serve the green mango curry at room temperature.

TOMATO AND TOMATILLOS IN A LIGHT TANGY GRAVY
Tomato Jhol

The concept of a tangy, light, sweet and sour gravy has been adapted in this recipe using local tomatillos. It turns out that the tangy green fruit is perfect for Bengali-style preparation and can fill in for the mango.

Prep Time: 10 minutes | **Cook Time:** 25 to 30 minutes | **Makes:** 10 servings

INGREDIENTS
4 tomatillos
2 tablespoons mustard oil
¾ teaspoon panch phoron (page 5)
3 or 4 red chilies
3 tomatoes, chopped
1 teaspoon turmeric
Juice of 2 limes
½ teaspoon salt
¾ cup sugar
2 tablespoons chopped cilantro

PREPARATION
Boil the tomatillos in about 3 cups water for 5 to 7 minutes. Drain and cool slightly and then chop coarsely, removing the central sticky and hard portion.

Heat the mustard oil in a wok or skillet. Add the panch phoron and chilies and when it crackles add the tomatillos, tomatoes, and turmeric. Cook the mixture for 3 minutes. Add the lime juice, salt, sugar, and 3 cups water. Simmer the mixture for 15 minutes. Garnish with the cilantro. This chutney is best served warm or chilled. It will keep well in the refrigerator for a couple of days.

FIERY MUSTARD AND LIME RELISH
Kasundi

I was first introduced to this mustard relish by my grand uncle Aseemmama, who actually introduced me to many a forbidden treat. It was not love at first taste, but over the years I learned to savor it. This usually accompanies the first course of greens and lentils and can take the place of ketchup or North Indian mint chutney with crisp Bengali meat chops. My recipe is modified for the electric grinder, but if you are using a traditional grinding stone you can reduce the amount of soaking time.

Prep Time: Overnight plus 10 minutes (mostly to soak mustard seeds)
Makes: ¾ cup

INGREDIENTS

8 tablespoons black mustard seeds
1 teaspoon salt
½ teaspoon sugar
2 cloves garlic
1 tablespoon ginger-cumin-coriander paste (page 14)
4 green chilies
Juice of 3 limes

PREPARATION

Soak the mustard seeds in 1 cup of water overnight.

Drain the seeds. Place the mustard seeds, salt, sugar, garlic, ginger-cumin-coriander paste, and green chilies in a wet grinder. Squeeze in the lime juice. Grind the mixture into a smooth paste. This will keep in the refrigerator for up to 2 weeks.

MUSTARD AND GREEN MANGO RELISH

Aam Kasundi

This is another traditional variation of the *kasundi*. It is usually prepared in early summer when tender green mangoes are plentiful. Green mangoes are used extensively in Bengali cuisine. The green mangoes traditionally used in Bengali cooking are the delicate wind-blown mangoes felled by the *Kal Baishaski* (northwesterly storms, see page 101). The large green mangoes that are available in Indian grocery stores in the U.S. are an acceptable substitute, though not as delicately sharp and fragrant in their flavor.

Prep Time: Overnight plus 10 minutes (mostly to soak mustard seeds)
Makes: ¾ cup

INGREDIENTS

8 tablespoons black mustard seeds
1 teaspoon salt
½ teaspoon sugar
2 cloves garlic
4 green chilies
1 green mango

PREPARATION

Soak the mustard seeds in 1 cup of water overnight.

Drain the seeds. Place the mustard seeds, salt, sugar, garlic, and green chilies in a wet grinder. Peel the green mango, cut the flesh into small pieces and place in the grinder. Grind to a smooth paste. This relish is ready to use right away but will keep in the refrigerator for 2 to 3 weeks.

MUSTARD, PINEAPPLE AND TOMATO RELISH
Tomato ar Anarosher Kashundi

In keeping with the concept of using nature's gifts in my cooking, I adapted the tomatoes that I find in plentiful abandon in my garden into this relish. The addition of the pineapple offers an interesting dimension of sweetness, and also gives this relish the consistency of a blended salsa. This can be served with some cheese and crackers if desired. Since this recipe does not use an entire pineapple, you can use frozen pineapple if you prefer, but then eliminate the sugar.

Prep Time: Overnight plus 10 minutes (mostly to soak mustard seeds)
Makes: ¾ cup

INGREDIENTS
8 tablespoons black mustard seeds
1 teaspoon salt
½ teaspoon sugar
1-inch piece fresh ginger, peeled
¾ cup fresh pineapple chunks
4 green chilies
2 ripe tomatoes, chopped

PREPARATION
Soak the mustard seeds in 1 cup of water overnight.

Drain the seeds. Place the mustard seeds, salt, sugar, ginger, pineapple, green chilies, and tomatoes in a wet grinder. Grind to a smooth paste. This will keep in an airtight jar.

TANGY FISH RELISH
Maacher Bhorta

This recipe is a simple way to use up extra fish. The flavor emphasizes tartness rather than fiery chilies, which are used in relative moderation. This relish is good with a side of steaming rice and lentils, but can also be used contemporary-style over toasted baguette slices. It will keep in the refrigerator for up to 2 weeks.

Prep Time: 10 minutes | **Cook Time:** 25 minutes | **Makes:** 1 cup

INGREDIENTS
½ pound white fish fillets (catfish or tilapia work well)
2 teaspoons salt
¼ cup mustard oil
¾ teaspoon cumin seeds
1 red onion, finely chopped
4 garlic cloves, pressed

1 teaspoon fresh ginger paste (page 13)
¾ teaspoon fenugreek powder
½ teaspoon cumin-coriander powder (page 17)
½ teaspoon turmeric
2 tomatoes, finely chopped
6 green chilies, finely chopped
Juice of 1 lemon
2 tablespoons finely chopped cilantro

PREPARATION

Place the fish, 2 cups water, and 1 teaspoon salt in a medium pot and bring to a simmer. Cook for about 10 minutes, until the fish is soft. Drain the fish and flake.

While the fish is cooking, heat the mustard oil in a wok or skillet on medium heat. Add the cumin seeds and cook for about 30 seconds. Add the onion, garlic, and ginger paste and continue cooking on low heat for about 7 minutes, until the onions have softened and are pale gold in color.

When fish is ready, add the flaked fish and remaining 1 teaspoon salt. Add the fenugreek powder, cumin-coriander powder, and turmeric and stir well. Add the tomatoes and chilies and cook the mixture on high heat for 10 minutes, stirring frequently to mash the fish and allow the liquid to dry out. Squeeze in the lemon juice and mix well. Stir in the cilantro. Let the flavors settle for at least 1 hour before serving. This relish is usually served at room temperature.

SPICY MASHED POTATO RELISH
Alur Bhorta

I love potatoes and this spicy, comforting relish is one of my favorite variations. It can be pureed further with a little yogurt. It tastes wonderful with pita chips, but is also an excellent accompaniment to the regular Bengali meal.

Prep Time: 10 minutes | **Cook Time:** 15 minutes | **Makes:** ½ cup

INGREDIENTS

2 large potatoes, boiled in their jackets
2 tablespoons mustard oil
2 dried red chili peppers, lightly crushed
½ teaspoon turmeric
¾ teaspoon salt
1 teaspoon cumin-coriander powder (page 17)
2 green chilies, finely chopped
Juice of 1 lime
1 tablespoon finely chopped cilantro

PREPARATION

Peel and mash the potatoes. Heat the mustard oil on medium heat and add the crushed red chilies and cook for 1 minute. Add the mashed potatoes, turmeric, salt, and cumin-coriander powder and mix well. Add the green chilies and squeeze in the lime juice. Stir in the cilantro and mix well. Cool and serve at room temperature.

LEMON, CHICKPEA AND CUCUMBER SALAD
Soshar Salad

I usually associated raita (a yogurt condiment) with North Indian cuisine, but lately I see it served in a slightly different variation with Bengali meals. Here I created a somewhat Bengali cross between the raita and a cucumber salad.

Prep Time: 45 minutes (including time to drain cucumbers)
Makes: 10 servings

INGREDIENTS

3 Kirby cucumbers
1 teaspoon coarse salt
Juice of 1 lemon
½ cup Greek yogurt, whipped
1 teaspoon sugar
½ teaspoon cayenne pepper powder
½ cup cooked chickpeas
1 tablespoon chopped cilantro (optional)

PREPARATION

Peel the cucumbers and grate them coarsely. Place in a colander and sprinkle with the salt and allow to drain for about 30 minutes.

Squeeze lemon juice into a bowl and add the yogurt, sugar, and cayenne pepper powder. Gently stir in the chickpeas and drained cucumber. Mix in the cilantro, if using, and serve as a condiment.

Chapter Thirteen:

Drinks
Jol Pan

Bengalis love their tea done just right. I have to confess this is a passion that I share and find it extremely frustrating when I cannot find a decent cup of well-brewed tea. I will accept a good blend of Darjeeling and Ceylon or Assam in the morning for my breakfast choice, but most of the time it has to be a good cup of well-brewed tea.

Outside the general social circuit, you have the more sophisticated well-heeled crowd who tend to enjoy alcohol to unwind. Alcohol, which is not something one would see gracing a festival or wedding table, is not really taboo—in fact, there are several references to the elite and their love for alcohol. The modern Bengali gentleman in post-colonial Bengal has acquired a taste for scotch, usually nursing his Johnny Walker as the evening settles. And beer is the drink of choice on weekend afternoons. There is, of course, the poorer man who gets his share of libation by indulging in cheaper home brews that are almost as potent, leaving them the butt of several jokes. The women tend to be more discreet in their choices, opting for colorful cocktails that are more subtle. Wine is a newer trend in India, suggesting a modern taste and foodie sophistication. Both in West Bengal and India in general, people are beginning to enjoy it.

Juices and smoothies are very traditional and something that my grandmother would painstakingly prepare for us when we were little. Most of the cocktails in this chapter are inspired by some traditional fruits drinks, and just for fun I gave them Bengali names. Adding alcohol to these drinks is absolutely optional—they stand perfectly well in their virgin form. All things being said, I will emphasize that for a good Bengali meal, serve a drink alcoholic or otherwise as an optional choice, but always make sure that there is cool water on the table.

PAPAYA AND GINGER COCKTAIL
Malobika – Ada Pepe Diye Shorbot

The papaya tree is another common fixture that dots the landscape of Bengal, though for some reason it is given a little less importance than the banana tree. Papayas are savored in both ripe and unripe forms. The general taste of this drink should not be too sweet. I prescribe a small amount of sugar, however, please do adapt the sweetness to suit your palate. This can either be served as a virgin drink or as a cocktail.

Prep Time: 15 minutes | **Makes:** 4 servings

INGREDIENTS
1 medium papaya, peeled, seeded, and cubed
1½-inch piece fresh ginger, peeled
¼ teaspoon black peppercorns
2½ cups milk (can be low-fat)
3 tablespoons dark brown sugar or powdered jaggery
½ cup coconut rum (optional)

PREPARATION
Place the papaya, ginger, black peppercorns, milk, and sugar in a blender. Blend for a good 5 minutes to ensure a nice smooth consistency. Add the rum, if using, and blend again. Place ice cubes in serving glasses and pour over the cubes and enjoy.

GREEN MANGO COOLER
Ahona – Aam Pora Shorbot

The last time I made this mango drink was on a sultry summer afternoon at my parents' home. Once I was done roasting, charring, and peeling the green mangoes, I was very tired and hot. I pureed the drink and set it aside in the fridge. Later when I drank the chilled tangy cooler, I was refreshed like the first dawn of light (called *Ahona* in Bengali, thereby giving the drink its name). It was later that I tried cooking the mangoes in the oven and on an inspiration added a shot of vodka, making the drink just right for parties.

Prep Time: 10 minutes | **Cook Time:** 1 hour (mostly unattended)
Makes: 6 servings

INGREDIENTS
5 small to medium green mangoes
¾ cup powdered jaggery or dark brown sugar
1 teaspoon black salt
½ cup vodka (optional)

PREPARATION

Place the mangoes in a 375 degrees F oven (there is no need to pre-heat the oven) and roast them for about 45 minutes (test them with a toothpick, when inserted it should sink right through). Change the temperature to a high broil and broil for about 5 minutes; then turn the mangoes and broil for another 5 minutes (the objective of this process is to char the skin of the mangoes as this imparts a smoky taste to the fruit).

Remove mangoes from the oven and cool. Peel the charred skin and then carefully squeeze out the cooked pulp. (The best way to do this is to use your hands and gently press and push the soft cooked pulp over the seed.) Place the pulp in a blender and add the sugar or jaggery, black salt, and 3 cups cold water and blend until smooth. If adding the vodka, pour into the blender and blend again. Place ice cubes in serving glasses and serve the drink on the rocks.

FRESH KIWI RITAS
Aparna

This was something that I had dabbled with using the Indian gooseberry, unfortunately a fruit not very readily available in the U.S. I usually have kiwis around because they make a very attractive garnish, so I put them to use in this recipe. If you wish to make a mocktail out of this, add 3 tablespoons lemon juice and eliminate the alcohol.

Prep Time: 20 minutes | **Makes:** 4 servings

INGREDIENTS
6 kiwis, peeled and quartered
1 cup orange juice
½ cup sugar
1 teaspoon salt
½ cup tequila
½ cup triple sec
1 cup ice-cubes
Coarse salt for edging the rims of glasses, if desired

PREPARATION

Place the kiwis, orange juice, sugar, salt, and ½ cup water in a blender and blend for about 3 minutes until very smooth. Add the tequila, triple sec, and ice cubes and blend again for about 2 to 3 minutes.

If you are salting the glasses, lightly moisten the rims and place inverted on a bed of salt. Shake off the excess salt. Carefully pour the slushy mixture into these glasses and enjoy.

WATERMELON, CARDAMOM AND COCONUT COCKTAIL
Balika Badhu (The Young Bride)

I don't use syrups in any of the other drink recipes in this book, because I don't think they do much more than add an extra layer of sweetness and calories. For this drink, however, cardamom-infused simple syrup is a lovely addition.

Prep Time: 25 minutes | **Cook Time:** 20 minutes | **Makes:** 4 serving

INGREDIENTS
1½ cups water
1 cup sugar
16 bruised cardamom pods
5 cups seeded cubed watermelon (about half a medium watermelon)
1 cup light coconut milk
¼ teaspoon black salt
1 cup watermelon vodka

Preparation
Place the water, sugar, and cardamom pods in a cooking pot and simmer for about 20 minutes. Cool and strain the syrup.

Place the sugar syrup, watermelon, coconut milk, and black salt in a blender and blend for 2 minutes. Add the vodka and blend again for 2 minutes. Pour over ice cubes in glasses and serve.

Snack cart on the streets of Kolkata

Chapter Fourteen:

Snacks
Jol Khabaar

Given all the elaborate formalities and options for main meals, you might wonder how the Bengalis makes time for any snacking in between. When it comes to food, however, the Bengali does not compromise on anything. Dinner is usually eaten later in the evening so the time after work or school is spent unwinding and enjoying an assortment of snacks, available in endless flavors in either the home kitchen or a cornucopia of shops. People also tend to pay social visits that call for snacks in the evening. Lunch and dinner tend to be meals that are shared by invitation. However, it is unheard of to visit a Bengali household and not be served any snacks, both sweet and savory.

This chapter also attempts a nod to street food and some of the original street snacks that are popular in West Bengal, namely the *phuchka* (page 251).

CHICKEN TENDERS WITH WHIPPED EGG COATING
Kabiraji Cutlets

Any Bengali worth their *panch phoron* is excited about Durga Puja. Growing up with Dida (my maternal grandmother), the four days of Puja entailed getting up, fasting till *Anjali* (floral offering to the Goddess), and then eating the *bhog* (the meal cooked for Durga or the Goddess). The *bhog* consisted of vegetarian offerings, usually *khichuri* and other fried *bhajas* cooked family-style.

In the evenings, the city was transformed into a magical wonderland! Each block had its own Durga idol, decorated and designed differently. (Making these *protimasr* [clay images] is a full-time occupation for the designers. While Durga Puja is the largest festival, there are religious festivals with similar images all through the year.) The evenings were enjoyed by visiting the different *pandals* and, of course, eating wonderful street food—*phuchkas*, rolls, and cutlets. A Bengali cutlet is usually a fish or meat fillet, well-spiced, coated with breadcrumbs, and fried. A *kabiraji cutlet* is a special variation, where the coating is made of eggs along with the breadcrumbs.

Prep Time: 3 hours (mostly to marinate chicken) | **Cook Time:** 25 to 30 minutes
Makes: 6 servings

INGREDIENTS
10 green chilies
1 medium red onion
Juice of 1 lime
2 tablespoons ginger-cumin-coriander paste (page 14)
1 teaspoon salt
½ teaspoon turmeric
1 pound chicken tenders
3 eggs
2 tablespoons flour
1 tablespoon cornstarch
2 tablespoons breadcrumbs
Oil for frying

PREPARATION
Put the green chilies, onion, and lime juice in a blender and blend to make a paste. Mix with the ginger-cumin-coriander paste and add the salt and turmeric. Add the chicken tenders and toss to coat. Place in refrigerator and marinate the chicken for at least 2 hours.

Separate the eggs (whites from the yolks). Whip the whites till fairly stiff. In a separate bowl, mix the yolks with the flour, cornstarch, and breadcrumbs. Gently fold this mixture into the egg whites.

Heat some oil in a wok or skillet on medium heat till hot. Coat the chicken tenders well with the egg batter. Gently lower some of the batter-coated chicken tenders into the oil and cook until crisp and puffy. Remove from the oil and drain on paper towels. Continue cooking the remaining tenders. Serve hot.

WELL-SPICED CRISP BREADED SHRIMP
Chingrir Cutlets

This is one of my favorites recipes, and it can be made with chicken tenders as well.

Prep Time: 4 hours (including 3 hours of marinating)
Cook Time: 15 to 20 minutes | **Makes:** 25 cutlets

INGREDIENTS
25 extra-large shrimp
1 medium onion, coarsely chopped
1-inch piece fresh ginger, peeled
4 green chilies
¼ cup loosely packed cilantro leaves
Juice of 2 limes
1 teaspoon salt
2 eggs
2 cups dry breadcrumbs
Oil for frying

PREPARATION
Shell and de-vein the shrimp carefully, leaving the tails intact. Butterfly them carefully without cutting through. Pound the shrimp to flatten. Put in a bowl and set aside.

Place the onion, ginger, chilies, and cilantro leaves in a blender. Squeeze in the lime juice. Add the salt and blend the mixture to a paste. Pour over the shrimp and mix well. Set aside in the refrigerator for about 3 hours.

Remove the shrimp from the refrigerator. Beat the eggs in a separate bowl. Spread the breadcrumbs on another plate. Dip each piece of shrimp (with the spice paste clinging) into the egg and then carefully coat with the breadcrumbs, flattening out to a nice flat heart shape. Place the coated shrimp on a tray and put in the freezer for about 15 minutes.

Heat some oil in a wok or skillet on medium heat for 3 to 4 minutes. Carefully lower 2 to 3 shrimp cutlets into the oil and fry until nice and crisp. Remove and drain on paper towels. Continue frying all the shrimp. Serve hot.

GRILLED MARINATED LAMB KABABS
Kababs

There are several variations of kababs in the Indian culinary repertoire. In my Bengali variation, I add mustard oil to the marinade and season the lamb with *panch phoron* while it is cooking. This provides the dish with a very interesting flavor and pretty appearance. These morsels are great for both main dishes and for snacking.

Prep Time: 4 hours (mostly to marinade) | **Cook Time:** 30 minutes
Makes: 15 appetizer servings

INGREDIENTS
2 pounds boneless lamb cubes
Juice of 2 limes
2-inch piece fresh ginger, peeled
2 cloves garlic
2 small red onions
1 teaspoon salt
¼ small green papaya, peeled (about 3 to 4 inches long)
2 green chilies
1 green bell pepper
4 tablespoons mustard oil
½ teaspoon nigella seeds
½ teaspoon panch phoron (page 5)

PREPARATION
Place the lamb cubes in a mixing bowl. Squeeze the lime juice into a blender. Add the ginger, garlic, 1 red onion, salt, green papaya, and green chilies and blend until smooth. Pour over the lamb and toss to coat. Marinate the lamb for at least 4 hours in the refrigerator.

Cut the remaining onion into eighths and then separate the layers. Cut the bell pepper into pieces that match the size of the onion pieces. Thread the lamb and the onions and peppers, alternating pieces on the skewers.

Heat the grill. Brush the kababs generously with the mustard oil and place on the grill. Cook for about 10 minutes on each side. Brush with mustard oil again and sprinkle with the nigella seeds and panch phoron and cook for another 5 to 7 minutes on each side. Serve hot!

SPICY SALT FISH CAKES
Shootki Maacher Chop

Maacher chop or *maacher bora* is a very Bengali creation. The fish cakes are coated in breadcrumbs and then fried. This version using salt cod is one of my signature recipes that many have tried to mimic and simplify, sometimes with good results. My friends have shied away from using the salt fish though, so if you want a quicker alternative you can substitute fresh cod and skip the soaking step.

It is not uncommon for Bengalis to salt and dry their fish, and this practice is more prevalent in East Bengal. The only difference is that the Bengali dried fish tends to be done with smaller fish and are possibly not very suitable for this recipe. But I find the salt cod (baccala) a good compromise.

Prep Time: 24 hours (mostly to soak and drain the fish)
Cook Time: 25 to 30 minutes | **Makes:** 25 cakes

INGREDIENTS
1 pound dried salt cod
2 large Idaho potatoes
1 red red onion, peeled and chopped
3 green chilies, finely chopped
1 teaspoon salt
2 tablespoons chopped cilantro
3 tablespoons chickpea flour (besan)
1 tablespoon cornstarch
1 egg
Oil for shallow frying

PREPARATION
Place the salt cod in a large bowl and add cold water to cover. Soak the cod for 24 hours, changing the water every 4 hours. (To do this faster you can soak it for 18 hours, changing the water every 2 hours.)

Wash the potatoes, quarter them, and boil in water to cover for about 20 minutes, till cooked through but not mushy. Drain the water. Peel the potatoes and place in a mixing bowl and mash.

Place the cod in a pan of hot water and simmer for about 10 minutes. Drain, cool, and flake into pieces. Add the fish to the potatoes along with the onion, chilies, salt, cilantro, chickpea flour, and cornstarch. Mix well. Beat the egg and add to the mixture and mix well. (I personally think that this mixing works best using one's hand.)

Shape the potato mixture into twenty-five 3-inch cakes. Add some oil to a skillet to about 1-inch depth and heat on medium heat till almost smoking. Place some of the cakes in a single layer in the hot oil and cook for about 4 minutes on each side until the cakes are nice and golden brown. Remove and drain on paper towels. Continue frying the other fish cakes. Serve hot.

VEGETABLE CROQUETTES
Bhegetabil Chops

The Bengali language does not have the "v" sound in its lexicon, often leaving the native speaker to substitute an exaggerated "bh" sound in its stead. This has lead to the street vendors christening this particular vegetable creation, "*bhegetabil chop.*" This is a relished winter treat since it is made of root vegetables like beets and carrots. The blanched peanuts used in this and other recipes are commonly used in Indian food, and are available by the bagful in Indian stores.

Prep Time: 75 minutes (including 30 minutes refrigeration)
Cook Time: 45 to 60 minutes | **Makes:** 20 croquettes

INGREDIENTS
4 medium beets
2 medium carrots
2 medium potatoes
6 tablespoons oil
½ cup unsalted shelled peanuts
1 onion, very finely chopped
1 tablespoon fresh ginger paste (page 13)
1½ teaspoons salt
1¼ teaspoons sugar
¾ teaspoon cayenne pepper powder
1½ teaspoons bhaja masala (page 16)
1 cup all-purpose white flour
1½ cups dry breadcrumbs
Oil for frying

PREPARATION
Peel and quarter the beets and carrots. Quarter the potatoes. Fill a large pot with about 5 cups of water and bring to a boil. Add the beets and cook for about 6 to 7 minutes. Add the carrots and potatoes and cover and cook till tender but not mushy, about 20 minutes. Drain and cool the vegetables slightly. Peel the potatoes and mash into a smooth paste with the carrots and beets. Set aside.

Heat 2 tablespoons oil in a wok or skillet on medium heat. Add the peanuts and lightly roast until pale golden. Remove the peanuts with a slotted spoon. Add the remaining oil to the pan and heat for another minute. Add the onion and cook on low heat for about 3 to 4 minutes, until softened and beginning to turn pale gold. Add the ginger paste and cook for another minute. Add the mashed vegetable mixture and mix well. Add 1 teaspoon of the salt, the sugar, and cayenne pepper powder and cook on high heat for 5 minutes, until the mixture is a little dry. Stir in the bhaja masala and the reserved peanuts and turn off the heat and let the mixture cool.

In a separate bowl, mix the flour, remaining ½ teaspoon salt, and ¾ cup water and beat into a thick paste. Spread the breadcrumbs on a plate. Shape the cooked vegetable mixture into 20 small ovals. Dip the ovals in the flour mixture and then roll over the breadcrumbs until they are evenly and generously coated. Place the coated ovals on a tray and refrigerate for at least 30 minutes.

Put some oil in a wok or skillet and heat on medium heat for 3 to 4 minutes. Gently put 2 of the croquettes in the hot oil. Fry for about 3 minutes on each side until nice and crisp. Drain on paper towels. Continue to cook croquettes in the hot oil. Serve hot.

BANANA BLOSSOM CROQUETTES
Mochar Chop

This recipe is one of my mother's specialties. I have recently been asked for this recipe several times, so I am including it in my cookbook.

Prep Time: 60 minutes (including 30 minutes refrigeration)
Cook Time: 45 to 60 minutes | **Makes:** 10 to 15 servings

INGREDIENTS
2 tablespoons oil
1 red onion, chopped
1 cup prepared banana blossoms (page 131)
½ teaspoon cayenne pepper powder
1 teaspoon garam masala (page 17)
2½ teaspoons salt
1 teaspoon sugar
3 Idaho potatoes, boiled and peeled
½ teaspoon cumin-coriander powder (page 17)
1 cup all-purpose white flour
1½ cups dry breadcrumbs
Oil for frying

PREPARATION
Heat the oil in a wok or skillet on medium heat for about 30 seconds. Add the red onion and cook for 3 minutes, until softened and turning darker. Add the prepared banana blossoms, and stir well. Add the cayenne pepper powder, garam masala, 1 teaspoon of the salt, and the sugar and cook for 5 minutes, until the mixture is well-cooked and dry and fragrant. Remove from heat and let cool.

Mash the potatoes with 1 teaspoon of salt and the cumin-coriander powder. Take a small amount of the potato filling and shape into a lime-size ball. Make a dent to form a cup and fill with 1½ teaspoons of the banana blossom mixture and cover over with the potato filling and seal the ball and flatten. Continue this process until all the potato mixture is used up.

In a separate bowl, mix ¾ cup water, the flour, and remaining ½ teaspoon salt and beat into a thick paste. Spread the breadcrumbs on a plate.

Dip the prepared cakes in the flour mixture and then roll over the breadcrumbs until they are evenly and generously coated. Place the coated ovals on a tray and refrigerate for at least 30 minutes.

Put some oil in a wok or skillet and heat on medium heat for 3 to 4 minutes. Gently put 2 of the croquettes in the oil. Fry for about 3 minutes on each side until they are nice and crisp. Drain on paper towels. Continue frying the croquettes until all are cooked. Serve hot.

CRISP AND SPICY POTATO CROQUETTES
Alur Chop

The most basic of the "*chop*" creations, the simplicity and joy of this savory appetizer should not be underestimated. This is best served with a mustard-based condiment called *kasundi* (page 226). The simple potatoes are a nice backdrop to the sweetness of the sautéed onions and the sharpness of the green chilies.

Prep Time: 50 minutes (including 30 minutes of refrigeration)
Cook Time: 45 minutes | **Makes:** about 20 croquettes

INGREDIENTS
6 Idaho potatoes, boiled in their jackets
3 to 4 tablespoons oil plus more for frying
2 medium red onions, chopped
2 cloves garlic, minced
1 tablespoon fresh ginger paste (page 13)
1 tablespoon cumin-coriander powder (page 17)
1½ teaspoons freshly ground black pepper
3 green chilies, finely chopped
2 tablespoons chopped cilantro
1½ teaspoons salt
½ teaspoon black salt
2 teaspoons amchur
½ cup all-purpose white flour
1 egg (optional)
2 cups dry breadcrumbs

PREPARATION
Peel the potatoes and mash until smooth.

Heat the oil in a wok or skillet on medium heat for about 2 minutes. Add the onions, turn the heat down low, and cook for about 6 minutes, until soft and pale gold in color.

Add the garlic and ginger paste and cook for another 3 minutes. Add the cumin-coriander powder and cook for another minute. Turn off the heat and put the onion mixture in a mixing bowl. Add the mashed potatoes, black pepper, green chilies, cilantro, salt, black salt, and amchur and mash the ingredients well. Shape into 20 small 3-inch cakes.

Place the flour in a bowl and beat with the egg, if using, and enough water to form a thick batter, about ¾ cup. Spread the breadcrumbs on a plate.

Dip the cakes in the flour mixture and then roll over the breadcrumbs until they are evenly and generously coated. Place the cakes on a platter and refrigerate for at least 30 minutes.

Pour some oil in a wok and heat on medium heat for 3 to 4 minutes. Add 2 or 3 cakes and fry for about 3 minutes on each side until they are nice and crisp. Drain on paper towels. Continue frying remaining cakes. Serve hot.

POTATO AND CHICKPEA SALAD
Alu Kabuli

This simple recipe is symbolic of childhood and carefree times to a lot of Bengalis. It is a unique, traditional Bengali street food served on the leaves of the *shaal* tree, called "*shaal pata.*" While I can't comment on the cleanliness of the rest of the street food process, *shaal pata* cones are an amazingly hygienic and biodegradable contraption. The leaves are formed into cones and secured with a toothpick, and food such as *alu kabuli* (potato and chickpeas), and *phucka* are served in them.

These were a surreptitious treat for me during my college days, since I was not allowed to eat street food, mostly due to concerns about hygiene. Street food, however, is a rather essential part of the Kolkata food experience. For me street food is also synonymous with the rains that in Kolkata are magical and refreshing and stir up all the cravings for the tasty, tangy flavors of street food.

Prep Time: 2 hours (mostly to chill the salad) | **Makes:** 6 servings

INGREDIENTS
4 russet potatoes, boiled and peeled
1 tablespoon tamarind paste
Juice of 2 limes
1 teaspoon black salt
¾ teaspoon cayenne pepper powder
1 cup cooked chickpeas
1 red onion, very finely chopped
2 tablespoons chopped cilantro leaves
1 or 2 green chilies, finely chopped

PREPARATION

Slice the potatoes and place in a mixing bowl. In a separate small bowl mix the tamarind paste, lime juice, black salt, and cayenne pepper powder. Gently add the spice mixture to the potatoes. Add the chickpeas, red onions, cilantro, and green chilies and mix in lightly but evenly. Chill for 1½ hours. Serve as a light meal or as a salad with any other dish.

SPICY PUFFED RICE MEDLEY
Tel Muri

There are two versions of spicy puffed rice medley—this recipe that is the more homestyle variety and then the street version called *jhal muri*. Puffed rice is eaten in various ways, such as with milk, bananas, and sugar, much like a cereal.

When I began my first job in New York City, several people advised me against the suburban commute. So to test drive whether I liked city living, I spent two months spending the weekdays with my aunt and uncle, who live in Queens, New York. On returning from work every evening my uncle very diligently made this mixture for me.

Prep Time: 20 minutes | **Makes:** 3 servings

INGREDIENTS
1½ cups puffed rice (muri)
½ cup Indian snack mixture (*chanachur* or *dalmut*; sold in
    most Indian groceries)
1 or 2 green chilies, finely chopped
½ red onion, finely chopped
1 small tomato, chopped
½ teaspoon salt
3 tablespoons mustard oil

PREPARATION
Place the puffed rice and snack mixture in a mixing bowl and toss to combine.

Add the chilies, onion, and tomato and mix well. Add the salt and mustard oil and mix well with a wooden spoon. Serve right away to avoid the mixture getting soggy.

Dashami

The tenth or last day of the Durga Puja is called
Dashami or Bijoya Dashami, since this is the day the
Goddess was deemed victorious and returned home to
her husband. Images of Durga are decked with bangles and gifts of
vermillion (a traditional Hindu symbol of marriage) and immersed in
the Ganges. Married women usually anoint the Goddess with the
vermillion and later exchange vermillion and sweets as a sign of
celebration and promise of a long marriage.

The period between Dashami and Lakshmi Puja is also a period
when people take the opportunity to catch up with elders and
relatives by visiting them. There is usually a large preparation of
sweets and savories in anticipation of these visits. I remember my
mother preparing both the savory *nimkis* (page 249) and dough
sweets called *goja* for these events.

LIGHT AND CRISP SALTED PASTRY DISCS
Nimki

Lightly seasoned pieces of dough are popular as snacks all across India. They are cut into different shapes from region to region, and depending on the shape and spice combination, they have varying names. The most common variations in my house were the large triangular version seasoned with nigella seeds or the smaller diamond version in this recipe.

Prep Time: 90 minutes (including 30 minutes for resting dough)
Cook Time: 30 minutes | **Makes:** about 3 cups

INGREDIENTS
2 cups all-purpose white flour
1 teaspoon salt
¼ teaspoon baking soda
1½ teaspoons nigella seeds
4 tablespoons vegetable shortening
¾ cup ice cold water
Ghee for rolling and greasing
Oil for frying

PREPARATION
Sift the white flour in a mixing bowl with the salt and baking soda. Mix in the nigella seeds. Add the shortening and mix together with your fingertips until the dough is well moistened with the shortening. The dough should bind together when squeezed. Gradually add the cold water in small batches and mix together until a firm but manageable dough is formed. Let the dough rest for 30 minutes, covered with a wet cloth.

Lightly flour a rolling surface. Grease your hands with some ghee and form a round piece of dough. Roll out to a rough circle ¼-inch thick. Cut the dough circle into lengthwise strips 1-inch wide. Then slice across to form "diamonds."

Pour some oil into a wok and heat over medium heat till it reaches frying temperature.

Place 8 to 10 dough diamonds in the wok and fry on medium-low heat until pale caramel color. Remove with a slotted spoon and place on a wide plate to dry. Continue this process with the remaining dough. Cool thoroughly and store in an airtight container and use as needed.

BEATEN RICE PILAF
Chirer Pulao

As I write this recipe, I am reminded of Sravasti, a fellow schoolmate who was a day student while I lived in the hostel at my boarding school. I remember at one point having a craving for this simple beaten rice concoction, and she was kind enough to ask her mother to make it for me.

Beaten dried flattened rice flakes are re-hydrated and eaten as a meal in many parts of India. It is called *chirey* in Bengali and *poha* in some other parts of India. In fact, legend has it that this snack was Lord Krishna's favorite, brought to him by his friend Sudama. Other ingredients are flexible, but the potatoes and sliced onions are essential in this version.

Prep Time: 20 minutes | **Cook Time:** 25 minutes | **Makes:** 4 servings

INGREDIENTS
4 tablespoons oil
2 onions, thinly sliced
1 medium potato, peeled and cubed
1 cup cauliflower pieces
¼ teaspoon turmeric
1 teaspoon salt
1 teaspoon sugar
½ cup shelled raw (un-roasted) peanuts
1 or 2 green chilies, finely chopped
1 cup beaten rice (chirey)
1 tablespoon chopped cilantro
2 curry leaves, chopped (optional)
Juice of 1 lime

PREPARATION
Heat the oil in a skillet on medium heat. Add the onions and cook on medium heat for about 7 minutes, until they are pale gold in color. Remove half the onions and set them aside. Add the potatoes to the remaining onions in the pan and cover and cook for 3 minutes on low heat. Remove the cover and add the cauliflower and mix well. Add the turmeric, salt, and sugar and cover and cook until the vegetables are soft. Add the peanuts and green chilies and mix well.

In the meantime wash the beaten rice and soak in 2 cups of water for a couple of minutes to soften. Drain thoroughly in a colander. Mix the rice into the vegetable mixture and stir well. The mixture should be fairly dry and the rice should be soft. Taste and adjust salt if needed. Add the cilantro and curry leaves, if using. Mix in the reserved onions. Squeeze in the lime juice and serve hot.

CRISP PUFFY SHELLS WITH POTATO FILLING AND TAMARIND DIPPING WATER
Puchka

These tantalizing treats are popular across India with many variations and different names. The eastern Indian version is called *puchka*. The *puchka* stand is usually a portable straw basket filled with hundreds of these crisp delectable puffy crackers. Somewhere in other parts of his ware cart, the *puchka* seller has *ghugni* (spicy curried chickpeas), boiled potatoes, chopped cilantro, chopped green chilies, and spices. To balance all of this out is spicy water or "dipping water" that is stored in a large earthenware vessel to keep cool. This is what the whole concoction is really about—the quality of the spiced tamarind water.

It is not typical to make this treat at home, because a lot of this is about the experience of popping these spicy water filled crisps as they are placed in the *shaal* leaf cones by street vendors. But I make these at home and do a respectable job of the creation, though I cannot bring the spirit of the street to my table. So I encourage you to try making these for a fun experience and novel teatime treat that often becomes a weekend lunch for us.

Prep Time: 3 hours (mostly to chill dipping water) | **Makes:** 5 to 6 servings

INGREDIENTS
Filling
3 small potatoes, boiled, cooled, and peeled
¾ teaspoon black salt
½ cup prepared ghugni (page 75) or boiled chickpeas
2 tablespoons chopped cilantro
1 packet puchka shells (sold as pani puri in Indian stores)

Dipping water
6 cups water
3 tablespoons strained tamarind paste
¾ teaspoon black salt
½ teaspoon cayenne pepper powder
1 teaspoon bhaja masala (page 16)

PREPARATION
Mash together the potatoes, black salt, prepared ghugni, and cilantro. Cover and set aside.

Mix together the water, tamarind paste, black salt, cayenne pepper powder, and bhaja masala. Place in a pitcher and refrigerate for a couple hours to chill.

To serve, on each plate place a small amount of the potato mixture, about 6 puchka shells, and a cup with some of the chilled tamarind dipping water (stir the water well before pouring in cup). To eat, poke a hole in a shell and fill with the potato mixture, dunk this in the water and pop the whole thing into your mouth in one go.

INDO-CHINESE CHICKEN BREAD FRITTERS
Chicken Gold Coin

This is another delight from the ever-popular Indo-Chinese repertoire. It is a snack version and can be made with shrimp or even mixed vegetables and paneer if desired. It tastes good with a chutney, and is also often served with ketchup and a very basic condiment of sliced green chilies marinated in vinegar.

Prep Time: 25 to 30 minutes | **Cook Time:** 25 minutes | **Makes:** 6 servings

INGREDIENTS
1 pound boneless skinless chicken thighs
1 tablespoon soy sauce
2 scallions
1-inch piece fresh ginger, peeled
½ teaspoon sesame oil
2 green chilies
2 tablespoons chopped cilantro
15 slices of 2-to-3-day-old bread (white or multigrain)
2 eggs
2 tablespoons cornstarch
1 teaspoon salt
Oil for frying
Sesame seeds to garnish

PREPARATION
Place the chicken, soy sauce, scallions, ginger, sesame oil, and green chilies in a food processor and blend until very smooth. Mix in the cilantro.

Cut the bread slices into 2-inch circles (about 2 per slice of bread), if you want you can cut them into triangles as well. Spread a comfortable amount of the chicken topping (about 1 teaspoon) on each bread circle. Beat the eggs, cornstarch, and salt and mix well.

Put some oil in a heavy-bottomed skillet and heat on medium heat for about 3 minutes. Dip each chicken-coated bread piece in the egg mixture and then carefully place in the oil bread side down (working in batches). Cook for about 3 minutes and carefully turn and cook for about 3 minutes on the other side until nice and golden. Drain on paper towels. Sprinkle with some sesame seeds and serve.

ROASTED OR FRIED LENTIL WAFERS
Papor

The *papor* (*papadums*) used on the Bengali platter are a simple light version, usually fried. The plain variety of *papor* (*papadums*) can also be cooked in the microwave as a healthier alternative. I buy these ready-made and then microwave or fry them.

Prep Time: 2 minutes | **Cook Time:** 15 to 20 minutes | **Makes:** 4 to 6 servings

INGREDIENTS
15 to 20 small plain lentil wafers (papadums, available in Indian grocery stores)
Oil for frying if using the frying method

PREPARATION
Microwave Method
Place the papadums on a plate (they should be separated not on top of each other, so I do 2 at a time) and microwave on high for 20 to 30 seconds (the wafer should darken a little and turn blistery and crisp).

Frying method
Heat oil in a wok or frying pan on medium heat. Add the lentil wafers a couple at a time, the wafer will soften and crinkle. They need to be removed in less than a minute. They turn crisp once removed from the oil.

Chapter Fifteen:

Sweets
Mishti

To some the hallmark of a true Bengali is his proverbial sweet tooth. While there are many variations of sweets that grace the Bengali table, the most popular are milk-based. While I tried to select a good representative collection of dessert recipes, to truly do justice to this section on Bengali sweets one could provide more than double the fifteen given here and still have to leave some special recipes out. In fact, when I finished this chapter, I felt that I had only scratched the surface.

Many people believe that the art of curdling milk to make a cheese called channa or paneer (page 18) was taught to the Bengalis by the Portuguese and originated in the town of Bandel. Bengalis, however, wasted no time in putting their stamp onto it. Even the most basic home meal is incomplete without a finishing touch of *sandesh* (cakes made of channa) or sweetened yogurt. Seasonal specialties of the *sandesh* include varieties sweetened with the date palm jaggery called *notun gur*. This natural sweetener has also been very creatively fashioned into a date palm ice cream in some modern establishments. It is prepared much like maple syrup and I often use the latter as a substitute in my cooking if I don't have date palm jaggery.

Fritters or pancakes made of rice flour and coconut or another seasonal fruit called *pithey* also have a special place in the Bengali dessert universe. The rice-based varieties are especially symbolic of the harvest festival of Pous Parbon in winter. Since a large amount of the harvest in Bengal centers around rice, it is very fitting that offerings and celebrations of the harvest would include this grain.

I must confess that a lot of the sweets are still the sole domain of commercial confectioners. There are sweet shops on almost every block in Kolkata, and they are equally frequent in the surrounding suburbs. Certain sweets are considered distinct to certain regions of Bengal, for example, thin-shelled rosewater-filled *sandeshes* are the hallmark of the region of Burdawan, and sweet yogurt (*misti doi*) is considered better in Belur where my paternal grandparents lived.

COTTAGE CHEESE CAKES
Sandesh

When considering the rather simple number of ingredients for *sandesh*, it might seem easy to make, however it does take about fifteen minutes of precision to get good results. The first time I made it was on a festival morning, so you can call it the gift of the goddess or beginners luck, but it worked out perfectly.

What I have offered you is the simplest method of shaping these cakes. In Kolkata most people shape them using stone molds specifically for molding the cakes. This is the one thing that I have not been able to procure. Although recently I saw someone shape them using a cookie cutter, which if relatively small in size would work I imagine.

Prep/Cook Time: 2 hours (1½ hours for cheese to drain)
Makes: 12 lime-size balls

INGREDIENTS
½ gallon 2% milk
4 cardamom pods
½ cup natural tart yogurt or juice of 1½ limes
½ cup sugar
1 tablespoon rosewater

Garnish
Chopped dried cranberries
Ground pistachios

PREPARATION
Place the milk and cardamom pods in a heavy-bottomed pan and bring to a boil on medium heat. Stir in the yogurt or lime juice and wait for the milk to separate into milk solids and whey. Turn the heat off, drain the solids into a cheesecloth, tie and hang the cheesecloth for about 1½ hours to let the water drain out.

Remove the solids from the cheesecloth and place in your food processor with the sugar and process for about 2 minutes. (The cheese actually begins to gather into a ball at this point.)

Place in a heavy-bottomed (preferably non-stick) pan and cook on medium-low heat for about 8 minutes. (The mixture begins separating from the pan at this point.) Remove from heat and let cool. Sprinkle with rosewater.

Shape into lime-size balls, top each with a piece of chopped cranberry, and dust with pistachios and serve.

BAKED ORANGE-FLAVORED CHEESECAKE
Bhapa Sandesh

This recipe is something that I adapted from a steamed variation that my grandmother made for me. I am not sure how she combined the ingredients precisely, because she did not cook or teach from measurement. She probably used homemade paneer cheese and steamed this on the stove top.

What I have developed here is rather different from any technique that my grandmother would have used. If the proof of the pudding is in its taste, however, this version is pretty close to what I remember from my childhood, resulting in an easy and very elegant Bengali cheesecake using ricotta cheese.

Prep Time: 45 minutes (some time for cooling) | **Cook Time:** 30 minutes
Makes: 12 servings

INGREDIENTS
Clarified butter or ghee for greasing the casserole
1½ cups low-fat ricotta cheese (about 30 ounces)
¾ cup sweetened condensed milk (about 12 ounces)
½ teaspoon saffron strands
6 tablespoons fresh orange or tangerine juice

Optional garnishes
Orange sections
Slivered almonds
Chocolate shavings

PREPARATION
Pre-heat the oven to 325 degrees F. Grease an 8 by 12-inch cake or casserole pan and set aside.

In a mixing bowl, beat together the ricotta cheese and condensed milk. Stir in the saffron strands. The objective is to get a streaked effect rather than uniform coloring. Pour into the prepared pan and bake for 30 minutes.

Drizzle with the orange juice and let cool in refrigerator for about 30 minutes.

Carefully invert the prepared cheesecake on a flat surface. This can be cut into shapes using a cookie cutter or rolled into walnut-size balls.

Serve garnished with orange sections and almonds or rolled in or sprinkled with chocolate shavings. Chill and serve.

COTTAGE CHEESE DUMPLINGS IN SAFFRON SYRUP
Kesar Rasogolla

These delectable dumplings are quite the specialty when it comes to Bengali sweets. Neighbors from the state of Orissa, however, claim that this dessert was hijacked from them. *Rasogolla* did actually originate in Orissa but is omnipresent on most Bengali tables.

A good *rasogolla* is a ball of cottage cheese poached in flavored syrup till it gets nice and spongy. It is a temperamental dessert and in my opinion tastes best when warm. The recipe I have provided here does cheat a little with the addition of ricotta cheese, but I have found that it works well.

Prep Time: 3 hours and 15 minutes (including 3 hours for draining of channa)
Cook Time: 30 minutes | **Makes:** 8 servings

INGREDIENTS
1 cup fresh homemade channa (see recipe page 18)
3 tablespoons whole ricotta cheese
1 tablespoon semolina

Syrup
1½ cups sugar
1 or 2 cardamom pods
½ teaspoon saffron strands or rosewater

PREPARATION
Hang the channa to drain the whey out very thoroughly, about 3 hours (it is important to allow enough time for this or you will not get the right texture for this recipe).

Mix the channa with the ricotta and semolina. Knead the mixture like bread dough for a good 20 minutes, rolling and shaping it into a round. It should be one well-formed mass and feel a little greasy to touch. (To aid this process you can begin by placing the cheese mixture in a food processor and pulsing for 1 minute, till the mixture forms a ball; it can then be removed and kneaded for another 5 minutes by hand.)

Break the cheese mixture into balls about the size of a small walnut and place on a flat surface. Cover with a moist cloth and let the balls rest for about 25 minutes.

Meanwhile prepare the syrup: In a pressure cooker, mix the sugar and 5 cups water and simmer for about 10 minutes. Add the cardamom pods.

Gently lower the channa balls into the syrup (make sure there is plenty of room, since the balls swell up; I do this in two batches). Cover and cook on high till the pressure cooker reaches full pressure, then lower the heat and cook for 8 minutes. Remove from heat and let cool slightly. Remove from pot with a slotted spoon and place in a bowl. Sprinkle with the saffron strands and let cool slightly. Serve warm.

COCONUT-FILLED SWEET POTATO DUMPLINGS
Ranga Alur Pithe

These delectable sweet potato dumplings are an autumn treat. Interestingly enough, the first time I made these for someone from India, they were not sure what I was serving! I realized the reason was that Indian sweet potatoes are lighter in color, giving the dumplings a totally different appearance.

Prep Time: 25-30 minutes | **Cook Time:** 40 minutes
Makes: 15 servings

INGREDIENTS
Dumplings
2 sweet potatoes or yams
½ cup rice flour or all-purpose white flour
¾ cup frozen or fresh grated coconut
½ cup sugar
Oil for frying

Syrup
1½ cups sugar
1 or 2 cardamom pods

PREPARATION
Cut the sweet potatoes into quarters. Place in a large pot, add water to cover, and bring to a boil and cook until soft. Cool the potatoes and peel them. Mash the potatoes with the rice flour. Cover and place the mixture in the refrigerator to chill while cooking the coconut filling.

Place the coconut and sugar in a heavy-bottomed saucepan and cook on low heat, stirring frequently, till the coconut is aromatic, the natural oils are released, the color darkens, and the mixture is somewhat thick and sticky. Remove from heat and allow to cool.

Meanwhile, make the syrup: put the sugar, cardamom pods, and 3 cups water in a heavy saucepan on medium heat and cook for about 15 minutes, till a fairly thick (½ strand) syrup is formed.

Shape the cooled coconut mixture into small balls, using about 1½ teaspoons of the filling for each. Using a slightly larger amount of the sweet potato mixture, coat each coconut ball with some sweet potatoes. Flatten slightly into small cakes.

Heat some oil in a wok or skillet and gently add the sweet potato cakes a few at a time and fry till crisp. (This needs to be done with attention because sweet potatoes have a low caramelization point and brown very quickly and you need to cook them through without burning them.) Remove the cakes from the oil with a slotted spoon, draining the oil thoroughly, and add to the syrup and let soak for 3 to 5 minutes. Serve warm.

COCONUT AND CARDAMOM FUDGE
Narkol Khirer Borfi

Khir or *khoya* is solidified milk used for making fillings and fudges. It takes a long time to make at home and the texture does not often turn out right, but luckily it is sold in blocks in most Indian stores, greatly simplifying the dessert making process.

This recipe is a quick-fix that I often put together—it satisfies the sweet tooth, keeps well in the refrigerator, and can be made ahead for parties. I usually make this with commercial frozen coconut, making this even simpler—done in less than 25 minutes.

Prep Time: 2 hours (includes time to let the fudge set)
Cook Time: 20 minutes | **Makes:** 20 pieces

INGREDIENTS
1 pound commercial khoya (solidified milk)
1 cup grated coconut (can be frozen)
1 cup sugar
1 teaspoon crushed cardamom seeds
1 teaspoon ghee for greasing
2 tablespoons sliced almonds

PREPARATION
Place the khoya in a heavy-bottomed pan and melt over medium to low heat for about 7 to 8 minutes.

Once the mixture is a thick liquid mass, stir in the coconut. Add the sugar and cardamom and cook for another 5 minutes, until the sugar has melted and the mixture has thickened.

Lightly grease a flat heavy 12-inch plate or 9-inch cake pan with the ghee. Pour the coconut mixture into the pan and let cool slightly for about 15 minutes.

Top with the sliced almonds. Cut into squares or diamonds and then cool completely. This fudge will keep in the refrigerator for a couple of weeks.

ALMOND, MAPLE AND TAPIOCA PUDDING
Badam Doodher Payesh

This is a simple dessert that I enjoy making on winter mornings for an indulgent starter. It is quite nutritious and if you have a sweet tooth like me, you might enjoy this with your morning cup of tea. I use maple syrup as a substitute for jaggery in this recipe.

Prep Time: 15 minutes | **Cook Time:** 15 minutes | **Makes:** 4 to 6 servings

INGREDIENTS
2 cans (14 ounces each) evaporated whole milk (about 2½ cups)
½ cup blanched almonds
¼ cup tapioca pearls (sabudana)
1 cup hot water
2 or 3 cardamom pods
⅓ cup raisins
1 cup maple syrup

PREPARATION
Put 1 cup of the milk and the almonds in a blender and blend to a smooth paste. Set aside. Soak the tapioca pearls in the hot water for about 10 minutes, until the seeds are soft and swollen; drain.

Place the remaining 1½ cups of milk in a heavy-bottomed pan and bring to a simmer on low heat.

Add the drained tapioca, cardamom pods, raisins, and almond paste to the simmering milk and bring the mixture back to a simmer. Stir in the maple syrup and cook for another 3 minutes, till the tapioca is soft, the milk and almonds are melded through, and the raisins are lusciously swollen. This dessert is best served warm.

COTTAGE CHEESE PUDDING
Channar Payesh

This elegant variation of *payesh* is well-liked and savored on special occasions, usually events such as birthdays or weddings.

Prep Time: 20 minutes (plus 3 hours for chilling pudding)
Cook Time: 30 minutes | **Makes:** 10 servings

INGREDIENTS
1 cup sugar
1 cup channa or cottage cheese, drained for 2 hours (see recipe page 18)
1 cup whole milk
1 can (14 ounce) evaporated milk

2 or 3 cardamom pods
2 teaspoons rosewater

PREPARATION

Place half the sugar and ¾ cup water in a heavy-bottomed saucepan and bring to a simmer. Simmer for 20 minutes on low heat until a thick syrup is formed. Remove from heat and set aside.

While the syrup is cooking, knead the channa for about 20 minutes, until it is smooth and springy to touch. Break the channa into small pieces (they do not have to be uniform) and soak in the warm syrup.

Put the whole milk and evaporated milk in a heavy-bottomed saucepan and bring to a light simmer. Add the cardamom pods and simmer for about 20 minutes. Add the remaining ½ cup sugar and simmer for 3 to 4 minutes. Mix in the channa with the syrup and simmer for 2 to 3 minutes. Chill the pudding for at least 3 hours. Sprinkle with rosewater before serving.

RICE PUDDING WITH MOLASSES
Gur Diye Bhater Payesh

Thickened milk puddings called *payeshes* are a much-loved Bengali sweet. This particular version is traditionally made with date palm molasses called *khejur gur* and is considered a winter treat. It is not possible to find the real thing in the U.S., so as a substitute I use a blend of light molasses and jaggery. If this mixture is added to the milk when at full boil, it seems to curdle the milk, so I add it towards the end.

Prep Time: 10 minutes (plus 3 to 4 hours for chilling pudding)
Cook Time: 1 hour | **Makes:** 10 servings

INGREDIENTS
½ gallon whole milk
1 pint half and half
3 tablespoons kala jeera rice
¼ cup raisins
½ cup light molasses
½ cup powdered light jaggery

PREPARATIONS

Pour the whole milk into a heavy non-stick saucepan. Bring to a boil and then turn the heat to very low and simmer for about 30 minutes without stirring.

Stir the milk well to integrate the thick well-formed layer of cream on top. Add the half and half and rice and continue cooking the mixture for another 25 minutes, stirring the mixture frequently, until the rice is very soft and the mixture is nice and smooth. Stir in the raisins. Turn the heat off and cool the mixture for at least 1 hour.

While the milk is cooling, mix the molasses and jaggery together and cook in a separate pan on low heat until the jaggery has dissolved.

Gently stir the molasses mixture into the cooled milk mixture and chill for at least 2 hours before serving, stirring the mixture every 20 minutes or so to allow the molasses to uniformly dissolve.

BREAD PUDDING WITH RAISINS

A good steamed pudding made with milk, eggs, and raisins is a common dessert that I saw both my mother and grandmother make. They would steam the pudding on the stovetop, tightly enclosed in a stainless steel container with an engraved lid. This warm pudding, moist and well-flavored with plump raisins was sometimes a treat my grandmother made for me when I visited her. I keep my recipe simple as well, but I bake the pudding immersed in a deep pan of water and add a dose of alcohol to the raisins for a touch of fun.

Prep Time: 10 minutes | **Cook Time:** 35 minutes (plus 30 minutes cooling time in oven) | **Makes:** 10 servings

INGREDIENTS
½ cup large raisins
⅓ cup pineapple rum
4 eggs
¾ cup sugar
½ teaspoon vanilla extract
3 cups half and half
2 cups white bread cubes (the bread should be at least a couple of days old)
½ cup (1 stick) salted butter, melted

PREPARATION
Place the raisins in a small bowl, pour on the rum, and set aside to soak while preparing the batter. Pre-heat the oven to 350 degrees F.

Put the eggs and sugar in a bowl and beat with an electric mixer for 3 minutes until nice and thick. Add the vanilla extract and half and half and beat well.

Toss the bread cubes in the melted butter and place in a 10-inch to 12-inch square casserole. Pour in the rum and raisin mixture and mix lightly to distribute evenly. Pour the egg mixture over the bread cubes and mix well.

Place the casserole in a deeper ovenproof dish and fill with 2 inches of water. Place the pans in the oven and bake for about 35 minutes, until the mixture is golden and well risen. Turn off the oven and let the pudding cool in the oven for at least 30 minutes before serving.

VERMICELLI PUDDING WITH ALMONDS AND PISTACHIOS
Simoyer Payesh

This recipe is a classic Muslim *payesh* popular for the festival of Eid following the month of Ramadan. I have simplified it significantly by using pre-roasted vermicelli and evaporated milk.

Prep Time: 5 minutes (plus 3 hours for chilling pudding)
Cook Time: 30 minutes | **Makes:** 10 servings

INGREDIENTS
2 cans (14 ounces each) evaporated milk (about 2 cups)
½ cup sugar
4 cardamom pods, lightly bruised
⅓ cup raisins
1 package (12 ounces) pre-roasted thin wheat vermicelli
¼ cup chopped almonds
¼ cup chopped pistachios
2 teaspoons rosewater

PREPARATION
In a heavy pot, heat the evaporated milk and sugar. Add the cardamom pods and simmer for about 5 minutes to infuse the flavor into the milk. Mix in the raisins and vermicelli and cook for another 3 to 4 minutes, until the vermicelli softens.

Turn off the heat and stir in the almonds and pistachios. Pour into a bowl and chill the pudding for at least 3 hours. Sprinkle with rosewater before serving.

THICKENED MILK PUDDING
Rabri

The *rabri* is another sinful and decadent ode to milk and cream. It requires a little patience but the results are well worth it.

Prep Time: 5 minutes (plus 3 to 4 hours for chilling pudding)
Cook Time: 3 to 4 hours | **Makes:** 6 to 8 servings

INGREDIENTS
¾ gallon (12 cups) whole milk
1 cup heavy cream
⅔ cup sugar
2 tablespoons rosewater
2 tablespoons ground pistachios

PREPARATION

Pour the milk and cream into a heavy-bottomed pot and cook on medium heat until it reaches a simmer. Reduce the temperature and let the milk simmer gently until a thick layer of cream is formed. Gently stir the layer of cream back into the milk, keeping the layer intact. Continue this process every 20 minutes until the milk is reduced to a quarter of its original volume and there are solid layers of cream throughout, about 3 to 4 hours.

Stir in the sugar and mix until dissolved. Chill the pudding for several hours. Pour the rosewater over the pudding. To serve, place a little of the pudding with the solids in serving bowls and garnish with pistachios.

MILK CAKE
Kalakand

An interesting cross between a cheesecake and a milk fudge and aptly called milk cake, this dessert is exceedingly popular in many parts of India and is one of the first things I learned to cook.

Prep Time: 5 minutes (plus time to cool cake before serving)
Cook Time: 50 minutes | **Makes:** 8 servings

INGREDIENTS
1 can (14 ounces) evaporated milk
1½ cups ricotta cheese
¾ cup milk powder
¾ cup sugar
2 to 3 tablespoons ghee (clarified butter), plus additional for greasing
½ teaspoon cardamom powder
3 tablespoons coarsely chopped pistachios

PREPARATION
In a heavy-bottomed saucepan, put the evaporated milk and ricotta cheese and bring to a simmer. Continue cooking this mixture on low heat for about 20 minutes, stirring frequently, until the mixture has thickened considerably.

Add the milk powder and sugar, and continue cooking until the mixture has reached a soft fudge-like consistency, about 45 minutes or longer. (The key to getting this dessert to set is to make sure that it is cooked until most of the moisture has evaporated.)

Mix in most of the ghee (leave some for greasing the dish) and cook for an additional 3 to 4 minutes. Grease a deep 8-inch or 9-inch dish and pour in the cheese mixture. Let the mixture cool and solidify.

Cut the cake into 2-inch squares. Sprinkle with the cardamom powder and pistachios and serve when cool.

BAKED SWEET BENGALI YOGURT
Misti Doi

This thick, creamy, rich, and sweet yogurt is simple but yet another fantastic Bengali specialty. Traditionally this pink confection is made with thickened sweet milk and set in unglazed clay pots. The clay pots do two things for the dish— they impart a delicate flavor, and since they absorb some of the moisture, the yogurt that is produced is a smooth and rich textured creation. I bake the dessert rather simply using Greek yogurt and milk.

Prep Time: 10 minutes (plus 3 to 4 hours for chilling)
Cook Time: 35 minutes (mostly unattended) | **Makes:** 6 servings

INGREDIENTS
2 cups low-fat Greek yogurt
2 cans (14 ounces each) low-fat evaporated milk (about 2 cups)
¾ cup sugar

Optional garnish
3 tablespoons finely chopped cashew nuts

PREPARATION
Pre-heat the oven to 300 degrees F. Beat together the yogurt, evaporated milk, and sugar. Pour into a casserole (usually a loaf-shaped container works well for this purpose).

Cover and place in the oven and bake on low heat for 30 to 35 minutes until set. Turn off the heat and let it rest in the oven for about 30 minutes.

Place in the refrigerator and let chill for 3 to 4 hours before serving. Serve small amounts in glass or steel bowls and garnish with the cashew nuts if desired.

ANGLO-INDIAN FRUIT CAKE

I shy away from calling this recipe plum cake (or "palm cake" as my grand-mother mispronounced it). That dark moist fruit cake is a Christmas regular in the multiple cake shops that dot Kolkata. This recipe is close, but something about it falls just a little short of the taste I remember, possibly because nostalgia, unlike vanilla extract, cannot be bottled and infused in a cake batter to complete the flavors as the mind remembers them.

Prep Time: 20 minutes (plus a week to a month for soaking the fruit)
Cook Time: 45 minutes | **Makes:** 10 servings

INGREDIENTS
1 cup large mixed raisins
½ cup chopped candied citrus peel
¼ cup chopped dried cherries or cranberries
1 cup rum
2 cups all-purpose white flour
¼ teaspoon salt
1½ cups (3 sticks) unsalted butter, softened
¾ cup loosely packed light brown sugar
¼ cup granulated sugar
¼ cup robust molasses
4 eggs, well-beaten
1 teaspoon baking powder
¾ cup milk
1 teaspoon vanilla extract
½ cup shredded coconut

PREPARATION
Place all the fruits in a non-reactive bowl. Add the rum and cover and set aside for at least a week,or for best flavor, for a month.

Grease an 8-inch to 10-inch loaf pan or a 12-inch round cake pan and pre-heat the oven to 350 degrees F. Drain the fruit when you are ready to use and reserve the soaking liquor, if any.

Sift together the flour and salt. Sprinkle about a ¼ cup of the flour mixture over the drained fruit and toss to coat.

Cream together the butter, brown sugar, and granulated sugar. Stir in the molasses. Add the beaten eggs to the mixture and beat to combine. Add the baking powder to the remaining flour mixture and add to the batter in batches, alternating with the milk, and beat until well combined. Beat in the vanilla extract. Stir in the shredded coconut. Stir in the floured fruit. Pour batter into prepared pan.

Bake the cake for 40 to 45 minutes, until a toothpick inserted into the center comes out clean. Cool slightly.

Invert the cake onto a plate and pour any reserved soaking liquor over it. Allow to sit to absorb the liquor. This cake can be served warm or alternately wrapped and stored and served when needed.

Christmas in Kolkata

The third most prominent religion in the state of West Bengal is Christianity. Like for all the other festivals in Kolkata, Christmas is much fuss and action. Owing to its colonial legacy, Kolkata has a nostalgic relationship with Christmas. Christmas, although a Christian holiday, takes on an entirely cosmopolitan dimension here. For Kolkatans, Christmas is synonymous with yummy cakes and pastries from established city bakeries such as Flury's, Nahoum's, or Kathleen; Santa Claus replicas in New Market; and glittering decorations along Park Street. There are lights and decorations across the city and people go through a spree of baking and buying fruit cakes. Church services, most notably the one in St Paul's Cathedral, are attended by many non-Christians who want to revel in the magic of community and the moment.

There was a sheer joy in being able to get to New Market to pick up the assorted candied fruit and peels to make the plum cake that my grandmother referred to as "palm cake." My father is also nostalgic about the traditional fruit cake, since he remembers his father picking one up to mark the occasion (this is an interesting illustration of the love of celebration to the Bengali). If you attended a parochial influenced school such as mine, you would close for the Christmas holidays after putting on an annual Nativity play. Christmas carols and their Bengali counterparts usually dominate the radio stations to add to the spirit. I recently thrilled my daughter when I was able to complete the words to some of her favorite Christmas carols in Bengali.

COCONUT TOFFEE BALLS
Narkoler Naru

This dessert is the symbol of the festival of Lokkhi/Lakshmi Puja, and typically is seasoned with a pinch of camphor, which is difficult to find so I make do with cardamom. Lokkhi Puja is very much a domestic festival, celebrated in most households in a simple way. Lokkhi is the Goddess of Wealth and is therefore invoked by business communities in all parts of India. She is depicted as a peaceful, compassionate, and flighty Goddess who thrives in an atmosphere of calm and cleanliness. Most households also pray to this Goddess on Thursdays by fasting and then breaking their fast with simple fruit offerings to her.

For Lokkhi Puja, houses are swept and washed clean and then decorated with *alpona* (a traditional floor design of rice paste). Among other things the symbolic patterns include sheaths of rice paddy and pairs of feet for Lokkhi to walk on. The floor in my grandparents' house was made of red stone and showed off the lovely white designs well. I was constantly chided by my Dida if the feet were not delicate enough, saying this would be off-putting to the Goddess and she would not enter our house.

The first time I tried making the *naru* I was disappointed because the results were drier and less chewy than I remembered. Recently I tried again and realized that the problem was patience. They need to be cooked on very low heat and stirred frequently to release the natural oils of the coconut.

Prep Time: 15 minutes | **Cook Time:** 30 minutes | **Makes:** 20 small narus

INGREDIENTS
2 cups grated coconut (I use the frozen variety)
¾ cup powdered jaggery
½ teaspoon cardamom powder

PREPARATION
In a wok or skillet on very low heat, cook the coconut, stirring frequently, for 15 to 20 minutes. The coconut should begin turning light brown and aromatic and begin releasing some oil.

Add the jaggery and continue cooking on low, stirring frequently, until the jaggery is melted and the mixture is well browned and very fragrant and toffee-like. (There should be plenty of coconut oil glistening on the mixture.)

Stir in the cardamom powder. Remove from heat and let cool until able to be handled.

Shape mixture into small balls. These balls keep well for a couple of weeks at room temperatures up to 70 degrees F, or refrigerated. If refrigerated, they should be brought to room temperature before serving.

MY FATHER'S FAVORITE MOLTEN LEMON AND MANGO CAKE
Bapir Cake Pudding

I adapted this recipe from one of the first cookbooks I owned. It was a step-by-step illustrated English publication from Hamelyn gifted to me by my aunt. I am not sure of its exact name, something like, "My Fun to Cook Book."

I played with this recipe for many years, the most prominent adaptation being the addition of the mango, and it became one of my father's favorites. I had not made it for a while, but dug it up from the recesses of my memories for the purposes of this book. My father named it cake pudding, which is apt given its cakey topping and pudding-like base.

Prep Time: 20 minutes (plus 1 hour cooling time) | **Cook Time:** 25 minutes
Makes: 6 servings

INGREDIENTS
1 tablespoon melted ghee (clarified butter)
4 eggs
½ cup sugar
4 tablespoons all-purpose white flour
Grated zest of 1 large lemon
½ cup mango pulp (preferably from a fresh mango)
¼ cup fresh lemon juice
1 cup milk
¼ teaspoon salt
Confectioner's sugar, for dusting

PREPARATION
Grease 6 (6-ounce) custard cups with ghee. Pre-heat oven to 300 degrees F.

Separate the eggs and place the yolks in a large mixing bowl. Beat the egg yolks with the sugar until well mixed. Sift in the flour and mix well. Gradually add the lemon zest, mango pulp, and fresh lemon juice, beating well after each addition. Lastly beat in the milk and salt.

In a separate bowl, whip the egg whites with an electric mixer until soft peaks form. Gently fold into the batter.

Divide the batter evenly between the six custard cups. Place in a roasting pan and pour enough water into the roasting pan to come halfway up the sides of the custard cups. Bake for about 25 minutes, until puffy and lightly browned.

Cool for about 1 hour. Dust with confectioner's sugar and serve.

CRISP COCONUT FRITTERS DUNKED IN SYRUP
Gokul Pitha

At the heart of the desserts called *pithey* is a sweetened coconut mixture. This sweetened filling is usually encased with something soft or crisp to make the *pitha* work. In this variation, the *pitha* is battered, fried, and coated in syrup.

Prep Time: 20 minutes | **Cook Time:** 40 minutes | **Makes:** 12 servings

INGREDIENTS
Syrup
1 cup Grade B maple syrup
½ cup water
2 to 3 cardamoms

Fritters
1 cup fresh or frozen grated coconut
¾ cup grated jaggery or raw cane brown sugar
¼ teaspoon cardamom powder
1 tablespoon ghee (clarified butter)
1 cup all-purpose white flour
⅓ cup rice flour
½ cup milk
Oil for frying, such as grapeseed or canola oil

PREPARATION
In a small saucepan, bring the syrup, water and cardamoms to a simmer for 10 minutes until a thick syrup is formed.

While the syrup is cooking, in a separate pan heat the coconut, jaggery, and cardamom powder on low heat, stirring constantly, for about 15 minutes, until a fragrant sticky mixture is formed. Add the ghee and lightly fry the mixture until it turns pale golden. Remove from heat and allow it to cool.

Shape coconut mixture into walnut-size balls and flatten them slightly.

In a mixing bowl, beat the flours and milk into a thick batter, adding a little water if needed. (The batter should be thick enough to adhere to the coconut balls.)

Heat some oil in a wok on medium heat. Dip a coconut ball in the batter and place into the oil. Cook on medium-low heat until a golden, crisp coating is formed, turning once. (You can cook a few of the balls at the same time but don't crowd.)

Remove balls carefully with a slotted spoon and immediately dip into the syrup. Let the balls rest in the syrup for about 2 minutes, then remove and serve hot.

DELICATE SPONGY PANCAKES WITH PINEAPPLES
Anaras Diye Chanar Malpoa

This recipe is one that I learned from my mother. My mother's *malpoa* (fennel-scented pancakes) are remarkable. Recently, she made these treats for a family gathering when my cousins were visiting and we enjoyed them dunked in syrup. This dessert is simple, but should be served hot. I dressed her recipe up just a tiny bit by adding pineapples. You can also use other seasonal fruit of your choice, such as apples, pears, or mixed berries.

Prep Time: 15 minutes | **Cook Time:** 25 to 30 minutes | **Makes:** 4 servings

INGREDIENTS
Syrup
2 cups water
2 cups sugar

Pancake batter
¾ teaspoon fennel seeds
½ teaspoon cardamom seeds
1 to 2 whole black peppercorns
2 cups commercial evaporated milk (about 2 large cans)
¾ cup ricotta cheese
1½ tablespoons semolina
½ cup all-purpose white flour

Oil for frying
½ cup chopped or shredded pineapple (canned or frozen)
2 to 3 tablespoons chopped nuts

PREPARATION
Prepare the syrup:
Place the water and sugar in a heavy-bottomed pot and cook on medium heat until the mixture comes to a boil. Lower the heat and simmer for about 15 minutes until a nice thick consistency is reached.

Prepare the pancake batter:
Dry roast the fennel seeds, cardamom seeds, and whole peppercorns for a few minutes. Grind to a coarse powder. Blend the evaporated milk, ricotta cheese, semolina, and flour until a smooth batter is formed. (The batter should be a little thicker than buttermilk.) Stir in the roasted spices.

Heat some oil in a skillet. Add 2 tablespoons of the batter for each pancake and spread slightly. When golden brown (about the shade of toffee) with some paler spots on one side, turn over and brown on the other side. (The objective is to form pancakes that are crisp on the outside with a moist center.) Remove from pan and place into the syrup and let soak for 5 minutes.

Serve warm topped with a small amount of pineapple (or other fruit of your choice) and chopped nuts, allowing 2 to 3 pancakes per serving.

RICE FLOUR CREPES WITH COCONUT FILLING
Patisapta

These crepes are a much-loved recipe that is usually guaranteed to please most palates. Mention them to a Bengali and you are bound to receive a nostalgic look of delight. I felt that this traditional and lovely recipe would make the perfect finale for this book.

Prep Time: 15 minutes | **Cook Time:** 30 minutes | **Makes:** 5 to 6 servings

INGREDIENTS:
Coconut filling
1½ cups fresh or frozen grated coconut
1 cup powdered jaggery
½ cup powdered milk or khoya
¼ teaspoon cardamom powder

Crepes
½ cup all-purpose white flour
½ cup semolina
½ cup sifted rice flour
1 cup whole milk

½ cup canola oil
2 tablespoons melted ghee (clarified butter)

PREPARATION:
Make the coconut filling:
Put the coconut in a heavy-bottomed pan and roast for about 5 minutes until the coconut is nice and fragrant. Add the jaggery and continue cooking on low heat until the jaggery melts. Stir in the powdered milk or khoya. Gently mix in the cardamom powder and ½ cup water and cook for about 10 minutes until the mixture is nice and sticky. Turn off the heat and set aside to cool.

Make crepes:
Place all the ingredients for the batter in a mixing bowl and beat to form a nice smooth pancake-consistency batter, adding more or less flour as needed. In a separate bowl, stir together the oil and ghee.

Heat a flat skillet or crepe pan (I have found using a non-stick hard anodized pan works best for this purpose) on medium heat for about 2 minutes. Add 1 teaspoon of the oil/ghee mixture and spread. Add a ladleful of the batter and spread this evenly over the pan and let the crepe cook gently for about 2 to 3 minutes. Place a small amount of the filling across the center of the crepe. Gently fold the crepe in half (it should be off-white with plenty of pale golden spots). Carefully remove from pan. Cook all the batter in this manner and allow about 2 crepes per person as a good serving size.

Acknowledgements

It is never possible to thank all the people who offer support and inspiration for a project like this one. I would, however, like to mention a few people who come to mind and have been instrumental to its conception and completion.

I start by thanking Priti Chitnis Gress, without whose initial suggestions I would not have begun working on this book. Working with her has been a personal and joyful intellectual experience, just what one would want for a personal project such as this one. Along with Priti, I thank the rest of the Hippocrene team including Barbara Keane-Pigeon, whose meticulous attention to detail helped this book move to its finished state.

A special mention for Monica, for instilling enough confidence in me to even think of getting a proposal out, otherwise this book would have been a collection of recipes that I could never find when I needed them. Many thanks to Liz Johnson, who created the wonderful food community that we in Westchester County, New York, live and create within, a community that includes all my students whose enthusiasm brings me to the kitchen again and again.

I always need Julianna, my sounding board for many of my writing projects who keeps me grounded with her attention to detail and neutral perspective.

Thanks to Shapna, who has been there for me, from sharing many an enthusiastic comment on my blog to providing some traditional recipes from her collection to help me offer context to the East Bengali side of the culinary heritage that Bengali cuisine offers.

Special thanks to my beloved sibling Khokan, who has also assisted with the tasting of recipes and is my special gift and touchtone in life and has also been helpful with compiling and assisting with the quality of many of the photographs.

I would like to thank several migrant Bengalis, including Priti Moudgill, whose enthusiastic memories of Bengali food have made me feel that this book would be much appreciated.

Home is where the hearth is, without home and family the food would not be the same and the words would not feel right. So as with all my culinary activities, the tasting driving and critiquing force is my husband, without whose objectivity these recipes would not be complete. He has had to patiently be the guinea pig but often had to wait to eat while the food was being photographed at all hours of the day. A special mention to my mother, who unknowingly contributed to several of the traditional segments of the book.

I am glad for my sisters-in-law Hema and Shweta for being such enthusiastic supporters of my cooking experiments and for helping me realize that Bengali food can certainly translate well for people with other regional palates. And I cannot forget my cousin Sharmilla, who is a genuine and true reader of my blog.

Lastly, I would like to thank my work colleagues, Ken and Ellie, without whose support for my "lunchtime" escapades my culinary world would not grow, and my supervisor Gerry, without whose enthusiasm for my cooking it would feel less complete.

References

Banerjee, Chitrita, *Eating India: Exploring a Nation's Cuisine*. Penguin Books, India, 2008.

Dasgupta, Minakshie, Gupta Bunny & Jaya Chalia, *The Calutta Cookbook: A Treasury of Recipes from Pavement to Palace*. Penguin Book, 1995.

POTATOES. *See also* <small>SWEET POTATOES; VEGETA-BLES (MIXED)</small>

Banana Blossom Croquettes (*Mochar Chop*), 244

Beaten Rice Pilaf (*Chirer Pulao*), 250

Crisp and Spicy Potato Croquettes (*Alur Chop*), 245

Crisp Puffy Shells with Potato Filling and Tamarind Dipping Water (*Puchka*), 251

Curried Cabbage with Potatoes and Green Peas (*Badha Kopir Ghanto*), 124

Dried Potato Curry with Garlic (*Shantipur Barir Aamish Alur Dom*), 127

Fiddlehead Ferns with Potatoes and Nigella Seeds (*Dheki Shaager Chorchori*), 110

Indian Cheese with Potatoes and Peas in a Creamy Sauce (*Channar Dalna*), 120

Julienne Pan-Fried Potatoes (*Alu Bhaja*), 85

Mashed Potatoes and Bitter Melon (*Alu Korola Sheddo*), 99

Mutton or Lamb Curry with Potatoes and Bell Peppers (*Alu Capsicum Diye Mandsho*), 204

My Father's Dry Egg Curry (*Bapir Dimer Dalna*), 147

Pepper-Spiced Bengali Vegetable Stew (*Doi Morich Diye Sobji Ishtew*), 122

Potato and Chickpea Salad (*Alu Kabuli*), 246

Potatoes with Poppy Seeds (*Alu Posto*), 122

Quick Spiced Potatoes and Cauliflower with Baby Shrimp (*Alu Kopir Dalna*), 134

Roasted Pork with Potatoes and Onions (*Pork Bhuni*), 215

Smoked Green Mangoes and Potatoes (*Kacha Aam Pora*), 101

Spicy Mashed Potatoes or Taro (*Alu ba Kochu Sheddo*), 99

Spicy Mashed Potato Relish (*Alur Bhorta*), 229

Spicy Omelet Curry (*Omelet Dalna*), 149

Spring Onions with Potatoes and Shrimp (*Piaj-Kolir Chorchori*), 107

Tempered Mashed Potatoes with Eggs (*Alu Dimer Bhortha*), 100

Whole Potatoes Cooked with Ground Chicken (*Keema Diye Alur Dom*), 188

POULTRY. *See* <small>CHICKEN; TURKEY</small>

PUDDINGS

Almond, Maple and Tapioca Pudding (*Badam Doodher Payesh*), 262

Bread Pudding with Raisins, 264

Cottage Cheese Pudding (*Channar Payesh*), 262

Rice Pudding with Molasses (*Gur Diye Bhater Payesh*), 263

Thickened Milk Pudding (*Rabri*), 265

Vermicelli Pudding with Almonds and Pistachios (*Simoyer Payesh*), 265

PUMPKIN. *See* <small>SQUASH</small>

RADISHES. *See also* <small>VEGETABLES (MIXED)</small>

Radish and Cabbage (with or without Fish Heads) (*Mulor Chechra*), 113

Yellow Split Peas with Cauliflower and Radishes (*Mulo ar Kopir Data diye Moto Dal*), 71

RELISHES

Fiery Mustard and Lime Relish (*Kasundi*), 226

Mustard and Green Mango Relish (*Aam Kasundi*), 227

Mustard, Pineapple and Tomato Relish (*Tomato ar Anarosher Kashundi*), 228

Spicy Mashed Potato Relish (*Alur Bhorta*), 229

Tangy Fish Relish (*Maacher Bhorta*), 228

RICE

about, 36-37

Anglo-Indian Rice and Lentil Pilaf with Fish (*Reclaimed Kedgeree*), 49

Beaten Rice Pilaf (*Chirer Pulao*), 250

Bengali Lemon and Yogurt Rice (*Gondhora Lebu Diye Doi Bhaat*), 54

Essential Bengali Festive Rice (*Ghee Bhaat*), 39

Fine-Grained Refined White Rice (*Kala Jeera Atap Chaal*), 38

My Grandmother's Festive Rice with Vegetables (*Didimar Fried Rice*), 40

My Mother's Fish Head Pilaf with Vegetables (*Muro Bhaat*), 43

Parboiled Rice (*Sheddo Chaal*), 38

Red Lentils and Risotto (*Masoor Daler Khichuri*), 51

Rice and Lentil Pilaf (*Bhuni Khichuri*), 48

Rice Pilaf with Chicken (*Murgir Nobabi Pulao*), 41

Rice Pudding with Molasses (*Gur Diye Bhater Payesh*), 263

Rice with Beets and Green Peas (*Beet diye Ghee Bhaat*), 45

ABOUT THE AUTHOR

Rinku Bhattacharya is an accomplished cooking teacher and author of the Spice Chronicles blog (www.spicechronicles.com). Her expertise and passion lie in combining the rich, healthy, and vibrant flavors of her Indian childhood with the local bounty of Hudson Valley. Rinku also enjoys exploring regional Indian cuisine, particularly foods from her native Bengal, and adapting recipes so that they remain authentic but are practical for everyday cooking.

A busy mother with two young children, Rinku makes sure that mealtimes in her household are a simple and sustainable family affair. She lives in Westchester County, New York, with her husband (an avid gardener) in a house with a vibrant backyard.

The Bengali Five Spice Chronicles was the winner of the Gourmand World Cookbook Awards 2013 for Best Indian Cuisine. Rinku is also the author of *Spices and Seasons: Simple, Sustainable Indian Flavors* (Hippocrene Books, 2014).

Rinku teaches out of her home-based cooking school, and also conducts classes in various public locations. She writes a weekly column, "Spices and Seasons," for *The Journal News* and is also a regular contributor to *Zester Daily* and *The Poughkeepsie Journal*.

Photo by Aadi Bhattacharya

Also by Rinku Bhattacharya

SPICES & SEASONS:
Simple, Sustainable Indian Flavor

"Rinku's goal is to help readers understand the essentials of cooking with Indian spices, whilst still maintaining a sense of simplicity and a sustainable approach to life. She beautifully combines the time-tested traditions of the Indian kitchen with a practical, modern approach to educate those of us ready to cook alongside her. The instructions are easy, and the ingredients just as easy to find online or with a visit to a spice market. We are left with no excuses for not cooking food that is as delicious and fresh as possible."

—From the foreword by Suvir Saran, "Top Chef" contestant and
author of *Masala Farm*

Gourmand Award-winning author Rinku Bhattacharya offers time-strapped home cooks a realistic way to cook healthfully and sustainably. Included are more than 150 family-friendly recipes with plenty of gluten-free and vegetarian options; detailed sections on spices, ingredients, and utensils; and "green tips" for making your kitchen eco-friendly.

ISBN 978-0-78181331-0 · $35.00

Cookbooks from Hippocrene

INDIAN INSPIRED GLUTEN-FREE COOKING
Alamelu Vairavan and Margaret Pfeiffer, MS, RD, CLS

"Alamelu's healthy style of cooking is a harmonious blend of flavors and freshness that makes the journey into the world of gluten-free Indian cooking approachable and exciting for everyone!"
> —Jason Gorman, Executive Chef, The Art Institute of Chicago

ISBN: 978-0-78181306-8 · $19.95pb

A New York Times Notable Cookbook
RICE & CURRY
Sri Lankan Home Cooking
S.H. Fernando Jr.

"A terrific introduction to a great culinary tradition about which egregiously little is known. Well-researched, authentic, and easy-to-follow recipes."
> —**Anthony Bourdain**

ISBN: 0-7818-1273-9 · $19.95pb

HEALTHY SOUTH INDIAN COOKING
Expanded Edition
Alamelu Vairavan and Dr. Patricia Marquardt

"Coconut-infused curries, brilliant vegetable dishes . . .What could be complex becomes relatively simple in Vairavan's approach . . ."
> —*Los Angeles Times*

ISBN: 0-7818-1189-9 · $35.00hc

THE KERALA KITCHEN
Recipes and Recollections from the Syrian Christians of South India
Lathika George

"Here you will find clear recipes for the best of Kerala's fine foods, written with great love by someone who has been a part of that culinary tradition since birth."
> —Madhur Jaffrey

ISBN: 978-0-7818-1184-2 · $35.00hc

MENUS AND MEMORIES FROM PUNJAB
Meals to Nourish Body and Soul
Veronica "Rani" Sidhu

"Sidhu has dipped into—and helped preserve—a rich culinary tradition that extends back hundreds of years."
> —Andrew F. Smith, food historian and editor-in-chief of
> *The Oxford Encyclopedia of Food and Drink in America*

ISBN: 978-0-7818-1220-7 · $29.95hc

Dictionaries from Hippocrene

Bengali-English/English-Bengali Practical Dictionary
13,000 entries · ISBN 978-0-7818-1252-8 · $24.95pb

Bengali-English/English-Bengali (Bangla) Dictionary & Phrasebook
978-0-7818-1218-4 · $14.95pb

Prices subject to change without prior notice. **To purchase Hippocrene Books** contact your local bookstore, visit www.hippocrenebooks.com, call (212) 685-4373, or write to: HIPPOCRENE BOOKS, 171 Madison Avenue, New York, NY 10016.